Loneliness

In recent years its medical implications have brought loneliness to the centre of attention of mass media, government agents, and the general public. However, as this volume demonstrates, loneliness is not merely a psychological, individual, or health issue. In multiple ways, it is a serious social problem as well.

Yang urges fellow researchers and scientists to broaden the existing definition and classification of loneliness, to measure loneliness with greater accuracy, and to establish more specifically the connection between loneliness and particular illnesses. Drawing on vast sources of data, including literary works, case studies, and large-scale sample surveys covering a broad spectrum of countries (Europe and beyond), the empirical research of this study produces and presents simple but effective evidence for the social nature and variations of loneliness.

Examining loneliness at higher levels, including ethnic groups, classes, national cultures, and societies, *Loneliness* will appeal to students and researchers interested in areas such as sociology, psychology, and mental health.

Keming Yang is an associate professor of sociology at Durham University, UK.

Routledge Advances in Sociology

The Sociology of Knowledge Approach to Discourse
Investigating the Politics of Knowledge and Meaning-making
Edited by Reiner Keller, Anna-Katharina Hornidge, Wolf J. Schünemann

Christianity and Sociological Theory
Reclaiming the Promise
Joseph A. Scimecca

Ageing, Diversity and Equality
Edited by Sue Westwood

Cinematic Tourist Mobilities and the Plight of Development
On Atmospheres, Affects and Environments
Rodanthi Tzanelli

Bicycle Utopias
Imagining Fast and Slow Cycling Futures
Cosmin Popan

Islamophobia in Muslim Majority Societies
Edited by Enes Bayrakli and Farid Hafez

Equine Cultures in Transition
Ethical Questions
Edited by Jonna Bornemark, Petra Andersson, Ulla Ekström von Essen

Loneliness
A Social Problem
Keming Yang

For more information about this series, please visit: www.routledge.com/Routledge-Advances-in-Sociology/book-series/SE0511

Loneliness

A Social Problem

Keming Yang

Routledge
Taylor & Francis Group

LONDON AND NEW YORK

First published 2019 by Routledge

2 Park Square, Milton Park, Abingdon, Oxfordshire OX14 4RN

52 Vanderbilt Avenue, New York, NY 10017

Routledge is an imprint of the Taylor & Francis Group, an informa business

First issued in paperback 2020

British Library Cataloguing-in-Publication Data
A catalogue record for this book is available from the British Library

Library of Congress Cataloging-in-Publication Data
A catalog record for this book has been requested

ISBN: 978-1-138-55302-6 (hbk)
ISBN: 978-0-367-66091-8 (pbk)

Typeset in Times New Roman
by Apex CoVantage, LLC

Contents

Figures and tables

Figures

Tables

Preface

In prefaces, authors explain why they write a particular book. Among social scientists the reason is usually either addressing an important issue, or producing a text required for students and others to understand an important subject, or both. The books, however, are not supposed to relate to the authors personally, at least not explicitly – a social science monograph should not be confused with a biography or a memoir. The topic of this book is a bit different, however: besides its timeliness and the need for it, which I shall explain here and in the first two chapters, it will be difficult for a book on loneliness, or any other personal experience, to escape the suspicion that the author is writing it out of personal experience and interest.

Yes, that is true in the case of this book. I do not want to hide it. As far as I can recall, starting from my primary school years, loneliness has been a familiar experience to me, on and off with irregular frequencies, durations, and intensities, although I might not consciously use the word 'loneliness' to describe the feeling at a particular moment: loneliness because no other children went home together with me after school, loneliness when I found nobody at home after school, loneliness because I was the only one who could answer a difficult question in class, loneliness every time I changed school, loneliness when I could not find anybody to agree with me on something, loneliness every time I moved from one country to another, loneliness when my job applications or journal papers were turned down, and loneliness when I feel that no one else understands me . . . The list is long.

While loneliness is painful, I did not take loneliness as a serious problem until I read the academic literature about it. After studying sociology as my major subject, I have learnt from C. Wright Mills that although sociologists were encouraged to start their academic research by considering their personal experiences and feelings, they were obliged to study such experiences and feelings from the perspectives, and for the benefits, of the society as a whole. I started to realize that loneliness was not a personal and minor problem of my own when I learnt that many famous people, such as Princess Diana and Bertrand Russell, were very lonely, at least for some time. I also found that millions of people across the world were lonely; it is a common feeling among international students, mothers taking care of their babies, and older people, either living in private residences or nursing homes. My personal experiences did help me develop certain direct grasp of the issue, but this book goes beyond them in many ways and is written about, and for, every lonely human being and everyone who cares about them.

The prevalence of an issue may not be a sufficient justification for the production of a book about it. I still would not have a case for writing a book about loneliness if loneliness is not serious enough: what if it is only a transient and minor feeling without causing serious harms? As the first chapter demonstrates by summarizing the current research, loneliness could do seriously harm to our physical as well as mental health; but if not always, then when? What if loneliness could be even beneficial, as some have argued? It could even teach us something about ourselves and life in general, but how? If it is harmful, what are the causes and how could we prevent it? People of different social groups are vulnerable to different levels of risk to loneliness, so who are at a higher risk and why? These are important questions without well-established answers, at least not yet, which is another reason why a book such as this one is needed. So far most research on loneliness has been done by psychologists, psychiatrists, and researchers in medicine, health, and ageing. They are mostly interested in two questions: What does loneliness do to us? How to deal with it?

This book is about a connection logically prior to that: What makes people lonely in the first place? What kinds of people are most likely to experience it, and why? The premise of this book is that as loneliness is a mental reaction to unrealized, unsatisfying, or hostile social relations, it is inherently and essentially a social problem – hence the title of this book, and I write it to describe, illustrate, and explain why this is the case. This is not simply because I am a sociologist – I appreciate the work by researchers in the other fields, which advances our knowledge of the medical implications of loneliness, the risk factors for loneliness, and the effects of loneliness on people's quality of life. At the same time, I genuinely believe that loneliness is a serious social problem as well and therefore deserves serious attention from sociologists and other social scientists. My aim is to show how a sociological approach could help us expand our existing understanding of loneliness as an individual and psychological problem in regard to its meanings, sources, distributions, and remedies. The reader will not find grand or revolutionary theories of loneliness in this book; rather, I would be very happy if they could find the patterns revealed in my empirical investigations, my reflective criticisms, syntheses, and suggestions on specific issues useful for understanding, researching and tackling loneliness. It is my hope that together with the studies from psychology, medicine, public health, philosophy and religion, this book will help the reader develop well-rounded and deeper understanding of loneliness and effective strategies for tackling it.

With that aim in mind, I am writing this book firstly for fellow human beings who constantly feel lonely, and for those who care about them. I hope that this book will help them better understand and cope with their lonely experiences. Such understanding itself could alleviate the pain to a certain extent, and what researchers have discovered about loneliness could give them some ideas for improving their quality of life. Secondly, I write this book for a large readership that include students and academics interested in the social science studies of mental health in general and loneliness in particular, policy-makers and public health leaders, practitioners such as nurses, social workers, and counsellors, journalists and media staff members who report on mental health-related issues, and people in the general public who care about loneliness and want to do something to help the lonely. I have accordingly made the contents of this book as accessible as I could: jargon is either avoided or explained in plain English, statistical results are presented with (mostly) simple figures and tables, most key points are illustrated with stories and cases, and all technical details and academic references are presented as endnotes, while in the meantime, I hope, without diluting its academic rigor – the endnotes testify that the writing of this book draws on careful readings and analyses of a large amount of scientific research across several disciplines, for which I am extremely grateful.

I always admire those authors who have a long list of people they want to thank in the acknowledgements of their books, so long that sometimes they had to apologize if they missed anybody. My list is very short. Is this an indicator of my 'academic loneliness'? I simply cannot tell. Firstly, I would like to thank the lonely people who shared their personal experiences, whom I met in several different countries and on different occasions. It is their stories that motivated me to look into this issue seriously. I also would like to thank Christina Victor, who introduced the academic literature on loneliness among older people to me and collaborated with me on several papers. The idea of producing this book came to me when Pam Qualter and Kim Brownlee invited me to participate in a research retreat on loneliness with a few other scholars at University of Bath in the summer of 2016, and I am very grateful for their thoughtful feedback and encouragement. Finally, the production of a book usually means some unavoidable sacrifice that the author's family members must bear with. My wife Lixin, my daughter Marie, and my son Charles have already made enormous sacrifices for my research.

Chapter 1

Loneliness: is it a problem?

This book is about loneliness, and why it is a *social* problem, that is, why it is not merely an individual, psychological, or medical problem. Before answering those questions, we must be clear about what loneliness is, so that we know exactly what we mean when we use the word, and more importantly, we will not confuse it with other words. This remains necessary and useful particularly because loneliness is a word used in the daily language and it is an emotion that most people are familiar with – our 'natural' language is rich and vivid but not always accurate. Everyone with proper vision knows what the word 'sunlight' means, but not so many know how sunlight differs from other lights and what it does to our body. People who have felt lonely many times might not take their feelings seriously; if they see loneliness as a 'normal' part of their life, they would not pay much attention to the medical implications that loneliness has for their physical and mental health. But if we accept loneliness as a normal feature of life, there would be no need for scientific research on loneliness. Something that happens to us constantly and regularly should not mean that we should accept it as normal. The rapidly growing academic publications have demonstrated serious consequences that loneliness could bring to us, and I shall present a selection of key scientific findings as a way to show how it poses serious threats to our health. In addition, I shall also present some statistics about loneliness so that we can have a good idea of how serious the problem is in terms of its prevalence. All this evidence, however, may still be insufficient to a small number of people for treating loneliness as a problem. In fact, some religious scholars, philosophers, and psychiatrists see loneliness as an opportunity to grow spiritually because, as they argue, it urges us to examine our inner self and reveals our relationship with the external world and the divine entity. The meaning of such 'spiritual' or 'existential' loneliness is different from that used in daily life and in the scientific literature. Like many other concepts in life and social science research, loneliness has not one but multiple meanings.

What is loneliness?

It should be safe to assume that loneliness, like many other emotions such as joy or sadness, is universal among human beings. In other words, the percentage of people who have never felt lonely should be very low, although it is expected to vary greatly across different groups of people and from one time point to another. We shall learn more about these later in this chapter and the rest of the book. In this section, our aim is to explore and define the meaning and nature of loneliness: if it is so commonly experienced, then people should know what they mean when they say 'I am lonely' even though they may not be able to provide a clear definition. Here are some of the 'common elements' of the meaning of loneliness in daily languages: it is unpleasant to feel lonely, you are alone when you do not want to be, you cannot be with the person you love or want to be with anymore, you feel something separating yourself and others apart, or others around you do not accept you as one of them. The *Oxford English Dictionary* (hereafter OED) defines loneliness, when used for describing a human being rather than a place, as 'Want of society or company; the condition of being alone or solitary' and 'The feeling of being alone; the sense of solitude; dejection arising from want of companionship or society.' According to this definition, you are lonely when you are *socially alone*; it does not matter whether you are physically alone; you are lonely when you feel sad about not being part of companionship or society. When we are lonely, we are clearly aware that we are alone, but we do not like such aloneness because the society or company we want is missing; therefore, a sad emotion of dejection arises in us, which we call 'loneliness.' In academic circles, the most widely cited definition of loneliness was produced by Daniel Perlman and Letitia Anne Peplau in 1981: 'loneliness is the unpleasant experience that occurs when a person's network of social relations is deficient in some important way, either quantitatively or qualitatively'.[1] For convenience, we shall refer to this as the PP definition of loneliness.

There are two important, albeit subtle, differences between these two definitions (OED and PP). The first relates to the difference between aloneness and loneliness: by defining loneliness as 'the condition' or 'the feeling' of being alone, the OED definition runs the risk of confusing loneliness with aloneness. Researchers of loneliness have long urged people not to confuse loneliness with aloneness – the former is an emotion and therefore subjective, while the latter is a physical situation and therefore objective. More importantly, although it may have become common sense now, it is still worth pointing out that aloneness may or may not cause loneliness. People can be alone but not lonely, particularly when they choose to be alone. Conversely, people may feel lonely while they are not alone, such as being surrounded by a large crowd that they cannot relate to or feel close to. What remains not much common sense is the following question: if aloneness and loneliness do not have any certain corresponding relationship, when will aloneness lead to loneliness? Put differently, if aloneness by itself does not necessarily make people lonely, what other factors must there be so that the feeling of loneliness will arise? We shall examine these complex situations in the following chapters.

Furthermore, although aloneness and solitude have been used interchangeably in many situations, as in the OED definition, to be conceptually clear, in this book I shall define 'solitude' as chosen, voluntary, or preferred aloneness. But if solitude is the desirable state of aloneness while loneliness is the painful state, then what does it take to achieve solitude or transform loneliness to solitude? Throughout human history, a number of philosophers and religious scholars have reflected on this practically important question, and in the later chapters we shall learn their advice in connection with the recommendations that researchers of medicine and health have offered.

The second subtle difference between the two definitions is that while they share the same idea of tracing the source of loneliness to the absence of desired social relations (companions or communities), the PP definition covers a relatively broader set of situations (deficient social relations), which include not merely the absence of desired social relations but also the presence of undesired (deficient) ones. In this sense, besides describing what loneliness is, both the OED and the PP definitions are actually theories of loneliness as well; that is, they explain why loneliness occurs. However, the explanation is implicit, and it implies a key cognitive mechanism: deficient social relations do *not directly* lead to loneliness; *the perception and the interpretation* of such deficiency are the intermediary mechanisms that connect deficient social relations and loneliness. Therefore, this explanation is consisted of three steps in a logical sequence: certain social relations (objective state) → perception and evaluation of these social relations as being deficient or unsatisfactory (cognitive state) → loneliness as emotional reaction to the perceived deficiency of social relations (emotional state). In reality, few would pay much attention to these mental processes, let alone reflecting on them carefully, because these processes usually occur at a very high speed in people's minds. One reason that loneliness is a serious social problem is because these mental states and processes involve social relations and interpretations of social relations; obviously, social relations and their interpretations are social phenomena beyond individual control, even though it is down to the individual to interpret and evaluate their social relations. The reader will find further elaborations on this point in the next chapter.

Breaking the loneliness experience into the above three steps helps us to better understand why loneliness is both universal and specific. Loneliness is universal because social relations are everywhere and always changing in human life. Loneliness is specific because there are a large number of types of social relations, and the interpretations of social relations will change from one person to another and from one time point to the next. For loneliness as a negative emotion to arise, it requires both the objective existence of social relations and the subjective interpretations and evaluations. The large number of sources and representations of loneliness make it a complicated phenomenon to study despite the fact that most people have encountered it at some point in their life. As human life starts and ends with social relations, and as these social relations are bound to change, the probability of finding a desired social relation missing or being involved in an undesirable social relation must be very high, which is why loneliness is a universal emotion – parents cannot stay with their babies all the time, children leave their families for schools, young people start new jobs, adults marry and divorce, older people retire and die, people move from one place to another for a variety of reasons, new members join or leave a family, an organization, or an informal group, for a variety of reasons. As long as human beings live in social relations and social relations sooner or later terminate, there is no way to escape from loneliness.

While social relations keep coming and going, the minds of those involved are busy responding to these changes, consciously or otherwise. It is reasonable to expect at least some of them to become lonely because, as Cacioppo and Patrick claimed, 'Our brains and bodies are designed to function in aggregates, not in isolation. That is the essence of an obligatorily gregarious species.'[2] It is thus safe to assume that human evolution has programmed our minds so that they would react negatively when we perceive social relations that we value missing or disappearing. The study of loneliness therefore leads us to some fundamental issues about human nature and social life in general: What do we mean when we say human beings are 'social animals'? How do social relations affect who we are? How do social relations change across time points, places, groups and societies? Are members of a society all obliged to help those who feel lonely? These are difficult sociological and philosophical questions.

The case for loneliness as a problem

By definition, loneliness must be a problem – it is an unpleasant emotion, and it usually comes with other unpleasant emotions, such as sadness, emptiness, desperation, grief, anxiety, hopelessness, and depression. It is thus difficult to imagine that the emotional reaction to the perceived lack of desirable social relations could be positive, although we shall see in the next section some people do think so. In this section we focus on the reasons why loneliness *is* a problem, that is, an undesirable experience.

So the first reason for loneliness as a problem is obvious: by itself it is a painful psychological experience. Few have expressed the pain of loneliness more powerfully than Bertrand Russell in 'To Edith' (his fourth wife, Edith Finch), the opening poem of his *Autobiography*:[3]

> Through the long years
>   I sought peace,
> I found ecstasy, I found anguish,
>   I found madness,
> I found loneliness,
> I found the solitary pain
>   that gnaws the heart,
> But peace I did not find.

Now, old & near my end,
  I have known you,
And, knowing you,
I have found both ecstasy & peace,
  I know rest,
After so many lonely years,
I know what life & love may be.
Now, if I sleep,
I shall sleep fulfilled.

Not only he suffered from loneliness, but also in his eyes the whole world is full of 'loneliness, poverty, and pain' which 'make a mockery of what human life should be'.[4] What loneliness does to the mind is what hunger and cancer do to the body. The most effective, if not the only, antidote to loneliness, as many have believed, is love. But as Russell lamented, love is so rare and elusive, which is why love is so precious and loneliness so persistent. If love is the most powerful antidote to loneliness, the elusiveness, the rarity, and the temporality of love are the sources of loneliness.

A less obvious reason for loneliness as a problem is that it is much more than a psychological pain – as demonstrated below, loneliness could lead to a variety of harms to our mind and body. The causal chain between loneliness and these harms remains long and uncertain, however, which is why these harms usually escape ordinary people's attention. Although the effects of loneliness, isolation, or deprivation of intimate social relations on physical as well as mental health did not escape the attention of medical scholars, it was mostly since the end of the Second World War that medical researchers could have the peace and the resources for studying such effects rigorously. To make a case as strong as he could, Dr James Lynch compiled a large amount of evidence for 'The Medical Consequences of Loneliness' in two volumes, published in 1977 and 2000, respectively.[5] In Russell's poem, he was simply employing a metaphor when he was describing how 'the solitary pain' of loneliness gnawed his heart. According to Lynch, it was much more serious than that: loneliness 'can break the human heart', literally, because 'there is a biological basis for our need to form loving human relationships'.[6]

For the sake of clarity, I must point out that Dr Lynch used the word 'loneliness' in a rather relaxed manner. He did not draw on any direct and reliable measures of loneliness; rather, he used other indicators that he believed to be associated with loneliness, such as divorce, loss of loved ones, rejection, and so on, assuming that these experiences necessarily bring about loneliness. As I shall show in a subsequent section, carefully designed and rigorously tested measures of loneliness were not produced until the end of the 1970s, so it is understandable that Lynch did not make use of these scales in his first book, which is published in 1977. It is however puzzling that he did not use these scales and some of the large-scale sample surveys that included questions on loneliness in his second book, which was published in 2000. The use of proxy rather than direct measures of loneliness is not simply a technical issue because, while it is clearly sensible to expect those with the above stressful experiences to be lonely, it is an assumption to be tested and the relationship between these experiences and loneliness should be discussed in probabilistic rather than deterministic terms. Despite these conceptual and methodological issues, Dr Lynch observed an extremely important connection in many medical studies and his own practice: involuntary (or forced) severance of social relations, to which loneliness is expected to be a natural emotional reaction, is strongly related to many illnesses.

In more recent studies, other medical researchers tend to agree with him. For example, some have warned that loneliness is as bad as high blood pressure, lack of exercise, obesity, or smoking.[7] The negative effects of loneliness on health cannot be made more alarming than what John Cacioppo, a Chicago-based cognitive neurologist, has concluded:

> Our research in the past decade or so demonstrates that the culprit behind these dire statistics is not usually being literally alone, but the subjective *experience* known as loneliness. Whether you are at home with your family, working in an office crowded with bright and attractive young people, touring Disneyland, or sitting alone in a fleabag hotel on a wrong side of town, chronic *feelings* of isolation can drive a cascade of physiological events that actually accelerates the ageing process. Loneliness not only alters behaviour but shows up in measurements of stress hormones, immune function, and cardiovascular function. Over time, these changes in physiology are compounded in ways that may be hastening millions of people to an early grave.[8]

It would be neither possible nor necessary to enlist all major medical studies on this issue in this section. Instead, I shall present a summarizing but incomplete list of the medical evidence for the effects of loneliness on a number of serious physical and mental illnesses, which is meant to be illustrative rather than comprehensive:

- *Cancer*: Lynch cited the Alameda County Studies conducted by Dr Lisa Berkman and her colleagues in 1979, which found that 'In both sexes, the absence of close personal ties and the lack of perceived sources of emotional support were associated with a significantly increased risk of cancer. In women, this appeared especially true for the increased risk of developing breast cancer.'[9] This was later confirmed by subsequent studies on the population of Alameda.[10] On the other hand, many studies have shown that even if loneliness is not the culprit of cancer, the experiences of going through the treatments and fighting against the pain could make the patient lonely.[11] If so, then loneliness and the experience of suffering from cancer could evolve into a vicious cycle.
- *Heart disease*: Lynch showed evidence collected from studies conducted in the US, Sweden, and the UK, which suggest the following connections: the risk of suffering coronary heart disease in the US (1959–1961) is universally

higher among the single, the divorced, and the widowed, with gender and age being controlled.[12] That is, for people of the same gender and the same age, the risk of having heart attack is particularly high for the young (25–34) widowed (5.17 times more likely for females and 4.24 for males in comparison with the older and married groups), followed by the female singles (3.17) and the divorced (two to three times higher than the married). In contrast, those with emotional and social support enjoy a significantly higher chance of surviving heart diseases than those without such support. Another study reported that of the studied male heart attack survivors, the mortality rate among those of high social isolation scores was 14%, in contrast to 7% among those of low social isolation scores.[13] More generally, loneliness has been found a unique predictor of high blood pressure.[14]

- *Depression*: First of all, it needs to be made clear that there are at least two broad types of depression: clinical depression, by definition, means that it must be diagnosed carefully with specially designed instruments and treated by professional psychiatrists, while non-clinical depression refers to a much less but more commonly experienced emotion, as represented in daily languages such as 'being blue', 'feeling down', etc., although such distinction is not always followed in either media or academic reports. Loneliness is usually accompanied with a series of other negative emotions, including non-clinical depression. As Lynch pointed out, 'Depression is almost always accompanied by a tendency to withdraw from others, to reduce engagement with others, difficulties communicating, and with increased feelings of loneliness and abandonment', a connection found by other researchers as well.[15] In a more rigorously designed study employing well-tested measures and a longitudinal quota sample in Chicago, Cacioppo and his colleagues have found that 'The lonelier that people were at the beginning, the more depressive affect [non-clinical depression] they experienced in the following years', and depression also predicted loneliness longitudinally.[16] Thus, loneliness and depression seem to mutually reinforce each other over time.

- *Alcohol and drug abuse*: People in loneliness and other forms of mental suffering (depression, anxiety, etc.) tend to resort to alcoholic drinks and drugs (often illegal drugs).[17] Ironically, while the hope is to create a more enjoyable feeling to replace loneliness or other sufferings, the use of alcohol and drug only brings them deeper into the trap.

- *Bulimia nervosa*: People with bulimia nervosa, an eating disorder and mental condition, attempt to control their body weight but cannot control themselves for binge eating, so they will try to purge the food out from the body. Studies in the academic literature suggest that young adults and adolescents, particularly females, constitute the majority of patients. In a few small scale surveys, individuals with bulimia nervosa were found significantly lonelier and socially isolated.[18] The UK's NHS also confirms that bulimia nervosa is associated with low self-esteem, alcohol abuse, depression, and self-harm.

- *Dementia and Alzheimer's disease*: Like the relationship between loneliness and other health problems, loneliness and Alzheimer's disease (or other forms of dementia) could mutually reinforce each other, making it difficult to tell which causes the other. Researchers do find, however, that the lonely older persons were 1.6 to 2.6 times more likely to develop dementia than those who were not lonely.[19] In a longitudinal study on older people in Chicago, researchers found that the risk of having Alzheimer's disease was more than doubled in lonely persons compared with persons who were not lonely.[20]

- *Suicide*: As defined above, loneliness is an emotional reaction to perceived social isolation, so how the lonely person interprets the meaning of the experienced social isolation has implications for how the person reacts to it. If the loneliness is perceived as being forced and irrevocable upon the sufferer, then for the sufferer the purpose and the meaning of living in such social group or community or nation are lost. Such loss of purpose or meaning, once believed to be irreversible, will lead to suicide.[21] Sometimes loneliness leads to suicidal ideation through the use of drug.[22]

- *'Voodoo death'*: Walter Cannon published a paper with this term as its title in 1942 to describe the kind of sudden death caused by an emotional shock.[23] The specific case he studied was extreme fear among some aboriginal natives of natural phenomena. Later, the causes of voodoo death were extended to other situations and cultures, including extreme social isolations in modern societies. For example, by analysing the connection between people's birthdays and deathdays statistically, David Phillips found that people were more likely to die *after*, not before, a birthday or other significant anniversary.[24] James Lynch also observed that some isolated patients became fatally ill for no clearly identified reasons.

We could learn a few lessons from this collection of evidence. We should take loneliness seriously not only because it is a painful feeling but more importantly because it is responsible for a variety of physical as well as mental illnesses, although the direction of the causal relationship is not always clear and medical researchers are still in the process of discovering exactly how this happens. As some of these health problems are interconnected with each other, it could be difficult to specify the connection between loneliness and any particular illness. As I will argue in Chapter 9, a major challenge to researchers who work on the implications of loneliness for public health is to establish an accurate connection between a feature of loneliness (frequency, intensity, duration) and a particular illness. As a sociologist, I leave this task to medical researchers and concentrate on the social origins of loneliness in the rest of the book.

The controversy over loneliness as a problem

Despite suffering from the agony of loneliness for so many years, Russell lived for nearly one hundred years; even in his later years he was very active and productive. Other than the painful feeling, loneliness did not seem to have done any harm to the health of his mind or body, at least not in medical terms. He died of influenza, not heart attack, cancer, or any other major illnesses. For him, loneliness by itself is a problem because it is a psychological pain, a form of emotional suffering. His case suggests that loneliness does not necessarily cause major illnesses; in other words, it could be a psychological or emotional problem without medical implications.

For medical professionals, however, the reverse might be true: the psychological agony alone may not be a problem – no doctor would take patients who simply claim that they are lonely, although in the UK one in five older people were reported to see their GPs (doctors) in order to ease their loneliness by talking to the doctor rather than to seek treatment of any illness.[25] Even John Cacioppo, who has been conducting medical research on, and educating the general public about, the medical consequences of loneliness, wants to tune down the seriousness of loneliness as a psychological problem with a soothing message: 'loneliness itself is not a disease; feeling lonely from time to time is like feeling hungry or thirsty from time to time'[26] – we could imagine how strongly Russell and other sufferers of loneliness would disagree with such understatement, and 'Loneliness becomes an issue of concern *only when it settles in long enough to create a persistent, self-reinforcing loop* of negative thoughts, sensations, and behaviours' (emphasis added).[27] So for medical professionals, only a chronic and serious type of loneliness is a problem. However, to determine when loneliness becomes a medical hazard and how to distinguish it from other mental illnesses, such as clinical depression and anxiety, that psychiatrists will take seriously, remains an issue to be settled.

For at least two reasons, we cannot, and should not, dismiss loneliness as a serious problem. First, loneliness does not have to cause serious physical and mental diseases for it to be taken as a serious problem. The psychological pain itself makes loneliness deserve to be seen as a serious problem; that is, loneliness would still remain a problem had loneliness not induced the medical problems listed above, only that it may not be a problem for medical professionals; it is a problem for researchers in other academic disciplines, including psychology, sociology, public health, gerontology, education, philosophy, religious studies, etc. Loneliness could be a problem in multiple ways, each of which could make it a problem; it would become a more serious problem if it is identified as a problem in two or more aspects.

Second, the connection between loneliness and those medical problems must be understood as probabilistic rather than deterministic, meaning that not all lonely people will necessarily suffer from those medical illnesses, although the probability that they do is higher than those who are not lonely. Today's sciences still have a long way to go to pin down the exact conditions under which lonely people will *necessarily* develop a certain disease in their body or mind, but this probabilistic connection is sufficient for taking loneliness seriously. As Cacioppo and Patrick admitted:

> Looking at the question in a multivariate, multilevel way, we do not find a single, simple answer to the question of how loneliness causes ill health.

Instead, the most accurate assessment is to say that it is a grinding process of wear and tear that proceeds along five intersecting pathways. It so happens that these five pathways sum up much of the physiological data we have explored so far'.[28]

Here are the five pathways:

1   *Health behaviours*: put simply, the lonely are less likely to lead a healthy lifestyle but more likely to pick up habits that are destructive to their health.
2   *Exposure to stressors and life events*: the lonely are more vulnerable to stressors and more easily trapped in them.
3   *Perceived stress and coping*: the lonely perceive stressful events more severely and tend to look at the dark rather than the bright side.
4   *Physiological response to stress*: loneliness alters cells, genes, DNAs and damages the cardiovascular system.
5   *Rest and recuperation*: the lonely suffer from low quality of sleep and thus more easily experience fatigue during the day.

In other words, the causal chain from loneliness to a particular serious illness listed in the previous section is a rather long, complicated, and uncertain one. More importantly, changes to any one of the above five mechanisms, such as perceiving stressful events positively or taking actions to make oneself relaxed, could disrupt the connection and therefore make loneliness not so damaging. The uncertainty of the connection between loneliness and medical illnesses makes it more difficult to argue for a strong case for loneliness as a serious medical problem, but it should not lead us to believe that loneliness might not be the source of many illnesses and therefore that loneliness is not a problem.

For a categorically different reason, it may be very difficult to convince some people that loneliness is a serious problem. Perhaps the strongest case against loneliness as a problem comes from a certain albeit small number of philosophers, psychiatrists and religious scholars, who argue that researchers should not have treated loneliness as a problem in the first place. Let's try to understand their points of view.

The first important message that I have learnt from these scholars' writings is that loneliness in itself is not necessarily an undesirable experience; most of the times it is neutral, because it is simply a human experience, an attribute of humanity, a natural phenomenon of life. For example, while reflecting on his life of celibacy, Keith Clark, a Capuchin, realized that 'in and of itself, loneliness is simply one of life's moments'.[29] He sees loneliness in between intimacy and hostility, which are respectively positive and negative. As an emotional reaction, loneliness arises in our mind at the moments when our social relations naturally change, and Clark listed several of such moments: a young man returning to his empty house after the celebration of the birth of his daughter, a speaker returning to his hotel room after a long day of speaking and social activities, etc. These events are neutral as no one intends to hurt our feelings; therefore, although we naturally feel lonely while experiencing these events, there is no need to judge them, and the wisest thing to do is recognize it, accept it, and even welcome it. Clearly, the events Clark listed are mostly innocuous. But even for Cacioppo and Patrick, whose book *Loneliness* is full of examples and research results of the terrible things that loneliness can bring to our body, treated loneliness as a normal function of the human body in the end: 'Just as thirst is the prompt that reminds us to keep the body hydrated, loneliness is the prompt that reminds us how much we depend on one another.'[30] Loneliness is hardly more than an amber signal, a warning that something might be wrong with our social relations.

Nevertheless, I find it difficult to accept that loneliness should not be taken seriously as a problem simply because our life is inevitably and frequently full of lonely moments. Rarity should not be a criterion for defining a problem. Thirst does not cease to be a problem simply because we regularly feel thirsty. Moreover, an unpleasant experience remains a problem even though it motivates us to take actions to tackle it. Our awareness of being thirsty sends an ominous signal to our brain: the lack of water is threatening the health of our body! Over time, such a clear message evolves into an intuitive, even spontaneous, reaction, and there is no need to consciously remind ourselves with such clearly formulated messages. That loneliness is a trigger or a reminder of the forthcoming undesirable outcomes does not necessarily make it less painful or harmful. I believe this is why loneliness is almost always accompanied by some other negative emotions. In fact, Keith Clark pointed out that loneliness could be 'aggravated by fear, guilt, anxiety, depression, alienation, self-doubt or hostility', if it entered our life 'not in a healthy way'.[31] It is true that most human beings have to constantly deal with these negative emotions on a daily basis, but that should not mean that these emotions are not harmful, normal, and therefore there is no need to take actions to tackle them.

At a more abstract level, the idea that loneliness is an inherent feature of human existence is sometimes referred to as 'existential loneliness'. I cannot be certain that Clark Moustakas was the first who created this notion, but he made it very clear in the Preface of his book *Loneliness*:

> Loneliness is a condition of human life, an experience of being human which enables the individual to sustain, extend, and deepen his humanity. Man is ultimately and forever lonely . . . ultimately, in every fibre of his being, man is alone – terribly, utterly alone. Efforts to overcome or escape the existential experience of loneliness can result only in self-alienation.[32]

Several ideas are implied in such notion of 'existential loneliness'. To start with, it argues that the biological separation of one individual human being apart from another, as distinctive entities, is the origin of all forms of loneliness. Each human being has his or her own body and mind, which is not transferrable to another. While humans can and do share all sorts of experiences and emotions, either joy or sorrow, it is impossible for one person to experience the exactly same feeling as what another is experiencing. Loneliness due to such impossibility is existential because it makes people realize that sharing and understanding soon reaches a limit despite the fact that they all belong to the same species. With the invention of language, human beings are the most able of communicating mental states and contents to each other, but they soon realize that to express some of their feelings and experiences is beyond language or any tools of communication. No matter how painful or joyful your feeling is, it is *yours* and not others, at least not completely. Such inaccessibility of one person's feelings to another makes people feel lonely in the existential sense. It is most strongly felt when one approaches the end of life, thinking 'I am going to leave this world alone, and those around me are not.'[33] Perhaps this was why Qin Shi Huang, literally meaning the very first Emperor of China's first unified dynasty Qin, and some other emperors or kings wanted some people to go to the tomb with them: to leave this world alone is such a lonely experience!

The existential understanding of loneliness does not deny that loneliness could induce other negative feelings, including sadness, sorrow, frustration, depression, being forgotten or abandoned, etc.; or at least, loneliness comes with any of these feelings. What differentiates such understanding from the previously introduced medical and psychological notion of loneliness is whether these negative feelings should be taken seriously. For the existentialists, these feelings, although unpleasant, would bring a much worthwhile benefit to us: they remind us who we are, how dependent we are on other human beings, and what we should do in order to grow stronger mentally or even spiritually. 'I feel that', as the Jung psychiatrist Gilda Frantz claimed, 'loneliness is valuable and essential for human development'; for a child who feels lonely because of having nothing to do, 'he is on the verge of stepping over a threshold, growing up, changing'.[34] Carl Jung once interpreted chaos 'pregnant', a productive albeit painful process, so 'loneliness becomes a part of the birth process, part of the process of individuation that will bring forth new life'.[35] Similarly, Moustakas seized the opportunity offered by his loneliness to develop deeper appreciation of human bonds, life and nature: 'man's inevitable and infinite loneliness is not solely an awful condition of human existence but that it is also the instrument through which man experiences new compassion and new beauty.'[36] While they might not deny the unpleasant feelings arising from the awareness of being alone (i.e. loneliness), the philosophical or spiritual benefits from realizing this aspect of human existence have overwhelmed the painful feeling.

Some readers may have already found these points for or against the case that we should take loneliness as a problem confusing; it is therefore necessary and useful to clear them up. First of all, there should be no doubt that we must take chronic and intense loneliness as a serious problem as it leads to serious medical conditions; such loneliness is a problem by itself and a problem as the origin of other more serious problems. People's views start to diverge when they refer to transient, occasional, and mild loneliness in daily life. In itself, such loneliness is still painful; that is, it is still a problem, only that it is less severe. For two reasons most people do not tend to take such loneliness seriously: most people are expected to have the resilience and capacity to overcome the short-lived or mild loneliness, and the benefits brought about by such loneliness – the awareness of our relations and our existence in the universe – outweigh the pain.

What we must keep in mind, however, is the risk that the transient and mild loneliness could develop into the chronic and serious loneliness. Some actions must be taken to stop the bearable forms of loneliness from developing into what we may call 'clinical (or medical) loneliness' as well as to deal with the serious forms of loneliness with all sorts of therapies. In the fortunate situation when loneliness stays mild and bearable, people need to learn to develop an awareness of its existence, reflecting and meditating on such experience in attempt to turn the initially painful experience into a spiritually and mentally beneficial one. We shall discuss and develop these ideas further in Chapter 9.

How do we know how lonely someone is?

After identifying loneliness as a problem by discussing its impacts on people's physical and mental health, we could advance our understanding of how serious loneliness is as a problem by discovering how prevalent it is in different societies and population groups. However, to gauge its scale presumes a sensible measurement of loneliness, so we firstly need to know how loneliness is measured. This is more important than a technical issue of measuring, because our statements about loneliness rely on what kind (or which aspect) of loneliness is measured and how it is measured. For example, if loneliness triggers serious medical illnesses only when it becomes 'chronic', as Cacioppo suggested above, then how could we know someone is suffering from 'chronic loneliness' rather than a relatively temporary form of it?

To measure loneliness accurately, poems and verbal narratives of lonely experiences such as those cited previously, although rich and vivid, will not help anymore, because they are very different from one another in terms of the chosen words, the length of narrative, and other language features. As Cacioppo and Patrick admitted, there is consistency in people's sense of loneliness, but 'the consistency is situational and temporal' as 'the situation that causes you to feel most acutely lonely in childhood or adolescence will most likely be different from the situation that induces acute loneliness when you are a young parent or an older adult'.[37] However, the diverse situations that may trigger people's sense of loneliness obviously make it impossible, perhaps unnecessary either, for researchers to cover all or even most of them. In order to measure the prevalence of loneliness, we need something that is applicable to all of the subjects that we want to study, that is, a standard form of measuring loneliness is needed so that the results are comparable across a large number of people. By now the reader may have realized the tension between 'the universal' and 'the individual', an issue that social science methodologists have been struggling with for decades without being able to reach any consensus. In the practice of social science research, the principle that all researchers should follow is to report clearly how a particular concept is measured and be aware of its limitations. While recognizing the idiosyncrasy of individual experiences and cultural interpretations, we must accept that it is largely meaningful and sensible to measure an experience such as loneliness with an instrument (a survey question or a scale composed of multiple questions); otherwise, most of quantitative social science research is impossible.

Intuitively, perhaps the most 'natural' way to find out how lonely people are is to ask them directly. Such direct measure of loneliness that requests people to report how lonely they are is one of the most commonly used in academic studies on loneliness. For example, in the European Social Survey (ESS) – we shall present some of its results in the next section – the respondents were asked: 'please tell me how much of the time during the past week you felt lonely?', and they were expected to choose one from the following four options: 'none or almost none of the time', 'some of the time', 'most of the time', or 'all or almost all of the time'.[38]

There are several issues with such seemingly simple question, however. The first is that clearly the question is about the frequency rather than the intensity or severity of loneliness. The frequency of loneliness is doubtlessly very important, but the intensity, or *how lonely* people were when they were lonely, is no less important. Perhaps the researchers who formulated this question believed that the frequency and the severity of loneliness are interchangeable, an assumption I do not find sensible: it may well be that some people became lonely for a large number of times but each time the feeling was not very intense (very much bearable); or conversely, some people became lonely only once during the past week but it was very severe (hardly bearable). Therefore, it is not really appropriate to equate frequency with intensity of loneliness or any emotion in general.

Next, to aid the respondent answer the question, the ESS specifies a time frame of the respondent's loneliness experience as 'the past week'. Obviously, there is no 'perfect' time frame, and survey researchers usually do not have the luxury of asking as many questions as they like. One option is 'the past month', which however might be too long as people's memory of their feelings in such time period will become unreliable. On the other hand, 'one day' might be too short in order for us to see any temporal regularity. So it seems a reasonable compromise to set the time frame as 'the past week'.

There is an issue with the options in such time frame, however. Different survey researchers have adopted different classifications of time – some used five categories while others use four, some put 'often' and 'always' in the same category while others treated them as distinct. More importantly, respondents may have different understandings of the qualifiers 'some', 'most', and 'almost'. (The meanings of 'none' and 'all' should be sufficiently clear.) One may choose 'most' if he or she was lonely for three times or only once but it lasted for three days, while another person may choose 'often' to describe exactly the same experience. Without asking exactly how many times the respondents felt lonely and how long each episode lasted, the designers of the question seem to be prepared to accept a certain level of inconsistency in exchange for relatively comparable responses.

There is an even more fundamental issue with the question. It assumes that how loneliness comes about does not matter very much as the feeling must be the same. As we learnt in the previous sections, whether and how people feel lonely depends on the objective situation of their social relations and their subjective interpretations of these relations. Is the loneliness of a teenager who was rejected by his or her friends the same feeling as the loneliness of an old lady who cannot find someone to spend a long day together? Probably not. Designers of survey questionnaires would wish, I am certain, to take these differences into account for the purpose of measuring the diverse experiences of loneliness. But how many questions can they include in an already quite long questionnaire? It is a great challenge for social scientists to strike a subtle balance between achieving covering idiosyncratic and nomothetic attributes, and between academic and practical demands. By pointing out these limitations of the single question, I do not mean to suggest that we give up on such endeavour of measuring loneliness in this way; to the opposite, many quantitative analyses conducted in this book have relied on this instrument. I do hope, however, that the readers, particularly those not familiar with social science methodologies, appreciate the issues and challenges in such investigations. I would propose one scheme of classification of loneliness in the next chapter as a way of improving the quality of the measurement of loneliness.

Some researchers, particularly psychologists, are not contented with the single measure and prefer to use a battery of questions, which are usually referred to as 'loneliness scales'. In my view, although they could tap into multiple aspects or meanings of the lonely experience, they are not able to resolve the issues mentioned above. The most widely used is the scale developed by Daniel Russell and his colleagues at University of California at Los Angeles; hence 'the UCLA loneliness scale', which asks survey respondents about how strongly they agree with each of the twenty listed statements.[39] Another is produced by Jenny de Jong Gierveld and her associates, referred to as 'de Jong Gierveld loneliness scale', which contains 38 items.[40] Both scales were created at the end of 1970s, and both teams have revised their scales and developed shorter versions later so that the scale could be included in questionnaires that already contain many questions on other issues.

It is claimed that such scales have two major advantages over a single item measure such as the one used in the ESS. The first major advantage of multi-item scales is that none of the statements in any scale contains the word 'lonely' or 'loneliness'; rather, loneliness is measured indirectly with the words that are thought to represent the feeling of loneliness, such as 'left out', 'no one to talk to', 'no companion', etc. It is advantageous to do so because respondents may not want to directly refer to their lonely experiences in front of a stranger (the survey interviewer), no matter how legitimate the stranger's status and the study might be, due to the concern of the stigma that there must be something wrong with the lonely. The question is: how do we know that the respondents mean 'lonely' when they are not using the word? Good scale developers would take care of this by carrying out investigations to discover that the results from the scale are strongly correlated with those of the single item measure, although such investigations are usually conducted in small scale pilot surveys or experiments. The other advantage of using multiple items in a scale rather than a single question is that these items could tap into different aspects and forms of loneliness, so multiple questions are needed in order to cover these aspects or forms of loneliness. Clearly, this requires that the researchers have already developed certain sub-types of loneliness before the survey is conducted.

Finally, an important difference between the above two scales deserves our attention. The UCLA loneliness scale assumes that all of the statements measure a single entity (i.e. loneliness in this case). In contrast, de Jong Gierveld believed that the different ways of expressing the sense of loneliness actually suggest different components or types of loneliness. More specifically, the de Jong Gierveld scale was designed to discover whether the respondent was suffering from 'emotional' or 'social' loneliness, a distinction initially made by the sociologist Robert Weiss.[41] While we shall go into the details of these conceptual differences in the next chapter, suffice it here to explain that the difference lies in the nature of the missing relationship: emotional loneliness comes from the lack of at least one intimate personal relationship, such as the relationship between a child and the mother, while social loneliness refers to not belonging to a wider social network or community, for example, an immigrant finds it very difficult to fit into the hosting country's culture. Clearly, underlying each way of measuring loneliness, or any concept more generally, is a certain conceptual or theoretical choice.

Does it matter which measure is used when studying loneliness? The answer, unfortunately, is not a simple one: some researchers argue that it does, others not; sometimes, the results from two different types of measures are indistinguishable, but in other times they are, depending on the context and contents of the study. I do not think we need to concern ourselves with them here. The rule of thumb is that we must report how loneliness was measured in a particular study. All analyses conducted and presented in the remaining chapters of this book use the single-item measurement of loneliness, and the reader can find further details for each analysis.

How prevalent is loneliness?

One way to gauge the seriousness of the loneliness problem is to measure how prevalent it is. If the following statements are true, then loneliness is inevitable as a part of life and so should be highly prevalent everywhere human beings live: (1) human beings develop strong attachments to certain social relations as these relations have become the source of their welfare over time; (2) for a variety of reasons, social relations are bound to dissolve sooner or later; (3) an unpleasant emotion will emerge in human brains as reactions to the perceived disappearance or severance of social relations. If we look around, loneliness does seem quite common: celebrities such as Princess Diana, writers such as George Orwell, philosophers such as the aforementioned Bertrand Russell, psychiatrists such as Sigmund Freud, musicians such as Tchaikovsky, Rachmaninov, Sibelius, and Wagner, and many others have all openly reported lonely experience in their own lives. Loneliness is also a key theme of a long list of literary works over time, with the following being among the best known: Daniel Defoe's *Robinson Crusoe*, Mary Shelley's *Frankenstein*, Thomas Hardy's *The Return of the Native*, Charlotte Brontë's *Jane Eyre* and *Villette*, Herman Melville's *Moby Dick*, Fyodor Dostoyevsky's *Notes from the Underground*, Gabriel García Márquez's *One Hundred Years of Solitude*, Franz Kafka's 'Metamorphosis', John Cheever's *The Journals*, Samuel Beckett's *Happy Days*, George Orwell's *1984*, and many others. The long list of literary and biographical works with loneliness as their key theme is in great contrast with the shortage of social science studies on loneliness. These literary works offer rich descriptions of diverse lonely experiences in a variety of settings. However, they remain fictional rather than truthful representations of people's feelings and social realities. It is high time for us as social scientists to add our contributions to the understandings and explanations for loneliness to the existing knowledge and insights produced by psychologists and health researchers.

In recent years, loneliness has become newsworthy for mass media agents as well. While helping academics increase the impact of their research, these media reports tend to ring a loud alarm. In reality, however, exactly how prevalent is loneliness? To answer this question requires well-designed and expensive research. In fact, not many reliable answers could be found, particularly for areas beyond the economically developed countries, indicating that we are still in the early days of dealing with loneliness scientifically for most parts of the world. Here, I shall present some simple but trustworthy statistics in order to give the reader an initial idea of the prevalence of loneliness among the adult population. Among empirical studies on loneliness, most target older people (aged fifty or above). In contrast, data for measuring the prevalence of loneliness among children and adolescents have rarely been collected. Chapter 3 will focus on loneliness at different age groups, and Chapters 4–8 on other social groups.

For the case of the USA, according to Cacioppo, 'The percentage of Americans who responded that they regularly or frequently felt lonely was between 11% and 20% in the 1970s and 1980s.'[42] Then in his book he cited two academic reports published in 1982 and 2006, respectively: 'at any given time, roughly twenty percent of individuals – that would be sixty million people in the U.S. alone – feel sufficiently isolated for it to be a major source of unhappiness in their lives.'[43] These figures, however, are unable to tell us whether the prevalence of 'frequent or chronic loneliness' has increased over the years in the US. Cacioppo's words seem to suggest that it remained at about 20% during the twenty-five years from 1982 to 2006. He then used the more recent figures collected in two studies on older adults, i.e., not all adults, in the 2010s by the American Association of Retired Persons (AARP) and University of California – San Francisco, respectively, which found the rate of frequent loneliness between 40% to 45%. These figures are much higher than those reported for most European countries.

Well-designed probability sample surveys are usually seen as the most reliable source of data for estimating the prevalence of any mental or behavioural states. Disappointingly, the well-established General Social Survey (GSS) in the US does not contain any question that directly measures the respondents' sense of loneliness. GSS is a repeated cross-sectional survey starting from 1972; that is, it draws a different sample for each survey although the researchers have tried to retain as many questions as they could. Instead, other questions believed to be able to represent loneliness, or proxy questions, have been used. Analysing the data collected in the GSS over the two decades from 1985 to 2004, three sociologists discovered that the number of people with no one to discuss important matters nearly tripled and the mean number of confidants decreased from 2.94 in 1985 to 2.08 in 2004.[44] This paper has attracted a lot of attention from media agents, who took the results presented in this paper as the evidence for increasing loneliness in the USA.[45] Note that such claims assume a necessary connection between the number of confidants and loneliness. While it is sensible to expect the former to be an important risk factor for the latter, it is somewhat presumptuous to treat them as cause and effect or even the same thing. There is still a shortage of reliable estimates of the prevalence of frequent loneliness in the US.

For the UK, the Mental Health Foundation conducted a survey on 2256 people in 2010. Only 22% of the respondents never felt lonely and a bit more than one in ten (11%) felt often lonely. Nearly half (48%) of those surveyed believed that people in the UK were getting lonelier and more than one third (37%) knew a close friend or family member who was very lonely.[46] Fortunately, for the UK and most other European countries, we now have access to the data collected in one of the best social surveys in the world, the European Social Survey (ESS). In Table 1.1 I present the statistics of the prevalence of loneliness by using the data from the most recent round of ESS (2014).[47]

We can make several interesting observations while reading this table. Perhaps the first and most remarkable result is the percentage of people who never or almost never felt lonely in the past week at the time of the survey – even for Lithuania, more than half of the people were never or almost never lonely. This is clearly at odds with the previous statement that loneliness must be a universal experience. It is next to impossible to find out, however, whether loneliness is not as universal as previously believed, or whether the respondents of ESS underreported the frequencies of their lonely experience, but we shall come back to this issue later in this book.

On the other hand, if we define 'chronic or frequent loneliness' in this particular context as feeling lonely 'most of the times' or even more frequently, then the penultimate column shows that Czech Republic, Hungary, Poland, and Portugal have the highest rates at about 11%. Recall that this is the same as the lowest end of the figures in the US in the 1970s and the 1980s, reported by Cacioppo above. Not surprisingly, northern European countries tend to enjoy the lowest prevalence

Table 1.1 Prevalence of loneliness in countries participating in ESS round 7, 2014.

Country	How often felt lonely last week				Frequently lonely (Most and all the time)	Sample size (n)
	None or almost none of the time	Some of the time	Most of the time	All or almost all the time		
Austria	73.42	20.59	4.20	1.79	5.99	1787
Belgium	74.04	19.57	3.85	2.55	6.39	1768
Switzerland	79.03	17.37	2.55	1.05	3.59	1531
Czech Republic	59.76	29.65	7.11	3.48	10.59	2125
Germany	79.92	16.75	2.44	0.89	3.32	3038
Denmark	83.03	13.89	1.74	1.34	3.07	1497
Estonia	65.91	26.24	5.74	2.11	7.85	2039
Spain	69.45	21.84	5.91	2.80	8.71	1928
Finland	81.18	15.79	1.49	1.54	3.02	2083
France	68.34	23.32	5.22	3.13	8.35	1917
UK	74.99	19.90	2.93	2.18	5.11	2251
Hungary	62.68	26.12	7.78	3.42	11.20	1696
Ireland	71.22	23.98	3.11	1.68	4.80	2377
Israel	71.62	21.26	5.51	1.61	7.11	2488
Lithuania	55.69	36.77	6.19	1.36	7.54	2214
Netherlands	81.87	15.37	1.88	0.89	2.76	1919
Norway	79.48	17.38	2.16	0.98	3.14	1433
Poland	73.39	14.78	8.20	3.63	11.83	1597
Portugal	64.79	24.60	5.06	5.54	10.60	1264
Sweden	72.71	22.37	2.96	1.96	4.92	1788
Slovenia	74.45	18.98	5.34	1.23	6.57	1217

of frequent loneliness, which stays around 3%. We shall see and discuss further related results about such discrepancies across nations in Chapter 8.

To sum up, loneliness is a psychological pain that many people have experienced in their lives, although it may not be a universal experience. By itself it is a not a medical problem, but it may be responsible for many illnesses. We still do not know much about how intense and how long loneliness has to be so as to cause these illnesses. To find out the specific conditions under which loneliness will become a serious health hazard should be a priority for scientific research. When those conditions are not met, loneliness appears to be bearable, which makes it possible for the lonely to transform the initially negative and painful emotion into something with the potential of bringing about cognitive and spiritual benefits. We must note, however, that such transformative processes are an experience distinctive to loneliness; it is a process of consciously dealing with loneliness after loneliness has already been experienced, which requires extra mental efforts, such as knowledge about the nature of loneliness, the will of turning the experience in the positive direction, and the resilience of taking actions. We know even less about who have successfully experienced such transformation and how they did it. Empirical studies on loneliness remain unsatisfactory as the measurement of loneliness remains crude and restricted. Available data show that the prevalence of loneliness varies greatly from country to country and from one human group to another. To explain these differences and the occurrence of loneliness in general, we must focus our attention on the social origins of loneliness, which is the topic of the next chapter.

Notes

1 D. Perlman and L. A. Peplau. 1981. 'Toward a social psychology of loneliness', in S. W. Duck and R. Gilmour (eds), *Personal Relationships in Disorder*. London: Academic Press, 1981, pp. 31–56.
2 J. Cacioppo and W. Patrick. 2008. *Loneliness: Human Nature and the Need for Social Connection*. New York: W. W. Norton & Company, p. 127.
3 B. Russell. 1975. *Autobiography*. New York: Routledge.
4 Ibid., p. 9.
5 J. J. Lynch. 1977. *The Broken Heart: The Medical Consequences of Loneliness*. New York: Basic Books; J. J. Lynch. 2000. *A Cry Unheard: New Insights into the Medical Consequences of Loneliness*. Baltimore, MD: Bancroft Press.
6 Lynch, *The Broken Heart*, p. xiii.
7 J. S. House, K. R. Landis, and D. Umberson. 1988. 'Social relationships and health', *Science*, 241: 540–545.
8 Cacioppo and Patrick, *Loneliness*, p. 5, emphases original.
9 Lynch, *A Cry Unheard*, p. 92. L. F. Berkman and S. L. Syme. 1979. 'Social networks, host resistance, and mortality: a nine year follow-up study of Alameda County residents', *American Journal of Epidemiology*, 109(2): 186–204. L. Berkman and L. Breslow. 1983. *Health and Ways of Living: The Alameda County Study*. New York: Oxford University Press. L. F. Berkman. 1995. 'The role of social relations in health promotion', *Psychosomatic Medicine*, 57: 345–254.
10 P. Reynolds and G. A. Kaplan. 1990. 'Social connections and risk for cancer: prospective evidence from the Alameda County Study', *Behavioural Medicine*, 16(3): 101–110. J. R. Marshall and D. P. Funch. 1983. 'Social environment and breast cancer: A cohort analysis of patient survival', *Cancer*, 52(8): 1546–1550.
11 L. Deckx et al. 2015. 'Loneliness in patients with cancer: the first year after cancer diagnosis', *Psycho-Oncology*, 24(11): 1521–1528. A. Marcus. 2010. 'The loneliness of fighting a rare cancer', *Health Affairs*, 29(1): 203–206. M. Wells and D. Kelly. 2008. 'The loneliness of cancer', *European Journal of Oncology Nursing*, 12(5): 410–411.
12 Lynch, *A Cry Unheard*, p. 108.
13 W. Ruberman, E. Weinblatt, J. D. Goldberg, and B. S. Chaudhary. 1984. 'Psychosocial influences on mortality after myocardial infarction', *New England Journal of Medicine*, 311: 552–559.
14 L. C. Hawkley, C. M. Masi, J. D. Berry, and J. T. Cacioppo. 2006. 'Loneliness is a unique predictor of age-related differences in systolic blood pressure', *Psychology and Ageing*, 21: 152–164.

15 Lynch, *A Cry Unheard*, p. 85. C. Segrin. 1998. 'Interpersonal communication problems associated with depression and loneliness', in P. A. Anderson and L. K. Guerrero (eds), *Handbook of Communication and Emotion: Research, Theory, Applications, and Contexts*. San Diego, CA: Academic Press, pp. 215–242. M. Wei, D. W. Russell, and R. A. Aakalik. 2005. 'Adult attachment, social self-efficacy, self-disclosure, loneliness, and subsequent depression for freshman college students: a longitudinal study', *Journal of Counselling Psychology*, 52: 602–614.

16 J. T. Cacioppo, M. E. Hughes, L. J. Waite, L. C. Hawkley, and R. A. Thisted. 2006. 'Loneliness as a specific risk factor for depressive symptoms: cross-sectional and longitudinal analysis', *Psychology and Ageing*, 21: 140–151.

17 I. Akerlind and J. O. Hornquist. 1992. 'Loneliness and alcohol abuse: a review of evidence of an interplay', *Social Science and Medicine*, 34: 405–414. A. W. Stacy, M. D. Newcomb, and P. M. Bentler. 1995. 'Expectancy in mediational models of cocaine abuse', *Personality and Individual Differences*, 19: 655–667.

18 D. Coric and B. I. Murstein. 1993. 'Bulimia nervosa: prevalence and psychological correlates in a college community', *Eating Disorders: The Journal of Treatment and Prevention*, 1: 39–51. K. J. Rotenberg, C. Bharathi, H. Davies, and T. Finch. 2013. 'Bulimic symptoms and the social withdrawal syndrome', *Eating Behaviours*, 14(3): 281–284.

19 T. J. Holwerda, D. J. H. Deeg, A. T. F. Beekman, T. G. van Tilburg, M. L. Stek, C. Jonker, and R. A. Schoevers. 2014. 'Feelings of loneliness, but not social isolation, predict dementia onset: results from the Amsterdam Study of the Elderly (AMSTEL)', *Journal of Neurology, Neurosurgery & Psychiatry*, 85: 135–142.

20 R. S. Wilson, K. R. Krueger, S. E. Arnold, J. A. Schneider, J. F. Kelly, L. L. Barnes, Y. Tang, and D. A. Bennett. 2007. 'Loneliness and risk of Alzheimer's disease', *Archives of General Psychiatry*, 64: 234–240.

21 S. K. Goldsmith, T. C. Pellmar, A. M. Kleinman, and W. E. Bunney. 2002. *Reducing Suicide: A National Imperative*, Washington, DC: National Academy Press. A. Stravynski and R. Boyer. 2001. 'Loneliness in relation to suicide ideation and parasuicide: a population-wide study', *Suicide and Life-Threatening Behaviour*, 31: 32–40. A. R. Rich and R. L. Bonner. 1987. 'Concurrent validity of a stress-vulnerability model of suicidal ideation and behaviour: a follow-up study', *Suicide and Life-Threatening Behaviour*, 17: 265–270.

22 D. A. Lamis, E. D.Ballard, and B. A. Patel. 2014. 'Loneliness and suicidal ideation in drug-using college students', *Suicide and Life-Threatening Behaviour*, 44(6): 629–640.

23 W. Cannon. 1942. 'Voodoo death', *American Anthropologist*, 44: 169–181.

24 D. P. Phillips. 1977. 'Deathday and birthday: an unexpected connection', in J. M. Tanur et al. (eds), *Statistics: A Guide to the Biological and Health Sciences*. San Francisco, CA: Holden-Day, pp. 111–125.

25 See the report by Emma Innes in the *Daily Mail* on 15 November 2013, available online at www.dailymail.co.uk/health/article-2507365/One-patients-visit-GP-LONELY-sick. html (accessed 21 January 2017), and related reports at that time.

26 Cacioppo and Patrick, *Loneliness*, p. 228.

27 Ibid., p. 7.

28 Ibid., p. 99.

29 K. Clark. 1982. *An Experience of Celibacy: A Creative Reflection on Intimacy, Loneliness, Sexuality and Commitment*. Notre Dame, IN: Ave Maria Press, p. 27.

30 Cacioppo and Patrick, *Loneliness*, p. 229.

31 Clark, *An Experience of Celibacy*, p. 27.

32 C. Moustakas. 1961. *Loneliness*. Upper Saddle River, NJ: Prentice-Hall.

33 S. Sirtio et al. 2016. 'Existential loneliness at the end of life: design and proposal of Existential Loneliness Detection Scale of (ELDS), preliminary results', *Psycho-oncology*,

25(SP, S3): 56–65. E. Ettema, L. Derksen, and E. Leeuwen. 2010. 'Existential loneliness and end-of-life care: a systematic review', *Theoretical Medicine and Bioethics*, 31(2): 141–169.

34 G. Frantz. 2014. *Sea Glass: A Jungian Analyst's Exploration of Suffering and Individuation*. Cheyenne, WY: Fisher King Press, p. 51.

35 Ibid., p. 55.

36 Moustakas, *Loneliness*, p. x.

37 Cacioppo and Patrick, *Loneliness*, p. 82.

38 There is an additional option, 'Don't know', which however is usually treated as 'invalid', although some researchers may argue that it is a valid indication of a certain mental state.

39 D. Russell, L. A. Peplau, and M. L. Ferguson. 1978. 'Developing a measure of loneliness', *Journal of Personality Assessment*, 42: 290–294. D. Russell, L. A. Peplau, and C. E. Cutrona. 1980. 'The revised UCLA Loneliness Scale: concurrent and discriminant validity evidence', *Journal of Personality and Social Psychology*, 39(3): 472–480. The third version was reported in D. Russell. 1996. 'UCLA loneliness scale (Version 3): reliability, validity, and factor structure', *Journal of Personality Assessment*, 66(1): 20–40.

40 J. de Jong Gierveld. 1978. 'The construct of loneliness: components and measurement', *Essence*, 2: 221–238. J. de Jong Gierveld and F. Kamphuis. 1985. 'The development of a Rasch-type loneliness scale', *Applied Psychological Measurement*, 9(3): 289–299. The most recent update on this scale can be found in J. de Jong Gierveld and T. van Tilburg. 2010. 'The De Jong Gierveld short scales for emotional and social loneliness: tested on data from 7 countries in the UN generations and gender surveys', *European Journal of Ageing*, 7(2): 121–130.

41 R. S. Weiss. 1975. *Loneliness: The Experience of Emotional and Social Isolation*. Cambridge, MA: MIT Press.

42 Reported in an interview by Laura Entis for *Fortune*, available online at http://fortune.com/2016/06/22/loneliness-is-a-modern-day-epidemic (accessed 22 January 2017).

43 Cacioppo and Patrick, *Loneliness*, p. 5.

44 M. McPherson, L. Smith-Lovin, and M. E. Brashears. 2006. 'Social isolation in America: changes in core discussion networks over two decades', *American Sociological Review*, 71(3): 353–375.

45 For example, J. S. Crouse, 'The loneliness of American society', *The American Spectator*, 18 May 2014, available online at https://spectator.org/59230_loneliness-american-society, accessed 23 January 2017).

46 J. Griffin, *The Lonely Society?* London: Mental Health Foundation.

47 I would like to thank the ESS research team for making the data available (ESS Round 7: European Social Survey Round 7 Data, 2014, data file edition 2.1, Norwegian Centre for Research Data, Norway – Data Archive and distributor of ESS data for ESS ERIC). The percentages were calculated with design weight; for each country, the percentages add up to 100.

Chapter 2

Loneliness as a social problem

Here are the key points that I tried to make in the previous chapter. First, although some have argued for the potential benefits loneliness could bring to human beings, such as alerting us to our dependence on others and helping us grow spiritually, loneliness is a serious problem not only as a painful psychological experience but more importantly as a trigger for a set of serious medical conditions. Second, loneliness is a common, if not universal, experience across people of all walks of life, and researchers in different disciplines could contribute to the study of loneliness. Third, we have a long way to go to understand different types of loneliness, the causes or conditions of each type, and their connections to any particular medical condition. The reader may have also noticed that the sources of evidence used in the previous chapter, albeit limited for the sake of saving space, mostly come from psychologists, literary authors, philosophers, and public health researchers; few sociologists have contributed to the study of loneliness as a serious problem. The ambition of this book is to start a new round of sociological research on loneliness. In this sense, this is the most important chapter of the book. In case someone raises the objection to my complaint on the shortage of sociological research on loneliness, I start this chapter by presenting the evidence to show that this is the case. That does not mean that no sociologists have ever paid serious attention to loneliness, of course; some have, but only a few. It is therefore necessary to take a look at what these few have said about loneliness. Once this review is done, I shall move on to identify a few important principles that constitute the sociological approach to studying loneliness.

The shortage of sociological research on loneliness

The shortage of academic research on any issue does not automatically justify the value of a new study on that issue – a mistake that social science students often make. It is only when an issue that deserves to be studied but has not been studied that a study on it is worthwhile. In the next section I will answer the question whether sociologists *should* pay serious attention to loneliness – if it is not any sociologist's responsibility to study loneliness, there is nothing to complain about the shortage of sociological research on loneliness. In fact, some sociologists *have already* treated loneliness as a serious social problem, but their number is very small, their findings need updating, and their research needs to be expanded both theoretically and empirically, a task that I shall take in the last section.

It is not difficult to demonstrate that compared with the research in psychology, neurology, gerontology, and public health, the sociologist's share in academic studies on loneliness is rather disappointing. Put bluntly, the growth of loneliness as a vigorous research area in psychology and public health parallels the decline of research on loneliness in sociology. While the number of academic papers on loneliness in other fields has increased dramatically, a search on sociology journals (198 titles) published in the English language on JSTOR (a database of journal papers in the social sciences and humanities) from 1980 to 2016 produced only a few papers directly related to loneliness. Another search on the database of *Social Problems*, the official journal of the Society for the Study of Social Problems, generated only one article with loneliness as the focus of writing. The two most widely used measures of loneliness introduced in the previous chapter, the UCLA loneliness scale and the de Jong Gierveld loneliness scale, were developed by psychologists. The useful distinction made by the sociologist Robert Weiss – emotional vs. social loneliness, which we shall discuss later in this chapter – has been taken up mostly by researchers in fields other than sociology. Perhaps currently the most influential monograph on loneliness, *Loneliness: Human Nature and the Need for Social Connection*, was written by the neuroscientist John Caccioppo, and it is mostly about the medical implications of loneliness rather than its causes. For the educated general public, the entry 'loneliness' in *Encyclopaedia Britannica* is classified as a topic of psychology and produced by the Chicago-based psychologist Louise Hawkley. Within sociology, 'the sociology of emotions' remains a marginal subfield. As loneliness is one of human emotions, it is reasonable to expect sociologists in this area to have done some serious work on loneliness. Disappointingly, they have done little – a recent volume showcasing a comprehensive summary of the area does not even mention loneliness.[1]

Since its birth sociology has rarely taken emotions, feelings, or any other mental states and processes seriously. It would be pretentious to claim otherwise. What 'the founding fathers' of sociology (Karl Marx, Max Weber, Emile Durkheim, Georg Simmel, etc.) were concerned about are grand socio-historical regularities and processes, such as social structure and mobility, social conflicts and struggles, and the relations among different parts of society as a whole (economy, politics, religion, and social groups). Compared with these issues, loneliness or any form of mental suffering is too individual and psychological to deserve the attention of a sociologist. This does not mean that these classical sociologists were not interested in the mental states of the people under their study: Marx and Engels were worried about how the workers felt when they were alienated from the production process, and Weber conducted a survey on peasants' mental state. Nevertheless, they were clearly far more interested in the large-scale historical processes, such as class struggles, proletariat revolutions, and the rationalization of social organizations.

Compared with Marx and Weber, Simmel and Durkheim made greater efforts of examining the effects of social structures and processes on people's mental wellbeing. Contrasting the social lives between the fast-paced but personally indifferent urban lifestyle with that of the slow but personally close rural social life, Simmel was speculating on how historical processes such as urbanization must affect the residents' mental wellbeing.[2] Durkheim made an even stronger case for the sociology of mental states: an action as individual and psychological as suicide has its social origins in social solidarity, religion, and positions in social structure. Durkheim's attention to the 'national dispositions' of mental states is the source of inspiration for my study on the effects of national and cultural characteristics on loneliness, which I shall present later in Chapter 8.

It was not until the 1960s that sociologists started to study loneliness directly. Among them, David Riesman and his associates' *The Lonely Crowd* (1965) is perhaps the earliest and one of the most influential. Riesman et al. classified the Americans into three groups in terms of their 'social character', a set of psychological treats shared by the members of each group such as desires and satisfactions: the 'tradition-directed', the 'inner-directed', and the 'other-directed'.[3] However, it is difficult to pin down exactly what Riesman et al. said about loneliness among members of these groups. First of all, their discussions focused on the latter two types of Americans, that is, the inner-directed and the other-directed. In connection to the understanding of loneliness, they seemed to imply that the tradition-directed Americans would not feel lonely as they were surrounded by people of close ties. Clearly, this is a strong assumption which might not be true – it is probable that people living within tight family circles could still feel lonely, as shown later in this book. For the other two types of Americans, it remains unclear which one would be more likely to feel lonely. By definition, the inner-directed are expected to be lonely as they are socialized to live in their own worlds – 'the fate of many inner-directed children is loneliness in and outside the home'.[4] In the meantime, however, Riesman et al. also emphasized that these inner-directed people had the capacity to be on their own: 'the inner-directed person is capable of great stability . . . even when the reinforcement of social approval is not available'.[5] As they are less dependent on other people's company and involvement, the inner-directed should be less lonely than the other-directed. However, Perlman and Peplau had a different reading of Riesman's theory: the other-directed should be more lonely as they rely too much on other people's attention and approval, so much that they cut off from their own feelings and desires. Perlman and Peplau believed that 'the lonely crowd' referred to these other-directed Americans, although they admitted that this was only implied in Riesman's work.[6] Regardless of its ambiguity, Riesman's theory established the central role of cultural norms in shaping people's sense of loneliness; by telling people whether their value comes from inner pursuit or other people's approval, cultural norms regulate people's emotional reactions to their roles in social relations, and one emotional reaction is loneliness.

Anomie is a phenomenon that sociologists focused on for some years and has been taken as something equivalent to loneliness. For example, in his introduction to the edited volume *The Anatomy of Loneliness*, Joseph Hartog explained that 'we have chosen to minimize the sociological orientation because there is already an impressive collection of books and articles on anomie and alienation, the social cousins of loneliness.'[7] For readers who are not familiar with anomie, some explanations are needed, although there is not the space here to go into the details of this rather complex concept.[8] Briefly, in two major sociological works, *The Division of Labour in Society* and *Suicide*,[9] Émile Durkheim used the term 'anomie' to refer to the chaotic and confusing situation in which the society could not offer moral guidance to its individual members anymore; in other words, anomie is the opposite of social solidarity and cohesion, and it arises when individual behaviours have lost their moral campus, or their principles of behaviour have become highly inconsistent with those laid out by the society. In the mid-1950s, Leo Srole proposed 'anomia' as the individual's experience of anomie.[10] I do not think, however, it is appropriate to treat 'anomie' or 'anomia' as the sociological equivalence to the psychological meaning of 'loneliness'. Anomie describes a situation of the society as whole; it is thus not an individual experience. Anomia refers to individual experience, but it is much broader and ambiguous than loneliness. Unless anomia is clearly defined as a special kind of loneliness, such as loneliness due to the moral disconnection to the society at large, an anomic person may not feel lonely in the sense of having no desired social relations. In principle, loneliness and anomia should not be treated as interchangeable.

Finally, alongside with non-sociologist authors, some sociologists claimed to have studied loneliness but what they actually refer to is a much broader and less accurate concept, such as 'aloneness', 'isolation', 'disconnection', or something else. These terms have been used interchangeably in many publications. Among sociologists, for example, in spite of the title of his book being *The Pursuit of Loneliness*,[11] Philip Slater never defined the meaning of loneliness, how it should be measured and how it was different from other concepts. More recently, some sociologists and social scientists (e.g. Robert Putnam[12] and Eric Klinenberg)[13] have lamented the weakening of social ties and the increasing level of social isolation, but the conceptual boundaries between aloneness, isolation, and loneliness are very much obscured. One thing social scientists could do to improve the status of social sciences is to stop confusing these concepts and offer definitions with clear boundaries. 'Aloneness' refers to an objective state and therefore should not have any implication or assumption for its effect on people's mental state. Nevertheless, one way or another in daily language it has been constantly assumed or implied that a person alone must be lonely; when people say 'I feel so alone', what they actually mean is 'I am so lonely', and such confusion must be avoided for clarity and rigor in scientific research. The word 'isolation' is not sufficiently clear either – it could refer to the physical state of being alone or the consequence of being excluded by other members of the society (social isolation). This is an important question that academics have not been able to offer a satisfactory answer: some people do end up being lonely even though being alone does not necessarily lead to loneliness, so the question is when aloneness leads to loneliness, or more generally, how do we help people square the circle of *living alone without feeling lonely*?

In 1980, Sadler and Johnson pointed out that:

> One of the challenges to the social sciences, sociology in particular, is to examine loneliness in the context of modern society and to explain how it has come to loom so large and how it affects different persons and groups. Why in the midst of population explosion, overcrowding, and frequent interaction are so many people so disturbed by loneliness?[14]

In 2018, sociologists still have a long way to go to meet this challenge.

Why is loneliness a social problem?

It should be clear by now that loneliness is a multi-faceted problem; thus, it should be studied from the perspectives of different disciplines. As researchers in psychology, neurology, public health, and other disciplines have made significant contributions, it is high time for sociologists to offer their share. Before going into the details in the rest of the book, it is essential to make it clear from the outset in what senses loneliness is a social problem, and why sociologists should take loneliness seriously. Me answer will take two steps: in this section, I identify five overarching reasons for which loneliness is a social problem, which hopefully would make a short but strong case for the sociological study of loneliness; then in the next section, I will spell out some specific principles representing the sociological approach to studying loneliness.

The first reason that loneliness is a social problem is clearly suggested in its definition. Besides the two definitions introduced in the previous chapter, here is Sadler and Johnson's definition of loneliness:

> loneliness is an experience involving a total and often acute feeling that constitutes a distinct form of self-awareness of signaling a break in the basic network of the relational reality of self-world.[15]

No matter how different the wordings are, there is a consensus among this and the previous definitions of loneliness: it is an unpleasant feeling that arises from the perception of unsatisfactory feature of social relations. In other words, *the social origins of loneliness make it a social problem*. Obviously, the number of concrete forms of the social origins of loneliness could be enormous, if not infinite; therefore, it would be impossible, perhaps unnecessary as well, to list all situations in which a particular feature of social relation (absence, disappearance, severance, deterioration, confrontation, exclusion, etc.) induces some people to feel lonely, although we could enlist a few most commonly encountered ones: an orphan longing for mother's love and care, a child finding it intimidating to join a new school, another child being excluded from a play group, an immigrant having nobody to communicate with in the hosting country, a gay couple within a community of heterosexuals, an atheist among highly religious relatives, and so on and so forth. It is saddening to realize the large number of situations our social relations could make us feel sad, fearful, disappointed, frustrated, lonely, or even scared. More importantly, certain social structures or societal events could be ultimately responsible for the rise of loneliness among the individuals living in that social structure; for example, mass immigrations, large-scale social conflicts, particularly violent confrontations and wars, economic and financial crises, and so on. We shall elaborate on this point with further evidence later.

The only non-social origin of loneliness that could possibly exist is neurological or generic; for example, Cacioppo believes that some people possess certain 'genetic dispositions' that determine their expectations of social relations[16]. At the moment, researchers still cannot identify the exact genes or neurological mechanisms that trigger loneliness independently of social relations; until they could demonstrate the causal process how these genes or neural functions work, we must assume that the overwhelming majority of the sources of loneliness are in people's social relations.

The second reason for us to take loneliness as a social problem lies in the fact that *the meaning of loneliness is social.* To themselves and to those around them, what does it mean for a human being to be lonely? From the definitions of loneliness we learn that the lonely experiences is a process consisted of three mental activities that reinforce one another: the first is a mental process that perceives one's social relations, followed by another cognitive process in which one evaluates these relations as either negative, undesirable, or even threatening, which in turn induces an emotional reaction to such evaluation, although such emotional reaction could be constrained with further cognitive activities. Clearly, these processes occur at a speed of lightening in a human brain, or they occur without clear awareness, so people do not usually realize them. It is in the second step that the social meaning of loneliness starts to emerge: the individual person starts to realize the social meaning of the connection between themselves and others: Who am I? Who are they? Why do I need them? How did we connect to each other before and how do we relate to each other now? What would happen to me if they stop being part of my life? These or similar questions force the individual to reflect seriously on the state of their social life, and more importantly, their reflections are already and inevitably shaped by how they have been socialized. A key function of socialization is to instil in the younger generation's mind which social relations are valuable to their life.

To those who live with the lonely person, loneliness could be a social problem in a different sense. How do the non-lonely see the lonely? How do the non-lonely interpret what is behind the loneliness? Do the non-lonely think it is their responsibility to help the lonely? These questions bring us directly to the issue of the stigma of loneliness. While it is constantly mentioned in media reports and lonely people's narratives, so far we do not have much reliable evidence for the existence, the prevalence, and the details of such stigma. In a particular society, how popular is the view that there must be something wrong with a lonely person and others should shun away from them? Or is this an unfounded illusion that more likely represents the fear of being socially excluded if being perceived to be lonely? Clearly, we need more research to answer these questions, but they do show that loneliness is much more than an unpleasant feeling; it is about the relations between the lonely and the non-lonely. A community or society usually constructs its own interpretation of loneliness, which in turn will instruct its members how the lonely should be treated.

The third reason for taking loneliness as a social rather than a purely psychological problem will become clear if we uplift the unit of our observation from the individual to a higher collective level. We shall find that *the prevalence of loneliness is significantly higher among some social groups than among others*, such as ethnicity and race, socio-economic status (or class), nationality, etc. These are socially important groups that are constantly studied by sociologists. At the highest level, as the sociologist George Homans pointed out, 'The civilization that, by its very process of growth, shatters small group life will heave men and women lonely and unhappy.'[17] On the one hand, psychologists, neurologists, and public health researchers tend to focus on individual factors, such as age, gender, living arrangement, chronic illnesses, etc., when they attempt to detect any regularity in the distribution of loneliness. In recent years, some researchers have started to pay close attention to the most socially important groups, but such research is still in its early days – as to be shown in the later chapters of this book, many important patterns in the distribution of loneliness across important social groups are to be discovered and understood. On the other hand, sociologists of health and illnesses have done extensive research on those social groups in order to identify evidence of social inequality measured by the prevalence of certain illnesses and their treatments. Unfortunately, as reported in the previous chapter, theses sociologists have not paid serious attention to loneliness, very likely because they would not count loneliness as a serious illness. It is my hope that the evidence presented in the previous chapter would convince them to take loneliness seriously and to start to do research on the social distributions and processes of loneliness. The research presented in Chapters 4–8 of this book will serve as a starting point.

So far it is largely because of its medical implications that loneliness has been taken as a serious problem of public health. While this progress must be acknowledged, it is clearly not sufficient. A fourth reason for taking loneliness seriously as a social problem is that *loneliness has serious social consequences as well*, and academic research on these social consequences, in sociology or any other academic discipline, remains sketchy. Broadly speaking, we could look at these consequences from two perspectives: the perspective of the lonely person and the perspective of the non-lonely. Here are some important questions from the lonely: how do they interpret their social relations, and what actions do they tend to take based on that evaluation? In their book, Cacioppo and Patrick describe the lonely people as being not merely lonely, but fearful too: loneliness 'is often about our fear of negative evaluation',[18] lonely individuals 'found positive social interactions to be less of an uplift than did their nonlonely counterparts'[19]. What are they afraid of? Cacioppo and Patrick believe that it is 'social failure' because they have 'little if any control over external circumstances'[20]. Cacioppo and Patrick did not clearly explain the meaning of 'social failure', although intuitively it should refer to the inability to establish, maintain, and enjoy interacting with other people, which in turn could entail further negative reactions from others. Perhaps this is why 'lonely players become much less trusting'.[21] According to his theory, an important social consequence of loneliness is that the lonely will become more fearful and distrustful in social interactions.

Even worse, Cacioppo and Patrick believe that the lonely will be trapped in a vicious circle of fear, social isolation, more fear, and more isolation: 'When our negative social expectations elicit behaviors from others that validate our fears, the experience makes us even more likely to behave in self-protective ways that spin the feedback loop further and faster toward even more isolation.'[22] Therefore, 'feeling lonely creates self-fulfilling prophesies'.[23] This sounds very pessimistic – it seems that once lonely, the lonely individual will be on a downward spiral and doomed to be lonely forever: 'when people feel lonely they are actually far less accepting of potential new friends than when they feel socially connected'.[24] We would think that the lonely would try to welcome new friends and become even more appreciative of social relations. However, Cacioppo and Patrick believe that the fear induced by loneliness would be so overwhelming that we become 'harsh and critical toward those we wish to be near',[25] thereby locking ourselves in the lonely situation.

I accept that some lonely people could indeed be trapped in such miserable situation, but to me it remains more a plausible theory for a specific group than a well-established fact for the majority of the lonely population, that is, we need reliable evidence to know how many of all lonely people become trapped in such situation and why. More importantly, I think that his theory is incomplete as it misses two important elements in the process. The first is the lonely individual's ability (or resilience) to grow out of the misery. Cacioppo's theory seems to assume that the lonely people have no such ability; otherwise, at least some of them may not necessarily be trapped in perpetual loneliness. The other missing element is the reactions by the non-lonely people to the lonely. While the lonely are understandably suspicious, fearful, and distrustful, such attitudes could change or even reverse its course if those surrounding them are highly friendly and understanding. This is a very important social consequence of loneliness: the lonely may unwittingly have exercised some pressure on the social circle or community for adjusting their behaviours and social relations. In short, loneliness is not just about the lonely; it is about the non-lonely as well, and in this sense, *loneliness is not merely a problem for the lonely but for the society as a whole.*

The final reason for loneliness to be taken as a social problem could be seen as a corollary of the first: if the origins of loneliness are social, then *the remedies and strategies for coping with loneliness must be social too.* These remedies and strategies could be classified at three levels: the individual, the community, and the society. While someday in the future when neurologists may be able to discover the neurological mechanisms of loneliness it would be possible to develop a drug for curing chronic loneliness, at the moment people would not request for medical pills from their doctors for curing their loneliness. Instead, the remedies for individual loneliness must be social therapies, and usually they come in two general forms. The first, demonstrated by many self-help books, attempts to help the lonely individuals to understand the nature and the process of loneliness, which hopefully in turn will develop higher resilience to loneliness. The reasoning behind such helping hands is that once the individual accepts loneliness as a normal part, the newly gained understanding will lower what the individual will expect from their social relations and thus become less lonely or less likely to feel lonely.

The other general form of remedies at the individual level is to offer a list of actions the lonely individual could take to ease the pain of loneliness, such as owning a pet, developing a new hobby, or joining social groups. Clearly, some of these actions aim to help the lonely replace their lost relations with new ones or to expand their existing social networks, which obviously is a social solution. This leads us to the second level of remedies and strategies for coping with loneliness: for those lonely individuals who are unable to take initiatives to start new social relations, it requires the social communities in their life – family members, friends, neighbours, relatives, colleagues, etc., to intervene. One good demonstration of the community's power in helping those with mental health issues is the story of *Lars and the Real Girl*[26] – I am doubtful that any person in real life would be as lucky as Lars to have a supporting community anywhere close to the one in the movie! It seems that people, at least those in the West, have an increasing number of reasons for keeping their life to themselves rather than living a communal life. How to reverse this trend and enhance community life is a challenge that sociologists and the society at large must confront with.

Remedies and strategies initiated by a society as a whole or targeting societal sources of loneliness have gained the least amount of attention from not only the general public but also academic researchers. This is so because loneliness has been persistently understood as mostly an individual problem; if so, there will be no need for a society as whole to take any action. The lack of serious attention to societal sources of loneliness is most likely due to the habit of focusing on *the immediate, rather than the ultimate*, causes of loneliness. It is indeed true that people become lonely when they experience certain events, such as migrating to a new place, getting divorced or widowed, or being bullied by others around them. These seemingly individual experiences, however, could be traced back to something much higher or wider: why do they have to migrate to a new place in the first place? Why has the average life expectance of marriage declined so much in the past decades? Why have certain people been bullied more often than others? How could so many bullies go unpunished? How could we explain the fact that the prevalence of loneliness differs from one nation to another? The answer to each of these questions, at least partly, must be sought in social institutions, norms, and structures; and when we can locate these societal factors, we will know the societal remedies and strategies for tackling loneliness.

A sociological approach to understanding and studying loneliness

Indeed, loneliness is a multi-faceted experience. While psychologists, neurologists, and health researchers are concerned with the health conditions and consequences, sociologists should focus on the social origins, meanings, and implications for social groups and the society at large. The origin of loneliness is social in the sense that loneliness results from *the process of perceiving, understanding, and evaluating the social relations between the self and others*, a fundamental experience for human beings living in any group or society. Loneliness is a specific mental experience. However, as George Herbert Mead forcefully argued more than a millennium ago, the mind arises and develops 'within the social process, within the empirical matrix of social interactions'.[27] It seems to have become a truism of human nature that none would want to live alone but all prefer to be with others. As Aristotle observed in his *Politics*, only beasts and gods could be so self-sufficient as not to participate in any society. Monks, nuns, yogis, and other extremely religious people do choose to live in solidary confinements, but it requires extraordinary spiritual devotion and mental power to be completely solitary, and they know they actually rely on others and they could rejoin others if they want to; even within the monastic institution, many live together although they may not talk much to each other. As the solitude is chosen and voluntary, loneliness is transitory at worst and should not be a hazard to health.

In contrast, imposed or enforced solitary confinement aims to afflict pain to the body and the mind of the targeted human beings. That is, physical, social, or even sensual isolations were used as forms of severe punishment; for example, a Chinese emperor would lock up a concubine or even an empress who offended him so much as to be put in a 'cold palace', a palace not necessarily cold in temperature but in human connections; the intention was to inflict loneliness as a pain on the mind, while the concubine or the empress would live a physically comfortable life. A lot of research has been carried out for prison and military interrogators to find out how solitary confinement could make the inmates comply.[28] To the inmates, loneliness would be a blessing, not a pain, as what the enforced isolation aims to achieve is far worse: delusion, madness, hallucination, etc., are the common outcomes.

The vast majority of the members of a society live in between these two extremes, who have some but not complete control over the boundaries of their private and public lives. They find some of their social relations enjoyable but others irritating; they could do something to keep or even to improve social relations, but these relations may disappear or terminate without any warning; they may find themselves having no choice but to bear with new social relations. *The unpredictability, the uncertainty, and the uncontrollability of social relations are the ultimate sources of loneliness* for the vast majority of the members of a society. They were born into a set of social relations to which there is little they could do about and most of the times all they could do is to learn how to make use of them.

That humans are 'social animals' does not mean that everybody prefers to live with *any* other human being. The meaning of this well-known endowment is actually rather ambivalent: Is it simply a descriptive observation that humans normally live with others? If so, it is true but trite: everybody could see that. Does it mean that all human beings *prefer* to live with other human beings *regardless of who the other human beings are*? Clearly, we do prefer to live with others but *not any* others; we only prefer to live with *certain* others. We prefer to live with other human beings as we have long realized that we have to rely on one another to make our lives safer, easier and better, although it may not be the intention of some of the others to make our lives so. That is, we also realize that some other human beings may actually want to make *their* lives easier and better by taking advantage of *our* lives. Obviously, we would not want to be social with that kind of human being; in fact, we would try to stay away from them, perhaps even fight against them. In short, *human sociality is highly selective*; we prefer to live only with *certain* other human beings. It may sound simple, but *to live only with the desirable ones and not the undesirable others simultaneously* is, I would venture to claim, the holy grail of any social life. An ideal society is one whose members love to live together and enjoy a healthy amount of privacy (a certain kind of aloneness) at the same time; it is a balanced society in terms of the space of the private and the public, and whether its members could transit from one space to the other at will. A less ideal society would have members who would find the intrusion of their private and public spaces unpleasant but tolerable as they could somehow retreat to their limited private space. A society could be called 'ill' or in great trouble if its members do not want to live with each other anymore, because there is either too much or too little private (or public) life, which usually ends with either fight or flight. Loneliness is an emotional by-product of this endless process of evaluating, balancing and rebalancing the two spheres of life.

In a sense, socialization is a process of learning whom we should live with, whom we should stay away from, and how to achieve and maintain those situations. An important product of such process is the establishment of the connection between neurological and psychological reactions to the meanings of our relations with others. Loneliness is simply one example of such process and connection. We find the one we desire to live with while we grow up: those who directly make our lives safer and easier – those who give us food, shelter and fun, and later we could also recognize those whom we may not know personally but could indirectly or potentially support us – the workers and engineers who built the houses, the soldiers who fought wars for our safety, the technological innovators, the music composers, the authors, those who share beliefs with us, and many others. Consciously or unconsciously, some positive emotions will arise in our mind and attach to these human beings, with varying nature and degree, of course. By a large number of forces out of our control, our relations with these human beings we desire to be with will not stay the same over time, which in turn would make us suffer emotionally, and we call one form of such emotional suffering 'loneliness'. Our emotional attachment to the certain others only partly comes from physiological or psychological satisfactions that they bring to us. We also learn, by either active learning or passively being socialized, about what we can expect from the others, that is, what they will do to make us satisfied; conversely, we do the same to others. This process of learning takes a lot of energy from us, so the ideal would be that the process would complete as quickly as possible so that what we could expect from others and how we must behave recede to the back of our mind, that is, to become part of our unconsciousness, something we can assume, so that we could concentrate our limited amount of physical and mental energies on what we believe more important or enjoyable matters. Other than growing up into a competent member of a society, members of a society also benefit from this learning process by reducing the chance of becoming lonely – clear awareness and knowledge of the nature of the relations with others help avoid expected disappointment or even disheartening when any social relation becomes strained or terminated.

Strangely, few societies offer systematic and structured knowledge to their members about the appropriate ways in which the members establish, maintain, and terminate their social relations: what social relations they would have throughout their life, what each of the relations means to them and to others, how to establish a new social relation, how to maintain a social relation, what to do when a certain social relation comes to an end, and other related questions. Clearly, societies differ greatly in making such knowledge explicit, systematic and accessible to the younger generations, and within a particular society, whether and how much these questions are answered depend on the relation concerned. For example, in most modern societies, relations between married couples and between them and their children are usually clearly laid out in legal terms. Nevertheless, these laws, despite the fact that most of them are overwhelmingly detailed and carefully worded, cannot exhaust all interactions that couples and children conduct among themselves; often they prescribe solutions for resolving conflicts rather than pre-emptive instructions and expectations. For example, how often should they talk to each other or dine together? What if one family member does not want to participate in a family activity? In some societies, families, or rather the heads of family, such as those in China before the Communist Party took power, created their own 'family laws' to regulate family members' behaviours; for example, a son should not take a trip to a place far away from his parents. As the costs of violating these laws were high (physical punishment plus social ostracism), violations were avoided; thus, unexpected and unpleasant emotional reactions to violations were rare. Still, it is impossible, perhaps unnecessary too, for families or informal communities to cover every detail of a certain social relation in written regulations; therefore, it is inevitable for *knowledge and expectations of social relations to stay implicit, unspoken, tacit and ambivalent.* What should be done when one child refuses to play with another child anymore after the two have played for some time? How could a first-year university student know how to make new friends while violating the pressure of binge drinking? Why would a widow start to think that her changed marital status means all her social relations have changed? Why are so many elder ladies living alone reluctant to call their neighbours to have a chat or to initiate any other social activity? To most members of most societies, these are questions too trivial to think about seriously and therefore should be left to each member to deal with privately. So they answer these questions with their own interpretations, norms, or 'laws', and take actions accordingly, even though there is no evidence that other members of the society would concur. Questions regarding how to establish and maintain social relations are left unanswered perhaps intentionally, because they are deemed as private or trivial, or both. Individuals are expected to learn from specific incidents they experienced, from talking to others (family members, friends, etc.), from reading, from the mass media. This is why the socializing process for handling social relations is very much informal, private, sporadic, and unconscious. *It is widely recognized as an issue that should remain in each individual's private space.*

However, if it is each individual's responsibility to discover how to manage their social relations via their own experiences, there would be no hope for an individual to bring up loneliness to others as an issue, because it is merely a by-product of the individual's private life and therefore must be kept as such. In addition, the lonely individual would be very reluctant to resort to others for help with such private matter if the revelation of loneliness will bring negative social images to those suffering from loneliness. Although different cultures may interpret and react to a certain emotional experience with different meanings and interpretations, it is universal that no human beings would like to create negative images of themselves in the eyes of those around them, because we could safely assume that to keep dignity, confidence and respect is part of the human nature. As Fromm observed:

> A person who has not been completely alienated, who has remained sensitive and able to feel, who has not lost the sense of dignity, who is not yet 'for sale,' who can still suffer over the suffering of others, who has not acquired fully the having mode of existence – briefly, a person who has remained a person and not become a thing – cannot help feeling lonely, powerless, isolated in present-day society.[29]

No culture sees loneliness as a positive (desirable) psychological trait, and although the lonely may be stigmatized differently in different cultures, they are commonly seen as being weak, lacking confidence, unpopular or narcissistic, and it is their fault to carry this stigma. Had loneliness been perceived as a normal and neutral experience, it would have come up much more frequently in daily conversations and other discourses. As described and explained aptly by Riesman and his associates, this is how the Americans became 'a lonely crowd' – everyone wants to be popular and would become very unpopular if they share your unpleasant feelings with others, which in turn makes them even lonelier. Worse, they get into what James Lynch called 'the loneliness trap' – a vicious self-reinforcing process with no one talking about it and therefore no hope of getting out of it. It is worth quoting his powerful points here:

> many people – in fact, almost all people – recognize that loneliness exists in our society. And yet, in spite of all the talk about loneliness, the word 'loneliness' often seems to be completely detached form feelings, and especially detached from the idea that it produces suffering. 'If you don't tell me you're suffering from loneliness, then I won't tell you I'm suffering either.' . . . Many lonely people do not appear to be lonely at all – they do not look like they are suffering – and so the truly lonely individual is forced to believe that, as the only one suffering, he therefore shouldn't discuss his plight. Everyone believes he or she is the only one who feels lonely, and therefore we are forced to tell ourselves that loneliness must be a mirage. In our society, King Loneliness has no clothes, but we are afraid to acknowledge that fact.[30]

He called such situations 'loneliness traps':

> those who suggest that modern men and women should be totally self-sufficient and independent have woven an elaborate loneliness trap. Interpersonal freedom is the melody they play, and millions now march in step behind them. These pipers trap people because they make them feel guilty and ashamed for even admitting that they are lonely. They insinuate that it is a sign of weakness to admit publicly that a person really needs someone else. Yet, such an admission to another human being is frequently the catalyst allowing the other person to also admit that he or she is equally lonely.[31]

Now we could see a tension: on the one hand, we want to keep being ourselves; on the other, we suffer from not being able to relate ourselves to others in a way we value. How much self or privacy would we give up in order to obtain help and support from others? Is there a balance that we can strike between keeping our autonomy, independence and dignity on the one hand, and surrendering ourselves to others when we need them on the other? Few cultural and societal systems have attempted to answer these questions seriously.

Put differently, a key issue in the socialization and regulation of social relations is how to identify myself and others:[32] who am I in relation to a particular group of other human beings? Who are the others in a particular way? Do I see myself as 'one of them'? Do they recognize me as 'one of them'? Socialization is the process of finding answers to these questions. Answers to these questions constitute the social identity of a particular person. Initially, the answers must be explicitly stated; once they are found, the answers become part of our 'social intuition'. Our mind would be in peace if we have clear and satisfactory answers to both questions; and we hope that from then on we do not have to answer these questions anymore. When we have to go back to our answers to any of the questions and find that either we do not have an answer or have to find a new answer for any particular social relation, our mind starts to struggle, and the struggle could cause emotional pain; one of such pains is loneliness. As both the number of groups of others that the self could relate to and the number of ways in which the self could relate to a particular group of others can be large, the chance of obtaining satisfactory answers to questions of identities all the time could be quite low; conversely, the probability of feeling lonely is expected to be high throughout the life course. Those who could always find positive answers to the above questions – both the self and the others recognize each other as belonging to the same social community – should have very low risk of feeling lonely, while those who are lost with answers or find negative answers are at high risk of being lonely.

It could be derived therefore, that humans will feel the most severe loneliness at the moment of discovering that they could *identify* themselves *with no one else.* Extreme loneliness comes when the self could not identify any others so as to claim that both the self and these others all belong to the same set of something. Although the words 'lonely' or 'loneliness' were not used, the 'human' creature created by Frankenstein could be the loneliest of all:

> When I looked around I saw and heard of none like me. Was I, then, a monster, a blot upon the earth, from which all men fled and whom all men disowned? . . . I had never yet seen a being resembling me or who claimed any intercourse with me. What was I? The question again returned, to be answered only with groans . . . My person was hideous and my stature gigantic. What did this mean? Who was I? What was I? Whence did I come? What was my destination?[33]

This is 'the loneliness of sole identity'. It is an extreme form of loneliness because the word 'social' has completely lost its meaning, as there is no one of the same set that the self could possibly relate to; yogis know some other humans will come to them with food and other essentials, and criminals in solitary confinements knew other criminals and the guards were around. Note, however, that not belonging to the same species of those around is not the cause of the loneliness of Frankenstein's creature; it was the rejection, the exclusion, and the refusal that make the creature lonely. As the story is fictional, it should be appropriate to use a hypothetical situation: What would have happened had Frankenstein created an extreme beauty that no human beauty could match? The impossibly beautiful creature would not belong to any set of humans either, but it will not feel lost or lonely when all humans compete to be social with it. A difference of identity is a preliminary condition for loneliness, but it is *how those involved interpret the nature of the difference* that will determine whether the feeling of loneliness will arise. If we classify the interpretations into three categories – undesirable, neutral, and desirable, we could expect loneliness to be the most severe in the first situation, mild in the second, and none in the third.

The experience of Sigmund Freud offers a realistic case of loneliness as an emotional reaction to social rejection and exclusion. Loneliness never occurred to him until he found few academics would accept his new theories. In 1887 he had written to his family: 'One finds scientific support nowhere; rather there is an effort "not to give you a chance" which you feel is very disagreeable.' Seven years later, he wrote to Wilhelm Fliess: 'I am pretty much alone here in the elucidation of the neuroses. They look upon me as pretty much of a monomaniac, while I have the distinct feeling that I have touched upon one of the great secrets of nature.'[34] Later, he called that time 'those lonely years',[35] which he could triumphantly claim the loneliness 'splendid isolation'[36] as it allowed him to produce some of his most important works.

By now the complexities of loneliness may have become clearer to the reader: human beings feel lonely because they are involved in many social relations that are indispensable to their survival, but these relations are short-lived, or turn sour, or disappear for different reasons, which in turn depend on how the self identifies itself and others. One common way of classifying loneliness is to focus on the degree of closeness of the self to the others. Perhaps the simplest classification is the distinction between emotional and social loneliness, created by Robert Weiss several decades ago.[37] Emotional loneliness is the most common and easiest to understand: soon after being born, humans develop emotional attachment to the others who take care of them, and when these others disappear, we feel lonely. Later, our circle of social relations expands to other human beings, to whom we may develop emotional attachment as well but not as strong as to our carers. Rather, it is more a sense of belonging, membership, trust, and mutual commitment that becomes part of our mental state, and we will experience social loneliness if such sense is threatened. Shortly after Weiss published his classification, Sadler and Johnson published their scheme of loneliness along four dimensions: interpersonal, social, cultural, and cosmic.[38] Clearly, 'interpersonal loneliness' is very similar to Weiss's 'emotional loneliness', and Sadler and Johnson's 'social loneliness' is about the same as Weiss's. 'Cultural loneliness' stems from the deterioration or severance of an even more remote social relation: the relation between the self and those who belong to the same culture. The relation is much less personal now: the self may not even be able to identify specific persons of a particular culture, or the specific names do not matter anymore; what matters are the values and regular behaviours that represent that particular culture. Even more remote is the relationship between the self and the wider world and universe – could the individual person find a meaningful position in the world and the universe? This question may not come to the minds of all human beings, but some human beings start to search for an answer, and they will feel lonely if they cannot obtain a satisfactory answer. Sadler and Johnson also pointed out that the severity of loneliness would increase with the number of dimensions, that is, the loneliness experienced at two or more dimensions is more serious and unbearable than the loneliness experienced at one dimension.

As there are other ways of classifying social relations, there must be other types of loneliness. This is a relatively minor issue, however. More important to our understanding of loneliness is how a particular social relation becomes

strained or terminated. This is an important question because it affects how people determine how acceptable the changing relation is, which in turn will affect
how lonely they are, how long they will feel lonely for, and how often they will
feel lonely. Some social relations come to an end due to certain *natural forces*.
For example, victims of natural disasters (hurricanes, earthquakes, etc.) have
to leave their homes, thereby losing some of their relations at the same time;
widowers lose their spouses who died of advanced age or incurable diseases. As
these natural forces are very much out of the human control, the loneliness thus
induced should be more bearable than other types of loneliness. The intensity of
such loneliness is expected to be high, but the understanding and acceptance of
uncontrollable events could reduce the duration of the loneliness. The implication is that loneliness due to *human factors* should become less acceptable and
therefore less tolerable. And we could even distinguish the ways in which social
relations come to an end by identifying *who is responsible*, the self or the others, for the ending. The loneliness of a person whose spouse has decided to file a
divorce because of an affair with someone else is of a very different nature and
degree from the loneliness of a widower whose spouse died of a natural cause.
Similarly, the loneliness of a boy who has been repeatedly rejected by peers is
much more painful than the loneliness of another boy who has to move to another
place because his father has a new job there. Older people must feel much lonelier if they know that their children do not care to visit or call them than if it is
simply unfeasible for their children to do so. These examples suggest that it may
be insufficient to know what types of social relations are involved in causing
certain loneliness; we the researchers should pay serious attention to *the human
intentions and interpretations of the process* in which certain social relations are
believed to have caused loneliness.

If the general or ultimate origins of loneliness must be found in the changes
of social relations, we need to trace further to find the sources of these changes.
Where to look for the sources distinguishes sociologists from the researchers
in other disciplines. As loneliness has been a major research issue in psychology, neurology, and public health, individual attributes and life events – gender,
age, marital status, living arrangement, health conditions, number of confidants,
etc. – are the commonly identified 'risk factors' for loneliness. The principle guid-
ing such research is that a certain value of a particular factor would increase the
likelihood of feeling lonely, while the opposite value of the same factor would
reduce the likelihood. For example, age over a particular threshold such as 65
will make one person more likely to feel lonely. The sociological perspective to
studying loneliness goes beyond these individual factors and focuses instead on
factors at higher levels, such as group, institutions, societies, and cultures. A small
number of researchers have done some work on the effects of these higher level
factors, particularly national cultures, on loneliness, which shall be introduced in
the remaining chapters of this book. A key objective of this book is to develop
research on this front. Besides national cultures, we shall pay serious attention
to how social structures, such as inequality, social mobility, diversity in race and

ethnicity, etc., affect the prevalence of loneliness across different societies. Such sociological perspective also examines the effects of large scale social events as well, such as wars or collective conflicts, forced migrations, economic and financial crises.

In close relation to the inclination to focus on macro-level factors and events is the sociologist's interest in the distribution of fortunes and misfortunes across different social groups. As we see loneliness as a kind of misfortune, it is important for us to study loneliness across different social groups: Is loneliness more prevalent in some groups than in others? Does it mean the same to all social groups? Do the risk factors vary from one group to another? Studies aiming to answer these questions would show *the irony that while people are lonely individually, they are not lonely alone as there are many others as lonely as they are*. One function of a book like this one is to raise people's awareness of such situation, that is, *they are not lonely alone*, which itself could potentially reduce the intensity of their loneliness. Knowledge of the social distribution of loneliness would then beg the questions about what people living in the same society do and what they should do after learning this knowledge. What things do the lonely tend more likely to do that the non-lonely would not? What are the key differences between societies with high rates of loneliness and those with low rates? Which social institutions are most effective at reducing high prevalence of loneliness? *Loneliness, albeit individually experienced, is in fact a societal phenomenon, and thus should be treated and tackled as such.* This is perhaps the most important principle of the sociological perspective to studying loneliness.

Notes

1 J. H. Turner (ed.). 2011. *The Sociology of Emotions*. Cambridge: Cambridge University Press.
2 G. Simmel. [1903] 2002. 'The metropolis and mental life', in G. Bridge and S. Watson (eds), *The Blackwell City Reader*. Malden, MA: Wiley-Blackwell.
3 D. Riesman, N. Glazer, and R. Denney. 1961. *The Lonely Crowd: A Study of the Changing American Character*, abridged edition. New Haven, CT: Yale University Press, pp. 24–25.
4 Ibid., p. 24.
5 Ibid.
6 D. Perlman and L. A. Peplau. 1982. 'Theoretical approaches to loneliness', in L. A. Peplau and D. Perlman (eds), *Loneliness: A Sourcebook of Current Theory, Research, and Therapy*. Chichester: John Wiley & Sons, pp. 126–127.
7 J. Hartog. 1980. 'Introduction: the anatomization', in J. Hartog, J. R. Audy, and Y. A. Cohen (eds), *The Anatomy of Loneliness*. New York: International University Press, p. 11.
8 The concept of anomie gained some popularity among sociologists in the 1960s: see R. K. Merton. 1964. 'Anomie, anomia, and social interaction: contexts of deviant behaviour', in M. B. Clinard (ed.), *Anomie and Deviant Behaviour: A Discussion and Critique*. Glencoe, IL: Free Press. McClosky and Schaar later developed the concept to refer to 'a state of mind, a cluster of attitudes, beliefs, and feelings in the minds of individuals. Specifically, it is the feeling that the world and oneself are adrift, wandering,

lacking in clear rules and stable moorings . . . The core of the concept is the feeling of moral emptiness.' H. McClosky and J. Schaar. 1965. 'Psychological dimensions of anomy', *American Sociological Review*, 30: 14–40.

9   É. Durkheim. [1893] 1984. *The Division of Labour in Society*, translated by W. D. Halls. New York: The Free Press; É. Durkheim. [1897] 2006. *On Suicide*, translated by Robin Buss. London: Penguin Books.

10 L. Srole. 1956. 'Social integration and certain corollaries', *American Sociological Review*, 21: 709–716.

11 P. Slater. 1971. *The Pursuit of Loneliness: American Cultural at the Breaking Point*. London: Allen Lane.

12 R. Putnam. 2001. *Bowling Alone: The Collapse and Revival of American Community*. New York: Simon & Schuster.

13 E. Klinenberg. 2014. *Going Solo: The Extraordinary Rise and Surprising Appeal of Living Alone*. London: Gerald Duckworth & Co.

14 W. A. Sadler and T. B. Johnson, Jr. 1980. 'From loneliness to anomia', in J. Hartog, J. R. Audy, and Y. A. Cohen (eds), *The Anatomy of Loneliness*. New York: International University Press, p. 55.

15 Ibid., pp. 34–64.

16 J. Cacioppo and W. Patrick. 2008. *Loneliness: Human Nature and the Need for Social Connection*. New York: W. W. Norton & Company, p. 4.

17 G. C. Homans. 1950. *The Human Group*. New York: Harcourt, Brace.

18 Cacioppo and Patrick, *Loneliness*, p. 162.

19 Ibid., p. 163.

20 Ibid., p. 174.

21 Ibid., p. 175.

22 Ibid., p. 179; see also S. L. Murray, G. M. Bellavia, P. Rose, and D. W. Grifin. 2003. 'Once hurt, twice hurtful: how perceived regard regulates daily marital interactions', *Journal of Personality and Social Psychology*, 84: 126–147; M. T. Wittenberg and H. T. Reis. 1986. 'Loneliness, social skills, and social perceptions', *Personality and Social Psychology Bulletin*, 12(1): 121–130; J. T. Cacioppo and L. C. Harkley, 'People thinking about people: the vicious circle of being a social outcast in one's own mind', in K. D. Williams, J. P. Forgas, and W. von Hippel (eds). 2005. *The Social Outcast: Ostracism, Social Exclusion, Rejection, and Bullying*. New York: Psychology Press.

23 Ibid., p. 175.

24 Ibid., p. 180.

25 Ibid., p. 170.

26 *Lars and the Real Girl* is a 2007 film directed by Craig Gillespie, written by Nancy Oliver, and starring Ryan Gosling.

27 George Herbert Mead, 1934 [1967]. *Mind, Self & Society: From the Standpoint of a Social Behaviorist*, edited with an introduction by C. W. Morris. Chicago, IL: University of Chicago Press, p. 133.

28 For example, see A. Storr. 1988. *Solitude*. London: HarperCollins Publishers, ch. 4, 'Enforced solitude'.

29 E. Fromm. 1993. *The Art of Being*. London: Constable, p. 65.

30 J. J. Lynch. 2000. *A Cry Unheard: New Insights into the Medical Consequences of Loneliness*. Baltimore, MD: Bancroft Press, p. 333.

31 Ibid., p. 335.

32 Besides Riesman's *The Lonely Crowd*, the following sociological studies contain a large number of insights about the relationship between the self and others (or social structure in general) although they did not relate their points to the experience of loneliness, at least not directly: W. H. Whyte. 1957. *The Organization Man*. London: Jonathan Cape; H. Marcuse. 1964. *One Dimensional Man: Studies in the Ideology of*

Advanced Industrial Society. London: Routledge; Salter, *The Pursuit of Loneliness*; R. Sennet. 1977. *The Fall of Public Man.* Cambridge: Cambridge University Press; C. Lasch. 1979. *The Culture of Narcissism: American Life in an Age of Diminishing Expectations.* London: Abacus; R. Bellah et al. 1985. *Habits of the Heart: Individualism and Commitment in American Life.* Berkeley, CA: University of California Press; and K. Gregen. 1991. *The Saturated Self: Dilemmas of Identity in Contemporary Life.* New York: Basic Books. Thomson and McClay have both produced excellent critical assessments of this literature: I. T. Thomson. 2000. *In Conflict No Longer: Self and Society in Contemporary America.* Lanham, MD: Rowman & Littlefield; W. M. McClay. 1994. *The Masterless: Self and Society in Modern America.* Chapel Hill, NC: University of North Carolina Press.

33 M. Shelley. [1818] 1985. *Frankenstein.* London: Penguin Books, pp. 166–167, 174.

34 H. Gardner. 1993. *Creating Minds: An Anatomy of Creativity Seen through the Lives of Freud, Einstein, Picasso, Stravinsky, Elliot, Graham, and Gandhi.* New York: Basic Books, p. 61.

35 R. W. Clark. 1980. *Freud: The Man and the Cause.* New York: Random House, p. 141

36 S. Freud. 1963. *A History of the Psychoanalytic Movement.* New York: Collier Books, p. 304.

37 R. Weiss. 1975. *Loneliness: the Experience of Emotional and Social Isolation.* Cambridge, MA: MIT Press.

38 Sadler and Johnson, 'From Loneliness to Anomia'.

Chapter 3

Loneliness: a problem only for older people?

When being asked to put up an image of a lonely person in their minds, most people would have the following: a lady of an advanced age watching out of her room, alone. This stereotypical image of the lonely contains several perceptions of loneliness: that loneliness is a problem typically found among older people,[1] that older females are more likely to be lonely than older males, and that older people are lonely because they do not have much to do and have few people around them. In this chapter we carefully consider these statements and examine how true they are with available research findings and evidence. Essentially, these statements are general and ambiguous answers to some important questions about loneliness: At what age do older people become much more vulnerable to loneliness than the younger groups? Is it really true that older people, regardless of how they are defined, are always lonelier than *all* younger groups? Or more generally, is there a universal relationship between age and loneliness across different societies? Are female older people always more likely to suffer from loneliness than their male counterparts? It does not make much sense to say that people become lonely simply because their biological age has reached a certain point – age is only a numerical record of biological existence, which does not do anything to a person's mind. Clearly, what makes older people lonely are the events that come with an advanced age, so what are these events? The answers provided in the rest of this chapter may not be statistically the most sophisticated, but they should help the reader realize and appreciate some of the complexities in the relationship between age and loneliness.

Age and loneliness: theoretical models

If you had the above stereotypical image of lonely people in your mind, you are certainly not alone. That is not surprising because we know that some life events will more likely to occur to older people, which in turn will make them lonely: retirement from work comes with the severance of relations with former colleagues and others (customers, clients, etc.); children of older people, once having become adults, will sooner or later to live on their own, thus inadvertently shrinking their older parents' social circles; older people are more likely to suffer from chronic or serious health problems, and some even become disabled to a certain extent, which may make them less able to be social with others; finally, some older people, especially the so-called 'oldest old' (usually above 80), will leave this world, making their surviving spouses, partners, and other relatives feel lonely. With at least some of these events in mind, people would 'naturally' perceive loneliness as an experience almost exclusively confined to older people. To them, loneliness is an inevitable and thus normal part of ageing. This also explains why loneliness has become a vibrant research enterprise in all branches of gerontology, the study of the ageing process.

A related question is: Do the older people themselves think that loneliness is a problem particularly common among them? Available evidence shows some differentiated perceptions. Those in Europe seem to agree. The 1992 Eurobarometer Survey reported that 'Older people were more likely than those aged 15–24 to say loneliness or isolation is the main problem facing older people . . . '.[2] In contrast, older people in the US tend to think otherwise. In 2009, the Pew Survey on 'Growing Old in America' reported that 29% of those aged 18–64, compared with 17% of those aged 65 and over, expected loneliness to be a part of old age.[3] The importance of such perception among older people lies in the possible effect of self-fulfilling prophesy: if they believe loneliness is a 'natural' or 'normal' experience among older people, they will become lonely. A potential positive effect from the perception is that it makes older people more comfortable of revealing their lonely experience to others, which itself is an important first step towards healing the painful feeling. At the moment, however, this still remains a theory.

A more important question is: how true is the perceived connection between older age and loneliness? Or, is it true that loneliness is a serious problem *only* for older people? This question is important because different answers represent different theoretical models (or expectations) of the relationship between age and loneliness. Let's go through these models and see how plausible they are.

Perhaps the simplest and most naive is the linear model (Figure 3.1); consistent with the stereotype illustrated above, it says that people of an older age will always be lonelier than those of a younger age. It is simple because it assumes

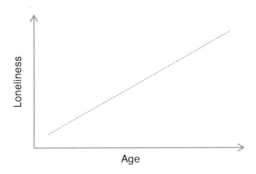

Figure 3.1 The linear model of loneliness increasing with age.

a universal connection of age to loneliness; that is, throughout the possible age range for human beings, on average, a person of a higher age is expected to be lonelier than another person of a lower age. And this is also the reason for its naivety: while it is still possible that this model represents the reality for a certain population at a particular point of time, it is difficult to imagine the painful process in which the risk of feeling loneliness increases at the same pace with the process of growing up and ageing, no matter how old you are!

What most people would expect in the relationship between age and loneliness is the shape represented in Figure 3.2, which we may call 'the loneliness at old age model'. It says that the prevalence (or the risk) of loneliness remains very much the same under a certain old age but increases significantly over that age point. Most people would find this model more acceptable as it is supported by life events listed previously, such as retirement, illness, living alone, etc. Where this age threshold is located is an empirical matter; that is, it depends on the place, the time, and the social group under study; for some populations, 50 may be enough; for others, one may have to be 60, or 65, or any other more advanced age. Note that the key difference between this model and the previous model lies not in the assumption of linearity of the relationship but in the existence of the age threshold. In effect, both models assume a linear relationship between age and loneliness, although Figure 3.2 argues that the relationship mostly exists for people aged above a certain point.

Now, some researchers have found the above argument problematic. They may not dismiss the prevalence of the loneliness among older people, but they would not accept that older people are the only group that is vulnerable to loneliness. They do not mean, however, that people of all age groups are equally vulnerable; in addition to older people, those at the other end of the age continuum – children, adolescents, and perhaps even young adults – are subject to the risk of being lonely as well. As early as 1982, Robert Weiss, one of the few sociologists who have taken loneliness seriously, suspected that 'Loneliness almost certainly is more common in adolescence than later in life, and possibly more intense as well, although we as yet lack the survey data that would provide conclusive evidence for this observation'.[4]

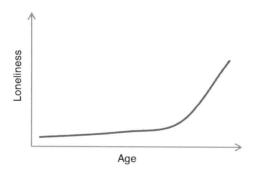

Figure 3.2 The loneliness at older age model.

Around the turn of the millennium, drawing on his own experience and studies conducted by Columbia University, James Lynch strongly believed that communicative difficulties and educational failures (drop-outs) would make children very lonely.[5] In the past two decades or so, we finally have more recent evidence for the prevalence of loneliness among children and adolescents. For example, data from New Zealand support the U-shaped model in that there is a non-linear relationship between age and loneliness, with reported rates of loneliness of 20% for those aged 15–24, decreasing to around 12–13% in midlife and increasing to 18% for those aged 65 and older,[6] a pattern nicely fitting the curve in Figure 3.3.

All the above three models assume a certain kind of relationship between age and loneliness, although they differ in the exact shape of the relationship. That assumption itself may not be true, at least for certain social groups or populations. For example, if loneliness comes from the lack of desired social relations, then loneliness will be an alien feeling to those who are lucky enough to have all of the social relations they wish to have. In an opposite situation, it is also possible that almost all members of a population felt lonely after a traumatic event, such as large-scale collective violence. If so, no socio-demographic attributes, including age, would show any connection with loneliness. While such groups or populations might be rare in reality, it is still helpful to put it down as a null or reference model (Figure 3.4).[7]

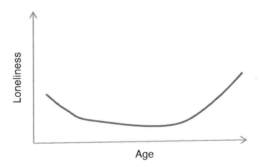

Figure 3.3 The U-shaped model of age and loneliness.

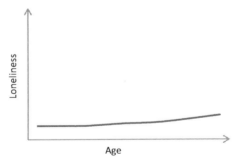

Figure 3.4 The flat model of age and loneliness.

Age and loneliness: variations across time and space

In this section I will identify and demonstrate which of the above models represent the relationship between age and loneliness in real life. At the same time, I will also present the variation of this relationship across countries and time periods, as it is almost certain that the relationship changes over these two dimensions. To do so will require data that contain relevant information, and I shall reply on the data collected from World Values Survey (WVS) and the European Social Survey (ESS).

To start with, I shall present graphs that demonstrate the age-loneliness relationship by analysing the data collected in the second wave of the WVS (1990).[8] Eighteen countries participated in this wave. However, only fifteen countries produced valid data for the question on loneliness. Slovakia had the smallest sample size (466), while the sample sizes of all other countries were much bigger, ranging from 924 for Czech Republic to 2736 for South Africa. Here is the relevant question in the survey: 'We are interested in the way people are feeling these days. During the past few weeks, did you ever feel very lonely or remote from other people?',[9] with two options: 1 = yes, 2 = no. The original age of each respondent has been recoded into eight groups: ≤19, 20–29, 30–39, 40–49, 50–59, 60–69, 70–79, ≥80. The relationship between the two will be shown with the percentage of respondents of each age group who answered 'Yes' to the above question. In order to facilitate comparison, the vertical scale representing the percentage of 'very lonely' has been made the same (0 to 50%). Figure 3.5 shows what the shape of the relationship in each country looks like.

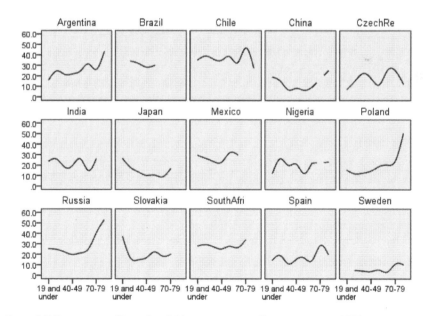

Figure 3.5 Percentage of 'very lonely' by age group in fifteen countries, 1990.

Many students of statistics have learnt the aphorism 'All models are wrong, but some are useful'. The four models presented early are all wrong as none of them describes any of the above relationships perfectly. Fortunately, that does not mean that we should give up using them; they are useful in several ways here. First, they summarize the relevant information so that we could see some patterns, connections, or common features. Second, some of them may come as a surprise to us, thereby revealing new information or bringing up new puzzles to us. Third, they help us make sense of the features of the reality because they represent our expectations, hypotheses, and theories.

The linear model (Figure 3.1) appears to fit the case of Argentina quite well – a straight line would fit the general linear trend with only a small amount of deviation and fluctuation.

The second 'loneliness at older age' model (Figure 3.2) seems to represent the situation in Russia particularly well: the percentages remain stable and pick up quickly after the age of sixty. Poland follows a very similar shape, although one could argue that it is a mixture of all three models: linear, older-age, and U-shaped.

The U-shaped model (Figure 3.3) represents the situations in China and Japan; and in a much milder manner, Mexico and Spain show a similar shape. We should take some caution here, however, as there were no respondents in the two oldest age groups (70–79 for China, 80+ for Japan, and both for Mexico). The problem of missing cases is the most serious for Brazil, whose survey failed to cover the youngest group (under 19) and the older three groups (60 and above).

If we could tolerate a certain level of fluctuations, the 'flat model' (Figure 3.4) could be used to represent several countries at different levels: Brazil (30–35%), Chile (30–40%), Czech Republic (10–25%), India (15–25%), Nigeria (10–25%), South Africa (25–35%), and Switzerland (5–10%). One could include Mexico here as well (20–30%). In these countries, the prevalence of loneliness hardly varies with the change of age, although the level of prevalence varies from country to country.

Slovakia is an outlier that does not fit any of the four models. Its age-loneliness relationship follows an 'L' shape, meaning loneliness was much more prevalent among the youth (under 19) than among the older groups. It is the only country in which the youngest group suffered from a higher prevalence of loneliness than all other adult groups. Again, we must be cautious here: there were only nineteen people in this young age group, and no respondents in the highest age group.

Putting these results together, how much support could we get for the claim that loneliness is a problem for older people? Of the fifteen countries, Argentina, Poland and Russia offer the strongest support, with people aged sixty and above suffering from a much higher rate of loneliness than all other younger groups. A few countries, including Chile, Czech Republic, Spain and Switzerland, show much weaker supporting evidence. Overall, we must accept an answer to the question with a strong reservation: *it depends on the country* we are talking about. As Christina Victor and I observed in a paper on this issue:

> We should consider the effect of age only after we have taken into account the effect of nationality. There is no consistent association between age and

the prevalence of loneliness across all of the nations studied. In fact, national differentials in terms of the percentages of frequent loneliness (all or almost all the time and most of the time) at any particular age level are substantial. It is therefore misleading to associate age with loneliness without firstly specifying the nation in which the association is examined.[10]

The reader may have already had a sense that this dataset is not ideal for several reasons: the year of study (1990) was nearly three decades ago, the number of countries with valid results was small despite that it was a worldwide survey, and the number of people in some age groups was perhaps too small to make the results reliable. It is therefore necessary to examine more updated and comprehensive data in order for us to develop a better grip on the issue. Below, I shall present the results produced with the analysis of the data collected from several rounds of the ESS. While it is a much reliable and larger dataset, the results produced are not free from limitations: they are only valid for the European countries that participated in the survey in any particular year (or wave), and children were not eligible participants. At the moment, I am not aware of any study that covers loneliness across the entire range of age. The ESS does have several strengths: in each wave it covers more than twenty countries in Europe; the survey design team is consisted of many specialists who employed the cutting-edge techniques to ensure the comparability of the results across the participating countries; the sample sizes are sufficiently big for statistical analyses, and each sample is statistically representative of its target population; and it included a question on loneliness in multiple waves so that we can have an idea of how the prevalence of loneliness has changed over time.

So far the ESS has released data from eight rounds, of which Round 3 (2006), 5 (2010), 6 (2012), and 7 (2014) contain the following question on loneliness: 'please tell me how much of the time during the past week you felt lonely?', and respondents were asked to choose one from the following four options: 1 = none or almost none of the time; 2 = some of the time; 3 = most of the time; 4 = all or almost all of the time.[11] Two important differences between this question and the one used in WVS are worth mentioning. The question used in WVS is designed to measure the *intensity* of loneliness of the respondent at the moment they were being asked the question. In contrast, the question in the ESS is about the *frequency* of the respondent's feeling. As pointed out before, these two aspects of loneliness should not be assumed to be equivalent or interchangeable. Both set up a time frame in order to help the respondent recall their experiences: for the WVS, it was 'during the past few weeks', and for the ESS, it was 'during the past week'. Clearly, respondents participating in the ESS would find it easier to answer the question as the time frame was shorter and clearer. These are not pedantic academic worries over wordings; they are important as they affect the quality of the data that we use for drawing out arguments and conclusions. By designing a better formulated question and sticking to it over several years and across more than twenty countries, the ESS provides us with much more reliable and meaningful data.

In Figure 3.6, the number of lines is also the number of rounds of the ESS that a particular country took a part. For countries that participated in more than

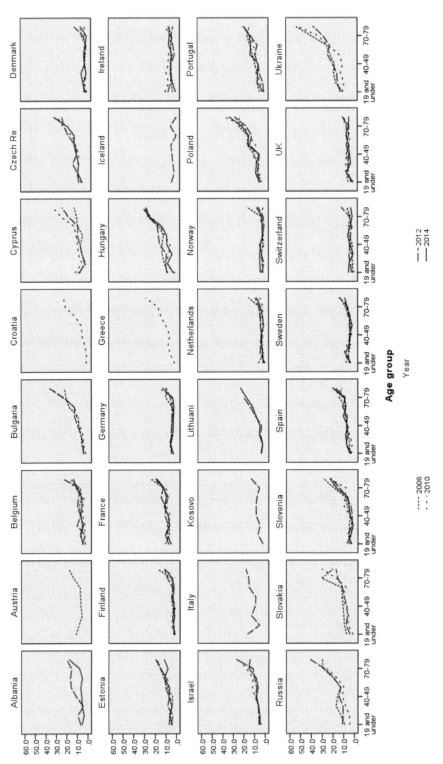

Figure 3.6 Percentage of 'frequently lonely' (most, almost all, and all the time) by age group, year and country in Europe.

one round, the lines could suggest the stability of the age-loneliness relationship over time. Lines clearly separated apart from each other mean low stability, while those hardly distinguishable high stability. Reading through the graphs across these thirty-two countries, we could make several interesting observations. For the overall shape, the following countries follow a basically linear relationship: Bulgaria, Croatia, Czech Republic, Estonia, Greece, Hungary, Israel, Lithuania, Poland, Portugal, Russia, Slovakia, and Ukraine. There are some variations within this group, in terms of the steepness of the lines and the stability over time. *These are the countries where loneliness is clearly a serious issue for older people.*[12] Few countries show a clear U-shaped curve; perhaps the countries whose pattern is closest to the U-shaped model is Austria, Cyprus, Italy, and to a milder extent, Sweden. Most of the countries in the western and northern parts of Europe follow an almost 'flat' shape: Denmark, Finland, Germany, Iceland, Ireland, Netherlands, Norway, Sweden, Switzerland, and the UK. Note that Kosovo follows a similar shape, although it has data only for one year. These countries enjoy the lowest levels of prevalence of loneliness in the world; in the meantime, they are also the countries where loneliness is a popular topic for academic research. It is interesting to note that for most countries in this group, the temporal stability has reduced for the older age groups, suggesting that *relative to other age groups in the same country*, older people seem to be vulnerable to somehow higher risk of feeling frequently lonely. That is, the majority of the adult populations in western Europe and Northern American countries are not lonely, and the rates of the 'often lonely' among the older people have stayed in the range of 5–10%.[13] This is reflected more strongly in the following countries, which we may put into a separate group, where the prevalence of the 'frequently lonely' changes very mildly but *picks up for the older age groups* (above 60), including Belgium, Estonia, France, Israel, Slovakia, Slovenia, and Spain.

To sum up, we could make the following qualified answers to the question whether loneliness is a problem for older people by looking at three groups of countries:

1   Of the nearly thirty European countries under study, a small number (Bulgaria, Cyprus, Czech Republic, Greece, Hungary, Poland, Russia, and Ukraine) show the strongest linear relationship between age and the prevalence of 'frequent loneliness', which offers clear evidence for the widely held perception that loneliness becomes a serious problem with the increase of age.

2   In the second group, the age-loneliness relationship in some European countries (Belgium, Croatia, Estonia, France, Israel, Lithuania, Portugal, Slovakia, Slovenia, and Spain) is also linear, but to a much milder extent. Older people in these countries are subject to higher risks of feeling lonely than the younger generations in the same country, but their absolute levels of prevalence of loneliness are much lower than those in the first group.

3   Most northern and western European countries show almost no ('flat') relationship between age and loneliness until age reaches a highly advanced point
('the old old' or even 'the oldest old'). Even for these groups, the prevalence
of frequent loneliness is much lower than that of the much younger groups in
other European countries, showing the effect of national context on the age-
loneliness relationship.

Loneliness among older people: a closer look

The previous section has described the overall age-loneliness relationship in
different national contexts. One cannot help but ask why loneliness is so much
more prevalent in eastern European countries than in the western and northern
European countries. This is a very important and difficult question, to which I
shall offer some theories and evidence later in Chapter 8. Here, let's stick to the
relationship between age and loneliness and take a closer look at it. Cacioppo
offered a physiological explanation for the increased risk of feeling lonely at
an older age: 'the physiological toll of loneliness likely becomes more appar-
ent with ageing. Since the body's stress hormones are intricately involved in
fighting inflammation and infection, it appears that loneliness contributes to
the wear and tear of ageing through this pathway as well'.[14] Given loneliness
is indeed a problem for older people in most of the countries, either absolutely across countries or relatively within a particular country, let's zoom in
and compare the older people with the younger generations on other aspects
so that we could have a sense of what make older people lonely in different
national contexts. Obviously, given the limited space on the one hand and the
large amount of data on the other, there is a limit to how close a look we can
take. We shall organize our comparisons as follows. To keep the contrasting
national contexts, we shall focus on two cases, each representing a different
age-loneliness relationship in a different region of Europe: The Netherlands
(the nearly flat shape with a gentle jump at older ages in northern Europe) and
Poland (the strong linear relationship in eastern Europe). Temporarily, as the
lines in Figure 3.6 follow a very similar pattern, it is appropriate to focus on
one year, and here we shall look at the most recent year with data, namely,
2014. For age, the graphs also suggest that it is sufficient for us to focus on
three groups: under 30, 30–59, and 60 plus.

At the individual level, we shall bring in a few factors that may affect the age-
loneliness relationship: gender,[15] marital status, number of people in household,
health conditions, and social life. Our overarching objective in this section is to
discover whether it is truly age, or one of these factors, or some combined effects
of two factors that might make people lonely. The results of our analyses could
also serve as a profile of the lonely in each country, although it will not be a complete one. It is worth repeating a point made earlier: loneliness is not a biological phenomenon; therefore, there is no reason to expect that people will become

frequently lonely once their age has reached a certain threshold; there is simply no biological mechanism that brings about that connection. The low percentage of 'frequent loneliness' in most western and northern European countries are clear and strong evidence for this observation. The same logic applies to gender as well: I am aware of no biological or neurological discoveries that offer a meaningful connection between gender and loneliness. We may observe that loneliness is more prevalent among females than among males, but that does not mean being female makes one lonely until certain neurological mechanisms are discovered. Health and social connections are different, however, as it makes sense to expect someone in poor health or not well connected with others to be lonely. As existing academic studies have shown, the number of 'risk factors for loneliness' could be very large across different demographic, social and economic groups; clearly, here we will be able to focus on only a small number of them. To make the results as accessible as possible to the readers, I shall avoid using sophisticated statistical models and only present simple tables.

Let's start by looking at the prevalence of frequent loneliness across the three age groups in the two countries. Each number in the first three rows of Table 3.1 represents, in each country, the percentage of people in the respective age group who felt lonely either 'most of the time' or 'all or almost all the time' (i.e. 'frequently lonely') in 2014. Together, they send us two clear messages: one, in both countries, the risk to loneliness increases with age – the older the people are, the more likely they will feel frequently lonely; two, the Polish are much more vulnerable to 'frequent loneliness' than the Dutch regardless of age – even the youngest Polish are almost twice more likely to feel frequently lonely than the oldest Dutch. In short, loneliness is a problem for older people, but the national context appears to have a much stronger impact.

Loneliness has also been perceived particularly as a problem for the females, the widowed, and the divorced. And these demographic attributes tend to relate to each other; for example, the percentage of the widowed is expected to be higher among older females, as some physiological laws dictate that they are more likely to outlive their male counterparts. Let's look at the relationship between each of them with loneliness and then put them together.

Table 3.1 Percentage of frequent loneliness by age groups, The Netherlands and Poland, 2014.

	The Netherlands	Poland
Under 30	2.1	7.3
30–59	2.6	9.2
60 +	3.7	19.4
n	1918	1598

The numbers in Table 3.2 confirm the expected relationship between gender and loneliness: in both countries, frequent loneliness is more prevalent among the females than among the males. Note, however, the percentages for the Dutch are so close that their difference, 0.2%, could be seen as negligible. In contrast, the corresponding difference is much bigger in Poland, 4.5%. Yet again, the national context has a more powerful effect than gender: frequent loneliness is so much more prevalent among Polish males than among Dutch females!

Now let's take a look at marital status. On the one hand, the data have confirmed our expectations: in both countries, the prevalence of frequent loneliness is the highest among the widowed and the lowest among the never married (or the singles, to use a word of daily language). Also, the least vulnerable group in Poland – here, the never married – is even more vulnerable (10.2%) than the most vulnerable in The Netherlands, the widowed (9.1%). Perhaps even more striking is that exactly one-third of the married Polish people (or with civil partners) were frequently lonely, almost the same as the widowed! Clearly, marriage has failed to shield the Polish from feeling lonely.

We could take an even closer look at these factors by putting them together, but note that we cannot always put age and marital status together; for example, there will be very few young people who are widowed on the one hand, and very few older people who never married. What we could do is to look the combined

Table 3.2 Percentage of frequent loneliness by gender, The Netherlands and Poland, 2014.

	The Netherlands	Poland
Male	2.6	9.4
Female	2.8	13.9
n	1918	1598

Table 3.3 Percentage of frequent loneliness by marital status, The Netherlands and Poland, 2014.

	The Netherlands	Poland
Married or in civil partnership	3.9	33.3
Divorced or separated	7.8	27.8
Widowed	9.1	34.3
Never married	2.2	10.2
n	882	690

Table 3.4 Percentage of frequent loneliness by age and gender, The Netherlands and Poland, 2014.

		The Netherlands	Poland
Male	Under 30	2.2	7.7
	30–59	3.2	7.9
	60 +	2.0	13.8
Female	Under 30	1.9	6.9
	30–59	2.0	10.4
	60 +	5.0	23.3
	n	1,916	1,598

attributes of age and gender, and marital status with gender. Table 3.4 shows the prevalence of frequent loneliness for the first combination.

The claim that loneliness is particularly a problem for older people gains much support for the females in each of these two countries: those aged 60 and above had a jump in the prevalence of frequent loneliness in comparison with their respective younger groups. In other words, the combined attributes of being female and aged above 60 would put these people much more vulnerable, although this is clearly much more the case if you were Polish – 5% of the Dutch females aged 60+ were frequently lonely, compared with 2% among younger females, while the discrepancy is much bigger among the Polish females, 23% among those 60+ versus 7% (under 30) and 10% (30–59). The Dutch males have given us a surprise: those aged 60 and above had an even lower rate of frequent loneliness than the other two younger groups, although the rates are quite close (about 1% difference). In contrast, Polish males share the same story as their female counterparts: the older they were, the more likely they would be frequently lonely, particularly for older people (above 60).

Now let's look at the combined effects of gender and marital status. Vigilant readers may have noticed that the percentages in Table 3.5 are much higher than those in Table 3.2 although both tables include gender. This is because the people in Table 3.5 are different from those in Table 3.2 – many people did not report their marital status in this survey and therefore they were removed from the analysis, which is shown by the sample size (*n*) at the end of the table. For those who did provide valid data, we can see that the percentage of frequent loneliness among a Dutch group is above 10%: the widowed males, 14.3%, which almost doubled the corresponding rate for Dutch widowed females. Keeping in mind that the Polish are much lonelier than the Dutch, widowhood seems to have hit Dutch males much harder than Dutch females, while this is not the case for the Polish – the widowed females are a bit more vulnerable (35%) than their male counterparts (31%). Another important difference between the two countries is the effect of divorce (or separation): again, it is surprising to see that for the Polish, the married group, a bit more so for males than for females, suffered from about the same rate of frequent

Table 3.5 Percentage of frequent loneliness by gender and marital status, The Netherlands, and Poland, 2014.

		The Netherlands	Poland
Male	Married or in civil partnership	3.7	33.3
	Divorced or separated	6.9	25.9
	Widowed	14.3	31.3
	Never married	2.9	11.1
Female	Married or in civil partnership	4.2	33.3
	Divorced or separated	8.4	28.8
	Widowed	7.6	35.0
	Never married	1.5	9.0
	n	882	690

loneliness as the widowed. For the Dutch, the two gender groups are different: for the Dutch females, divorce or separation is somehow more likely than widowhood to make them frequently lonely, but it is the reverse for the Dutch males.

We now move on to the combined effects of age and the number of people living regularly in the same household, expecting to see evidence for the following relationships: those living in one person households are more likely to feel lonely frequently, and older people tend to live in one person households, which is one reason why older people are more likely to be lonely. The number of people regularly living in the household has been simplified into three groups: one, two, three and above. To save space, I have put two sets of numbers into one table (Table 3.6).

The set of numbers outside the brackets are percentages of people of a particular age group who lived in one, or two, or three and more people households, for each respective country. The three numbers in each row for each country should add up to 100. For example, in The Netherlands, 16.7% of people aged thirty and under lived in one person households, much higher than the corresponding 5% in Poland. Reading through these numbers, we can see that the household sizes among the Dutch are much smaller than those in Poland; that is, the percentages of one or two person households in The Netherlands are consistently higher than those in Poland. Conversely, the percentages of households with three or more regular residents in The Netherlands are much lower than those in Poland. Perhaps the most striking difference is the percentage of older people (60+) living in three plus person households: it was only 4.6% in The Netherlands but 33.6% in Poland. Given these data, and if we accept the theory that those living with more people are less likely to often feel lonely, then we would predict that the Polish must be less likely to be frequently lonely, perhaps with the exception of those older people living alone. With the previous findings in mind, we are almost certain that this is not the case, but let's take a look at the numbers in the brackets.

Table 3.6 Age, number of people in household and frequent loneliness, The Netherlands and Poland, 2014.

	The Netherlands			Poland		
	One	Two	Three+	One	Two	Three+
Under 30	16.7 (7.5)	24.4 (2.4)	58.8 (1.0)	5.0 (22.2)	14.0 (10.0)	81.0 (5.9)
30–59	21.9 (7.5)	23.6 (2.5)	54.5 (1.6)	6.2 (22.9)	19.1 (11.0)	74.7 (7.7)
60+	36.0 (11.3)	59.4 (1.7)	4.6 (0.0)	22.5 (48.1)	43.9 (11.1)	33.6 (11.2)
n		1915			1598	

The set of numbers inside the brackets are percentages of people who were frequently lonely for that particular age and household type combination. For example, of the Dutch young people (under 30) who lived in one person households, 7.5% reported 'frequent loneliness' in the survey of 2014. If we look at only one country at a time, it is indeed the case that the more people in household, the less prevalent frequent loneliness will be. More specifically, in The Netherlands, the percentages of frequent loneliness are 7.5% for those under 60, increasing to 11.3% for those aged 60 and above who are the most vulnerable group in that country; and the story remains the same for Poland: of those aged 60+ and living in one person households, nearly half (48.1%) were frequently lonely, and the percentages decreased to around 11% and 7% for the households with more people. A big difference between the two countries is that for the Dutch, once they live with one or more people, old age is not a potential risk factor for frequent loneliness anymore, but this is not the case for the Polish: even for young people living with at least one more person, the rate of frequent loneliness was between 6% to 11%. All in all, those aged 60+ and living alone are indeed the most vulnerable, but the level of vulnerability varies greatly from country to country.

In a similar way, we could study the relationship between age, health, and loneliness. The expectation is that older people are more likely to suffer from poor health, which in turn leads to loneliness – poor health reduces one's abilities to communicate with others. However, our study on health is constrained by the data produced in the ESS; here, we shall only examine the effects of two factors related to health: the participants' own evaluation of their health and whether their daily life was hampered by any illness, disability, infirmity or mental problem. For the first factor, the original five values have been simplified into three: good and very good; fair; bad and very bad. Tables 3.7 and 3.8 present the results on these two factors, respectively.

The numbers in Table 3.7 depict an overall picture that is consistent with our expectation: if you read the numbers in the three columns from the 'bad or very bad' to 'good or very good' in each country, we can see that most of them decrease to a large degree. There are two exceptions, though. The first is the zero for the

Table 3.7 Age, subjective health, and loneliness, The Netherlands and Poland, 2014.

	The Netherlands			Poland		
	Bad or very bad	Fair	Good or very good	Bad or very bad	Fair	Good or very good
Under 30	0.0	6.3	2.1	11.1	24.0	5.9
30–59	16.3	5.4	1.4	24.3	15.7	5.6
60+	30.0	6.4	1.8	32.5	19.7	7.6
n		1394			1596	

Table 3.8 Age, immobility, and loneliness, The Netherlands and Poland, 2014.

	The Netherlands			Poland		
	Yes, a lot	Yes, to some extent	No	Yes, a lot	Yes, to some extent	No
Under 30	0.0	9.7	1.6	0.0	6.1	7.6
30–59	8.5	5.8	1.5	12.0	15.8	7.6
60+	20.7	5.9	2.1	31.6	21.0	12.6
n		1394			1585	

cell 'Bad or very bad' and 'Under 30' in The Netherlands, but this is a sampling issue – only one person under 30 reported bad or bad health, and that person happened to be not frequently lonely. The more serious violation to the overall picture is for the under 30 group in Poland who reported 'bad or very bad' health and 'fair' health – the latter had a higher rate of frequent loneliness (24%) than the former. The national contrast identified above remains: the prevalence of frequent loneliness for the Dutch with 'fair' health is about at the same level as that for the Polish who were in good or very good health. The percentage for the older Dutch people (60+) who reported 'bad or very bad' health did come as a surprise, which is 30%, almost as prevalent as among the same group in Poland (32.5%).

Similar observations could be made on the relationship between age, immobility, and frequent loneliness, based on the numbers in Table 3.8. Overall, frequent loneliness becomes less prevalent when immobility is less of an issue – the numbers become smaller from the column 'yes, a lot' to 'no', for each country. Again, there are a few exceptions. In both countries, no respondents were found who were both under 30 years of age and answered 'yes, a lot' to the immobility question, which is not surprising. For the 30–59 group in Poland, the prevalence actually increased from 12% to 15.8%, which is not consistent with our expectation. Also, we would expect the numbers of the same column to increase from top to bottom, that is, for the same immobility group, the prevalence of frequent loneliness should increase from a younger group to an older one. One group does not follow this pattern, though: the 'yes, to some extent' group in The Netherlands: the youngest group (under 30) had a percentage of nearly 10%, noticeably higher than the other older groups (nearly 6%). One possible explanation is that young people felt more frustrated and isolated even when they were mildly immobilized. But most importantly, for both countries, it was the older people entirely hampered in daily life who were the most lonely, more than 20% and 31%, respectively. When people are in old age and unable to move as they used to, the chance of feeling frequently lonely becomes very high.

In the last part of this section we take a look at the relationships between age, social life, and loneliness. Here, we use the following three measures of social life included in the ESS:

- How often you socially meet with friends, relatives or colleagues, with seven options: 1 = 'never', 2 = 'less than once a month', 3 = 'once a month', 4 = 'several times a month', 5 = 'once a week', 6 = 'several times a week', and 7 = 'every day'.
- How many people with whom you can discuss intimate and personal matters, with seven possible answers: 0, 1, 2, 3, 4–6, 7–9, and 10 and above, coded as 0 to 6 respectively.
- How much you take part in social activities compared to others of same age, with five possible answers: 1 = 'much less than most', 2 = 'less than most', 3 = 'about the same', 4 = 'more than most' and 5 = 'much more than most'.

As all three questions are about the respondent's social life, it is sensible to put them together as one index of how social they are. For each question, a smaller number indicates a lower level of sociality; therefore, for any particular respondent, a smaller number of the sum of the three choices also indicates lower level of social activity. The smallest number possible is 2, and the largest 18. For each country, the distribution of this summed score is fairly normal, so we could compare the means and the standard deviations: for The Netherlands, the mean is 11.62 with standard deviation 2.58, and for Poland, the mean is 9.57 with standard deviation 3.05. These numbers suggest that on average, the Dutch lived a relatively more active social life than the Polish in 2014, and the variation in terms of their social activity was higher among the Polish than among the Dutch. Recall that our concern here is with the relationships of age, loneliness, and social, and one way of studying them is to compare the average scores of social life across groups of age and loneliness (Table 3.9).

The numbers in Table 3.9 send several messages to us. First and perhaps most importantly, the numbers in the two columns of 'difference' are positive, which means that in both countries, those not frequently lonely had a more active social life than those frequently lonely. Social relations, represented here with being social with others, having a confidant, and feeling more social than others, do seem to relate to a lower chance of feeling frequently lonely. On the other hand, it is also

Table 3.9 Mean scores of social life by age and loneliness, The Netherlands and Poland, 2014.

	The Netherlands			Poland		
	Not frequently lonely	Frequently lonely	Difference	Not frequently lonely	Frequently lonely	Difference
Under 30	12.65	9.38	3.27	11.22	11.16	0.06
30–59	11.72	9.28	2.44	9.45	8.49	0.96
60+	11.35	8.11	3.24	8.86	7.94	0.92

clear that the differences appear to be more pronounced for the Dutch (2.44 to 3.27) than for the Polish (0.06 to 0.96); in other words, a more active or richer social life is more helpful for the Dutch than it is for the Polish in reducing the likelihood of feeling often lonely. We could compare the age groups by reading through the numbers of each column from the first row to the third. As they all gradually decrease from the younger group to an older one, it is clear that either frequently lonely or not, and for both countries, older people have a less active social life.

What these observations do not tell us is the prevalence of frequent loneliness for people of different age and levels of sociality. To compare the respondents in terms of age and social life without using more sophisticated statistical methods, I have classified the social life index into three groups: 2–6, 7–14, and 15–18. Now we can compare the percentages of feeling frequently lonely on age and social life.

Before interpreting the numbers, it is necessary to pay attention to the 50.0% for the group with '2–6' social life summed score and under 30 in The Netherlands – it is unrealistically high because there were only two respondents in that group and one of the two turned out to be frequently lonely. This occurs even when the number of rows or columns of a table starts to become moderately large, and when it is socially sensible for some groups to be either extraordinarily large or small. Here, as few Dutch scored 2–6 for the social life index, when we break them down even further into three age groups, the number of people in each combination of age and social life will become very small; for the other two age groups, there were only seventeen people in the group aged 30–59 and scored 2–6 on the social life index; for the 60+ and 2–6 group, there were twenty-four respondents.

There is another relatively unexpected number in Table 3.10: 37.5% of the Dutch respondents aged 60+ and scored 2–6 in the social life index were frequently lonely, which is much higher than the corresponding percentage for the Polish, 25.4%. It is difficult to explain away this figure with the above reason: twenty-four is not a big number, but it is not so small that would make the results so unreliable. In fact, we made a similar observation before. With some caution, we could come to the observation that having a very inactive social life or very few social relations for the older Dutch seems to dramatically increase their

Table 3.10 Prevalence of frequent loneliness by age and social life, The Netherlands and Poland, 2014.

	The Netherlands			Poland		
	2–6	7–14	15–18	2–6	7–14	15–18
Under 30	50.0	2.2	0.0	23.1	6.6	6.9
30–59	17.6	3.1	0.0	20.6	7.3	7.4
60+	37.5	4.0	0.0	25.4	16.7	6.3
n		1381			1523	

chance of feeling frequently lonely, a chance relatively higher than that among the older Polish people. Other than this particular group, the Dutch again were much less vulnerable to frequent loneliness than the Polish. Finally, for the Polish, once the social life score passes 6, it does not matter much anymore in reducing the prevalence of frequent loneliness.

Loneliness among children and adolescents

All results presented in the previous section are about adults, because children were not eligible of participating in social surveys. At least in today's Western countries, to carry out research on children, researchers must pass several rounds of administrative and ethical checks and approvals, which is responsible for the small number of studies on children. At the moment, large-scale social surveys that include people of all ages are unheard of – the age axis of the graphs presented previously started from eighteen.[16] Some researchers already strongly believed in the 1970s and early 1980s that loneliness must be a prevalent problem among adolescents. For example, Robert Weiss pointed out that 'Loneliness almost certainly is more common in adolescence than later in life, and possibly more intense as well, although we as yet lack the survey data that would provide conclusive evidence for this observation.'[17] At the same time, Tim Brennan made almost the same observation: 'Although there are no large-scale, systematic epidemiological studies of loneliness across different ages, the available evidence suggests that there is more loneliness among adolescents than among any other age group'.[18] In this sense, the relationship of age and loneliness depicted by the graphs and the tables in previous sections is regrettably incomplete. This chapter will not be complete without at least a brief discussion on the prevalence, the nature, and the causes of loneliness among children and adolescents. Is loneliness no less prevalent among children than among the adult population? How is loneliness among the youth different from that of the adults? Do children become lonely for reasons different from those for adults? Some researchers have produced answers to these questions, but they usually produced the answers by drawing on a much smaller set of data, some even replied on anecdotal evidence. They have used different ways of measuring loneliness, different sampling methods, and different analytical methods, all of which make it very difficult to put their research results together in a coherent manner in order to reach logical insights. In this last section of the chapter, I shall offer a brief discussion on the prevalence of loneliness by making use of some important existing studies and evidence available to me.

In the 1970s, Daniel Offer created the Offer Self-Image Questionnaire (OSIQ) as a tool for testing personality among adolescents in the US. Of the questionnaire's 130 items, one was created to measure loneliness: 'I am so very lonely'. Originally, the respondent could choose one of the six options as levels of agreement to this statement. In their analysis, however, the researchers simplified the results by collapsing the options into two categories: 'lonely' and 'not lonely'. The adolescents were classified into groups along several dimensions:

- Gender: boys and girls.
- Age: the younger (12 years to 15 years and 11 months) and the older (16 to 20 years).
- Normality: normal, disturbed, and delinquent.
- Nationality: US (Midwest suburbs), Australia, and Ireland.

I have re-analysed the results presented in their 1980 chapter[19] so that we could derive some answers and insights for our purposes.

First of all, as the authors did not present the data for older children of Australia and Ireland, it is impossible to compare all of the studied adolescents across the three countries. Focusing on the 'normal' American adolescents, the overall percentage of feeling 'very lonely' was 18.5%. This is remarkably high. In another study conducted at about the same time of over nine thousand adolescents aged 10–18 from ten US cities, 10–15% reported 'seriously lonely'.[20] If the reader could recall or go back to the graphs presented in the previous section for 1990 and 2000s, this is on par with the prevalence of 'frequently lonely' for older people in many countries, such as Argentina, India, etc., although lower than the rates for older people in Eastern European countries.

The authors, Ostrov and Offer, also expected a relatively higher prevalence of severe loneliness among the young than the older adolescents, because the older ones (16+) should be able to develop new relations with others, particularly those of the opposite sex. One statistic that is especially designed for testing these relations is the odds ratio. For females, the odds ratio is 1.8, and for males, it is 1.7. This means that of all female adolescents, the younger ones were 1.8 times more likely to feel very lonely than the older ones; similarly, of all male adolescents, the younger ones were 1.7 times more likely to feel very lonely than the older ones. Clearly, this is highly consistent with the author's expectation: regardless of gender, American adolescents under the age of 16 were 1.75 times more likely to be very lonely than those aged 16 and above.

Next, Ostrov and Offer zoomed in on the younger adolescents because they were more vulnerable to loneliness. The prevalence of feeling 'very lonely' among these adolescents varies across the three nations: 21.2% for the Americans, 18.4% for the Australians, and 16.7% for the Irish. Again, these figures are clearly higher than the percentages of 'frequent loneliness' among older people in most western and northern European countries in more recent years. If we could accept that at least in the 1960s and the 1970s Australia and Ireland were less 'modern' and competitive than the US, these numbers could also lend support to the two authors' claim that people in a more modern and competitive society were more likely to be lonely as well. Furthermore, the relationship between gender and loneliness is different across these three countries as well: as suggested above, gender did not appear to make a difference among the Americans, but it seems to make a slight influence among the Australians – girls were about 1.3 times more likely to be 'very lonely'; for the Irish adolescents, it is even more so: girls were about 1.8 times more likely to feel 'very lonely'.

In the UK, the Millennium Cohort Study (MCS) followed the lives of around nineteen thousand children born in 2000 to 2001. When they reached the age of 14, they were asked to complete a questionnaire that contained a question about loneliness. The question was how much they would agree with the statement 'I felt lonely', and they could choose one from the following three answers: 1 = not true; 2 = sometimes; 3 = true. Of the 11,286 (or 95.1% of the 11,872 total participants) 14-year olds who provided valid responses, 65.8% chose 'not true', 25.0% 'sometimes', and 9.1% 'true'. The 'True' category seems to be equivalent to the 'very lonely' or 'frequently lonely' used in other surveys discussed above. Note that fourteen is an age of the younger group (12 to 15) in the Ostrov and Offer study. If the survey questions and categories are deemed comparable, then loneliness seemed much less prevalent among the British young adolescents in 2014 than among their American, Australian and Irish counterparts in the 1970.

Overall, existing evidence does seem to suggest that at least in the US and western Europe, the prevalence of loneliness among children and adolescents may not be lower than among the adult populations. We shall come back to the issue of loneliness among the youth in Chapter 5 and Chapter 9.

Notes

1 Among academic researchers, there is no consensus on the criterion of 'older people'; therefore, I shall not give a universal definition. Each particular study has its own threshold, which is to be reported when the study is mentioned.

2 A. Walker and T. Multby. 1997. *Ageing Europe*. Buckingham: Open University Press, pp. 54–55.

3 S. Ayis, R. Gooberman-Hill, and S. Ebrahim. 2003. 'Long-standing and limiting illness in older people: associations with chronic diseases, psychological and environmental factors', *Age and Ageing*, 32(3): 265–272; National Council on Aging. 2006. 'Summary of the survey on attitudes to age (March, 2000)', available online at www.ncoa.org/content.cfm?sectionID=105&detail=43.

4 R. S. Weiss. 1982. 'Issues in the study of loneliness', in L. A. Peplau and D. Perlman (eds), *Loneliness: A Sourcebook of Current Theory, Research and Therapy*. New York: John Wiley & Sons, pp. 71–79.

5 To quote Lynch directly: 'My hypothesis is that repetitive early experiences with "toxic talk" – those childhood experiences that poison the child's capacity to expect or hope that language can be used in an effective manner to reach others, or developmental experiences that shatter a child's sense of self-worth – make all subsequent communications throughout life physiologically taxing. It leads to a bodily state I have labelled "physiology of exclusion" – a reaction to communicative stress that heightens loneliness, and increases the risk of premature death . . . In 1999, for example, the National Center on Addiction and Substance Abuse at Columbia University (now called simply the Center on Addiction) suggested that teenagers who had trouble communicating with their fathers were far more likely to use cigarettes, alcohol, and illegal drugs, than those whose families had two supportive and understanding parents.' J. Lynch. 2000. *A Cry Unheard: New Insights into the Medical Consequences of Loneliness*. Baltimore, MD: Bancroft Press, p. 120.

6 New Zealand Ministry of Social Development. 2009. 'Loneliness', in *The Social Report 2016 – Te pūrongo oranga tangata*, available online at www.socialreport.msd.govt.nz/social-connectedness/loneliness.html (accessed 15 August 2010).

7 For example, a publication by the Mental Health Foundation in 2010, titled *The Lonely Society*, reports an almost 'flat' distribution of loneliness across the age groups with little evident relationship with age.

8 In fact, there was a question on loneliness in the first wave of WVS (1981–1984), which appears to be better designed as it contains four rather than two valid options. The question is: 'Do you ever feel very lonely?' with the following five choices: 1 = 'yes, frequently', 2 = 'yes, sometimes', 3 = 'seldom', 4 = 'never', 5 = 'don't know'. I would love to analyse this set of results, but unfortunately relevant variables were not actually included in the data file I downloaded from the WVS website. It seems to be the case that the data were contained in the data file of European Values Survey (EVS). However, not only I could not access the data, there was also a warning that the data were only for replication. In the end, I abandoned the plan of analysing this set of data.

9 Strictly speaking, it is a flaw to include two different words, 'very lonely' and 'remote', in the same question. Questionnaire design specialists call such questions 'double-barrelled'. The assumption is that 'feeling very lonely' and 'feeling remote' are equivalent, which may not be true to some respondents; if it is indeed the case, the respondent will be unable to report their true feelings.

10 K. Yang and C. Victor. 2011. 'Age and loneliness in 25 European nations', *Ageing and Society*, 31(8): 1368–1388.

11 Respondents could also choose the option 'Don't know'. This question is one of a list of instruments designed to measure the respondent's subjective wellbeing.

12 Professor Richard Rose produced a report for Centre for the Study of Public Policy, University of Strathclyde in 2000, 'How much does social capital add to individual health? A survey study of Russians' (Studies in Public Policy series no. 329), in which he analysed data collected from the New Russia Barometer (NRB) surveys. The surveys adopted a multi-stage randomly stratified sample covering the adult populations (18 and above) in the whole Russian Federation, with the sample size 1904, from 6 March to 13 April of 1998. The relationship that he reported between age and 'emotional health in the past year', presented in the table below, followed about the same pattern (each row may not add up to 100% due to rounding):

	Very good	Good	Average	Poor	Very poor
18–29	5%	23%	60%	10%	2%
30–59	1%	14%	59%	22%	4%
60+	1%	7%	60%	26%	6%
Total	2%	14%	59%	20%	4%

13 Victor, Scambler and Bond demonstrated that in western Europe, North America and Australasia the prevalence of loneliness among those aged 65+ was about 8–10%, with approximately 20% classified as sometimes lonely and the majority of the population defined as 'not lonely'. For those aged 65+, it was in the range of 6–10% (according to Wenger in 1984) and 13–15% more recently (Victor, Scambler, and Bond's 2009 data). See C. Victor, S. Scambler, and J. Bond. 2009. *The Social World of Older People: Understanding Loneliness and Social Isolation in Later Life*. Buckingham: Open University Press/McGraw Hill Education; G. C. Wenger. 1984. *The Supportive Network: Coping with Old Age*. London: George Allen and Unwin.

14 *Science Daily*, 18 August 2007; see also J. M. Ernst and J. T. Cacioppo. 1999. 'Lonely hearts: psychological perspectives on loneliness', *Applied and Preventive Psychology*, 8(1): 1–22; C. Paul, S. Ayis, and S. Ebrahim. 2006. 'Psychological distress, loneliness and disability in old age', *Psychology, Health & Medicine*, 11(2): 221–232.

15 As gender has become a much more complicated concept and issue in public discourse, it seems advisable to make it clear that here I use 'gender' and 'sex' interchangeably although I am aware that gender carries more cultural and social intonations while sex is a more biological terminology. Also, other sexualities are not studied here for a practical reason: the data used did not include sexes other than male and female in their original design.

16 In some European countries, a small number of people under the age of eighteen participated in the survey, either because the legal age of adulthood is lower than eighteen or because the survey administers mistakenly allowed them to respond.

17 Weiss, 'Issues in the study of loneliness', pp. 76–77.

18 T. Brennan. 1982. 'Loneliness at adolescence', in L. A. Peplau and D. Perlman (eds), *Loneliness: A Sourcebook of Current Theory, Research and Therapy*. New York: John Wiley & Sons, p. 269.

19 E. Ostrov and D. Offer. 1980. 'Loneliness and the adolescent', in J. Hartog, J. R. Audy, and Y. A. Cohen (eds), *The Anatomy of Loneliness*. New York: International Universities Press, pp. 170–185.

20 The study was conducted by T. Brennan and M. Auslander, and the figures were reported in Brennan, 'Loneliness at adolescence', p. 271.

Chapter 4

Aloneness, loneliness, and solitude

To condemn, or to celebrate?

In his recent article 'How should we tackle the loneliness epidemic?', Mark Easton, the BBC's home editor, began with the following observation: 'One of the biggest changes to the way we live has been the big increase in the number of people who live alone.'[1] To illustrate, he then cited some official statistics: 'More than a quarter of all households in the UK contain just one person, around 7.7 million people, and this is predicted to increase by another two million over the next decade or so.' The two graphs he presented clearly show that the number of single person households, single family households, and single parent households, respectively, all gradually increased over the years from 1996 to 2017, and this trend is particularly pronounced for people aged 45 and above. Easton's message is clear albeit not completely explicit: blame the loneliness epidemic on living alone, and to stop the epidemic, stop people from living alone.

Others hold a radically different view. For Eric Klinenberg, a sociologist based at New York University, living alone is something to celebrate. In his book *Going Solo: The Extraordinary Rise and Surprising Appeal of Living Alone*,[2] Klinenberg presented further evidence for the ever increasing popularity of living alone in the US. For example, during the six decades since 1950, the percentage of single American adults increased from 22% to more than 50%, the number of Americans living alone increased from 4 million to 31 million, and the percentage of single person households went up from 9% to 28%.[3] More importantly, not only he tried to dismiss the worries in other social scientists' publications with the decline of communities and the increase of aloneness in the US,[4] but Klinenberg also tried to make a case with a list of reasons for why living alone was a sign of human progress (more details will follow in a section below), that is, something to celebrate and promote.

While Klinenberg was not particularly interested in the problem of loneliness, Easton was. Easton was also clearly aware of the complicated relationship between aloneness and loneliness – after presenting the statistics of living alone in the UK, he quickly came to the point that *by itself*, living alone may not necessarily lead to loneliness. To researchers of loneliness, that aloneness is not equivalent

Table 4.1 Loneliness and aloneness.

		Lonely?	
		Yes	No
Alone?	Yes	(1) Likely but not necessarily	(2) Solitude
	No	(3) Lonely among others	(4) Most common

to loneliness has been a common sense for many years. A little bit of logical think-ing with the aid of a simple table (Table 4.1) would make the point very clear. Suppose loneliness takes two values (yes and no), and so does aloneness, then we have four possible scenarios.

The first scenario in cell (1) – being both alone and lonely – is perhaps the reason why Mark Easton started his article with some facts about living alone and why researchers have repeatedly reminded the readers of their publications that the two are not the same, although people tend to expect some kind of strong connection. As one man admitted when being asked about the disadvantages of living alone, 'Well, you're bored, you're depressed, stressed, everything, you get lonely'[5]. On the one hand, the distinction between loneliness and aloneness is nec-essary because, as indicated by cells (2) and (3), it is possible that one is lonely but not alone (3) – that is, lonely among others, the focus of our discussion in the next chapter, or alone but not lonely (2), such as 'positive loneliness' that Mark Easton discussed in his article, which others refer to as 'solitude' and we shall discuss further later in this chapter and Chapter 9. The most common scenario, for most populations that we have studied, is the cell (4), that is, most people are neither alone nor lonely; obviously, this is a situation that we do not need to worry about.

If it is so clear and logical, then why is there still so much debate and contro-versy about the relationship between aloneness and loneliness? Before making any statement about this relationship in general, we must be clear about the fol-lowing point: we should not expect a kind of *deterministic* relationship between the two; rather, the relationship should be understood as *probabilistic*. Being alone is expected to increase *the chance* of feeling lonely, but not necessarily or automatically. This way, on the one hand we retain the expected causal effect of aloneness on loneliness, while on the other hand such probabilistic statement leaves some room for exceptional cases such as cells (2) and (3) in Table 4.1. Klinenberg could not deny the probability that solo living would lead to loneli-ness; as he admitted:

For many of us, the mere thought of living alone sparks anxieties about isola-tion, and not without reason. But although it's clear that for certain people, in certain conditions, living alone can lead to loneliness, unhappiness, sickness, or worse, it's also clear that it need not have such disastrous effects.[6]

Clearly, highlighting the connection between living alone and loneliness would weaken his overall argument for the benefits of living alone, so he is not interested in the kinds of people or the conditions under which living alone *will* lead to loneliness; but the reason that he *could* downplay the connection is because the connection is not deterministic but probabilistic. In other words, there are cases that defy the necessity that living alone will make people lonely. To resolve the controversy, we must estimate the probability in a particular context – if living alone has two possible outcomes, lonely or not lonely, then the question is which one is more probable than the other. For now, that living alone will increase the probability of feeling lonely remains a theory or a hypothesis, which we shall check with some empirical evidence later in this chapter.

In the rest of this chapter, we will first take a closer look at the historical trend of living alone, and again we shall do so by examining the trend across as many countries as the available data would allow. Once the connection between the two is established, our concern will shift from loneliness to aloneness, because the latter is one of the causal factors for loneliness; that is, we need to discover why more and more people live alone rather than with others. Note that living alone is one of the situations in which an individual person is physically alone; a person may stay alone in other situations, which we need to take a careful look. Finally, if being alone could lead to two opposite consequences, one painful – loneliness and the other desirable (or at least innocuous) – solitude, then it is important for us to find out how we could obtain the desirable situation (i.e. solitude). In Chapter 9, I shall try to discuss how solitude could be achieved.

The trend of living alone

Before determining whether living alone is worrying or not, we need to confirm that it is indeed true that more and more people live alone over time. We also need to find out whether the trend of living alone varies across different nations in the world. Employing a variety of sources of statistics, Klinenberg reported that one-person households experienced the fastest growth in three most populous countries in the world: China, India and Brazil, and for the whole world, the total number of people living alone skyrocketed from 153 million in 1996 to 202 million in 2006.[7] In their study on living alone, Lynn Jamieson and Roona Simpson compiled a table of one-person households as per cent of all households in forty-two countries for the years of 1950, 1980, 1990, 2000, and 2010.[8] As data for more recent years are available now,[9] I have updated their table with a new one (Table 4.2). It covers the three decades from 1980 to 2011. More recent data till 2015 are available but only for a small number of countries. Here, I have only included countries that have data for at least two years so that the temporal trend could be detected. The countries are ranked based on the percentage in 2011.

Across the countries, those in northern Europe (Finland, Norway, Denmark, Sweden, The Netherlands), plus Germany, Switzerland, Austria, Slovakia, and Estonia, have the highest percentages of one-person households of all households,

Table 4.2 Percentage of one-person households by selected countries and years.

Country	1980	1990	2001	2011
Finland	27.1	31.7	37.9	41.2
Norway	27.9	34.3	–	41
Germany	30.2	35	36.6	40.2
Denmark	–	34.3	37.2	38.6
Sweden	–	44.1	46.2	37.9
Switzerland	29	32.4	–	36.5
Netherlands	22.1	29.9	33.6	36.4
Austria	28.4	28	31.2	36.2
Slovakia	19.8	–	30	36.1
Estonia	–	–	30.8	34.9
Belgium	23.2	28.4	31.6	33.8
Luxembourg	20.7	25.5	29.3	33.3
Slovenia	17.1	18	–	32.8
Hungary	19.6	24.3	26.2	32.1
Lithuania	–	–	28.7	31.7
Bulgaria	18.2	19.7	22.7	30.8
Italy	–	–	24.7	30.1
United Kingdom	22	27	28.6	29
Canada	20.4	22.8	25.7	27.6
United States	22.7	24.6	26.1	27.6
Romania	–	17.1	–	26
Greece	–	–	19.7	25.7
Croatia	16	17.8	20.8	24.6
Poland	17.4	18.3	–	24
Ukraine	–	–	21	23.6
Spain	–	–	20.3	23.2
Serbia	13.2	15.1	–	22.3
Ireland	–	–	21.8	21.8
Portugal	–	13.8	17.3	21.4
Cyprus	10	12.6	16	20.8
Israel	14	15.4	17.7	17.7
Bosnia and Herzegovina	9.5	10.8	–	16.8
Georgia	–	–	12	15.2
Azerbaijan	11.6	9.1	6.8	6.8
Albania	–	–	4.8	6.4
Uzbekistan	–	–	4.1	3.2

Source: UNECE

from 35% to 42%. In addition, the prevalence of one-person households was on the rise in these countries in the three decades from 1980 to 2011, from around 27% to around 40%. The exception is Sweden: from 1990 to 2010, Sweden ranked the highest, with the percentages of one-person households increasing from 44% to 49%, but they dropped since then to 38%.[10] Following these countries, the US, Canada, most of the western and southern European countries (France, UK, Spain, Italy, etc.) have relatively lower rates of single-person households, from about 22% to 25% in 1990 to about 27% to 30% during the first five years of this millennium. While the percentages of single-person households in the remaining countries were between 15% and 25%, the prevalence of such households in Azerbaijan, Albania and Uzbekistan was dramatically lower (below 7%). A separate study has reported that from 1970 to 2005 in Japan, the percentage of one-person households rose from 11% to nearly 20%.[11]

In order to examine the trends over the longest period of time possible, I produced the graph shown in Figure 4.1 for a much smaller number of countries. What becomes clear from the examination of these figures is that it was the countries in northern Europe and Germany that witnessed both the highest rates of one-person households and the increases over time, and the decades of 1980s and 1990s saw the biggest increase of such households. In comparison with these countries, the US, some western European countries and Japan experienced relatively mild increases over time, although the trend of solo living in the US and western Europe has drawn the most attention and publicity in the media. In this sense, the temporal increase of one-person households in most of economically advanced economies is true, but we also need to keep the national variation in mind. In great contrast, the percentages of single-person households in some eastern European, Middle Eastern, and Near Eastern countries were

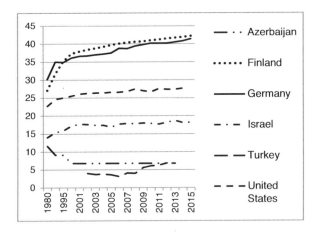

Figure 4.1 Percentage of one-person households, 1980–2015, selected countries.

consistently under 10%, including Albania, Azerbaijan, Israel, Tajikistan, Turkey, and Uzbekistan. We shall consider the reasons behind the temporal increase of solo living later in this chapter; for now, it seems sensible to suggest that the level of economic development, cultural, and religious factors are responsible for these regional variations.

Finally, we could also verify and learn more about the trend of living alone with the statistics produced from the European Social Survey (ESS). From the first round in 2002 to the latest round in 2016, the respondents of each of the participating countries in the ESS were asked to report 'Including yourself, how many people – including children – live here regularly as members of this household?'. Figure 4.2 shows the temporal change of the percentage of one-person households, calculated with design weight, in each of the countries that participated in the ESS for at least two years.[12]

Examining the country graphs in this figure, we can make several observations. First of all, it is generally the case that solo living has been the most prevalent in economically advanced states with generous welfare provisions, including most Scandinavian countries plus a few in western Europe. Finland is at the top over the years, with the percentage of single-person households at 23% to 26%, followed by Sweden, whose rates are stable at about 21%. Note that these are figures for the whole country; the percentages for the urban

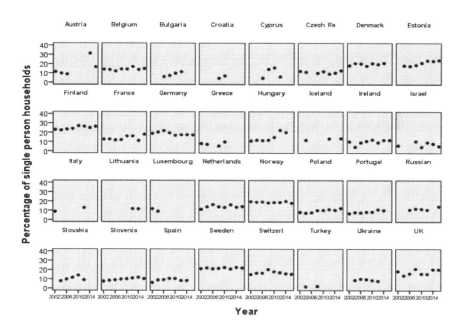

Figure 4.2 Percentage of single-person households by country and year in Europe, 2002–2016.

areas in these countries should be much higher. Following Finland and Sweden are a small group of countries whose percentages of solo living stay in the range of 15% to 20%, including Belgium, Denmark, Estonia, France, Germany, Norway, Switzerland, and the UK. Together, these are the countries in which solo living is both desirable and affordable, as Klinenberg argued in his book, although we should note that the prevalence has actually declined in both Germany and Luxembourg.

A few exceptions to the above overall pattern are noteworthy, however. Austria, Luxemburg, and The Netherlands are similar to the above countries in terms of level of economic develop, welfare provision, and perhaps individualism, but the prevalence of solo living in these three countries appears to be relatively low or have experienced ups and downs over time. Hungary is a very interesting case as well, whose rates of solo living continued to increase from about 11% to 20%, which seems to be following the country's overall trend of economic development and migration.

At the lower end of the spectrum are Turkey, Croatia, Cyprus, Greece and Israel, with Turkey having the lowest percentage of solo living at 2% and Cyprus experiencing some fluctuations.

The remaining countries could be classified into two groups whose rates of solo living are moderate. The prevalence of solo living in the first group is moderate as well as stable temporally, including Czech Republic, Iceland, Ireland, Lithuania, and Ukraine. Percentages of solo living in the second group of countries are moderate as well, but they showed a clear trend of going up over time: Bulgaria, Italy, Poland, Portugal, Russia, Slovakia, Slovenia, and Spain.

Overall, there is indeed evidence for the temporally increasing prevalence of single-person households in many parts of the world. However, I think it is too early to make the claim that this is a historical trend in the sense that countries in which solo living is currently not so popular will catch up over time with those countries with the highest rates of solo living. I also think it inappropriate to claim that solo living is necessarily a sign of better quality of life simply because the solo residents enjoy more autonomy and personal space. We shall continue our discussion on this issue in a section below.

Living alone and feeling lonely

Do we need to worry about the increasing prevalence of one-person households over time in Europe, North America, and some other parts of the world? By itself, living alone is a type of living arrangement and as such should not be necessarily worrying. It could become worrying, however, when the solo resident has other attributes. One situation in which it becomes worrying is when those dependent on others for daily life, such as children and people with disabilities, have to live alone. For normal adults, living alone is a problem if it is enforced rather than voluntary,[13] that is, the lone resident *prefers* to live with others but for some reason cannot. As a thirty-four year old British man confessed, he 'does get lonely at times', because he had no contact with his son or ex-partner, and he estranged from his mother:

> Well, Christ, I've sort of lost contact with a lot of people. Friends, like close friends, seem to have moved away from the area because they're in relation-ships . . . it's sort of like people you see in sort of pubs and whatever, it's not people I'd see going out, like doing anything . . . I don't actually like being in the house myself. I don't like . . . I don't like it.[14]

In some cultures, living alone is highly undesirable; for example, for most Koreans, the Spanish and the Italians, it is a very sad or even ashamed experience to have a meal alone. In almost all cultures, being a 'loner' is a symptom of utter social isolation, as the loner must be a social outcast, someone with a certain kind of mental difficulty, or someone with whom few would like to be associated, and it must be the loner, not those around them, who must take the blame. We shall come back to the stigma of aloneness and loneliness in the next chapter. In almost all cultures, living alone may be fine as long as it does not mean that the resident does not interact with others socially at all.

For our concern, whether living alone is a problem or not depends on whether it is closely associated with loneliness. If loneliness is no more prevalent among those living alone than among those living with others, then for our purposes, there will be no need to worry about whether living alone has become more prevalent or not. Most of existing studies of loneliness have focused on the older people and have found living alone a significant risk factor for loneliness and other medical condition even after controlling the effect of other risk factors such as marital status and health.[15] One of the most compelling is a meta-analysis on the effects of social isolation, loneliness, and living alone on mortality. Covering an academic literature from January 1980 to February 2014 in several databases, Julianne Holt-Lunstad and her colleagues found that with several confounds sta-tistically controlled, social isolation, loneliness, and living alone increases the risk of mortality by, on average, 29%, 25%, and 32% respectively.[16] Regardless of how living alone and loneliness are connected – either separately, or together, or living alone inducing loneliness firstly, it is difficult to ignore the detrimental effects of living alone on our health.

To expand the above analysis from older people to the general adult popula-tions in different national contexts, here I analyse the data collected from the sev-enth round (2014) of the European Social Survey (ESS). As explained above, the survey asked respondents about 'the number of people living regularly as member of household'. As we aim to compare those in one-person households with the rest, I have recoded the original variable accordingly. As a preliminary step, it is useful and interesting to examine the prevalence of one-person households in each of the participating countries (Figure 4.3).

In contrast to Figure 4.2 whose purpose was to demonstrate the temporal changes of single-person households over time in each country, Figure 4.3 compares the

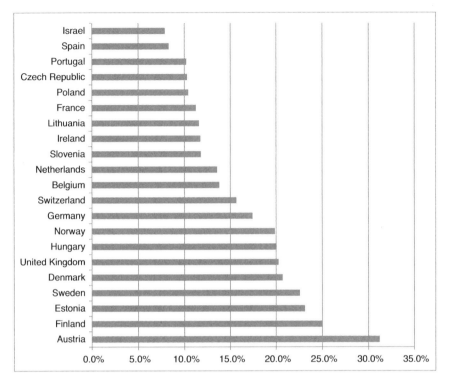

Figure 4.3 Percentage of one-person households in Europe, 2014.

Source: European Social Survey, Round 7.

Note: Percentage calculated with weights of design and population size.

countries in this regard at one particular time point (the year 2014). Furthermore, the percentages in Figure 4.3 are not completely consistent with those presented previously in Table 4.2 – while some northern European countries (Finland, Sweden and Denmark) still have the highest prevalence of one-person households, now Austria, Estonia, and the UK join them as the countries that have the highest rates. On the other hand, Hungary is exceptional among the countries in eastern Europe with a percentage of one-person households on par with the UK, which is in great contrast to the percentage of Slovenia, Czech Republic and Poland. In addition, the numbers here tend to be smaller than those in Table 4.2, which could be attributed to the following reasons: (1) the wordings are somehow different: in the ESS, it was the number of people 'regularly' living in the household, which could be different from the household owned or occupied by one person; (2) the samples were clearly different – the data for UNECE usually came from Labour Force Survey or other official statistics, while the data for the ESS were collected from a sample survey usually of a much smaller sample size; (3) the data were collected at different time points: the ESS data were collected in 2014, while the data for UNECE were collected in other years.

We have already met the loneliness question in the previous chapter: 'please tell me how much of the time during the past week you felt lonely?', and the respondent was expected to choose the one true to their situation from the following four options: 1=None or almost none of the time; 2=Some of the time; 3=Most of the time; 4=All or almost all of the time. Now we need to decide on how we want to simplify these four options into two, which can be done in two ways. The first is to collapse 2, 3, and 4 into one category, that is, the original question becomes a binary variable, with the following two values: 0=None or almost none of the time, and 1=At least some of the time. The second way of recoding is to focus on 3 and 4, which we call 'frequent loneliness', and to compare them with 1 and 2, a classification that we shall use in the rest of the book. As both are valid and interesting ways of categorizing loneliness, we analyse both of them here. Given both variables are binary now, we use the odds ratio to measure the strength of their relationship, the most effective statistic in such situation. Table 4.3 contains

Table 4.3 Odds ratio of living alone and two loneliness classifications by country, 2014.

Country	OR (Lonely)	95% CI	OR (Frequent lonely)	95% CI
Austria	3.5	(2.5, 5.1)	2.5	(1.3, 4.7)
Belgium	5.5	(3.7, 8.1)	5.8	(3.3, 10.0)
Switzerland	2.4	(1.5, 3.7)	1.4	(0.5, 4.0)
Czech Republic	2.6	(1.9, 3.6)	3.4	(2.2, 5.1)
Germany	3.4	(3.0, 3.9)	3.9	(3.0, 5.1)
Denmark	3.1	(1.8, 5.2)	4.1	(1.4, 12.0)
Estonia	2.6	(1.0, 6.5)	3.0	(0.8, 12.4)
Spain	4.1	(3.2, 5.2)	4.6	(3.5, 6.1)
Finland	3.6	(2.2, 5.9)	4.3	(1.4, 12.6)
France	4.0	(3.5, 4.5)	4.0	(3.4, 4.8)
UK	3.6	(3.2, 4.1)	3.7	(2.9, 4.6)
Hungary	6.7	(4.6, 9.8)	8.8	(5.5, 13.9)
Ireland	3.5	(2.1, 5.7)	3.0	(1.2, 7.3)
Israel	4.6	(2.8, 7.5)	3.5	(1.8, 6.7)
Lithuania	6.2	(3.0, 12.6)	4.9	(2.1, 11.4)
The Netherlands	5.0	(3.8, 6.5)	5.4	(3.0, 9.4)
Norway	3.9	(2.7, 6.5)	7.1	(2.3, 22.4)
Poland	6.9	(5.3, 8.4)	6.6	(5.2, 8.4)
Portugal	4.6	(3.1, 6.8)	6.4	(4.0, 10.2)
Sweden	3.7	(2.6, 5.3)	2.8	(1.5, 5.4)
Slovenia	3.9	(1.5, 9.9)	7.7	(2.1, 28.1)

the odds ratio and the corresponding confidence interval for each pair and for each participating country of this round of the ESS.

The term 'odds ratio' may sound to be a complicated jargon, but in fact its meaning is highly straightforward. For readers who are not statistically prepared, a brief explanation should be helpful. There are two steps of calculating an odds ratio: first, calculate the odds for each of the two groups you want to compare, and then, calculate the ratio of the two odds you just calculated in the previous step. So, if an odds ratio is bigger than 1, then it means the first odds is bigger than the second odds; otherwise, the second odds is bigger than the first. For example, 3.5 is the odds ratio for 'Not lonely' in Austria, which means that the odds of feeling lonely among the people living in one-person households is 3.5 times of the odds of feeling lonely among those living in two or more-persons households. As all odds ratios in Table 4.3 are above 1, we could say that this is the case for all of the countries listed here: *living alone is almost universally associated with a higher probability of feeling lonely, regardless of the frequency of loneliness and the national context.* Even in the Scandinavian countries, those living alone are several times more vulnerable to frequent loneliness than those living with others. Therefore, we should be worried about living alone as a potential risk factor for loneliness and cautious of celebrating solo living as an indicator of higher quality of life.

The two columns of '95% CI' contain the confidence interval of each odds ratio at the 95% level. If you have taken an introductory statistics course, you should have no difficulty of understanding these numbers; if you haven't, you could understand the two numbers in the bracket as capturing the true odds ratio – the odds ratios presented here are only estimates based on this particular sample – with about 95% chance. Now, two of the confidence intervals in the last column (for 'Frequently lonely'), one for Switzerland and the other for Estonia, contain the value of 1, meaning, the probability the odds ratio for the population is more than what we would like to tolerate (usually 5%); in such situation, we become suspicious that living alone and frequent loneliness are associated.

For 'Not lonely', Hungary, Lithuania and Poland have the highest odds ratios, above 6; on the other hand, the odds ratios for Belgium and The Netherlands are only slightly lower, in the range of 5 to 5.5. For 'Frequently lonely', Hungary, Slovenia and Norway's odds ratios are above 7, followed by Poland and Portugal (above 6), and Belgium and The Netherlands (above 5). That is, living alone does seem to have a consistent effect on loneliness among the Hungarians and the Polish, and to a relatively small extent on the people in Belgium and The Netherlands.

The advantage of odds ratios is that they give us a straightforward measure of the strength of the relationship between two things, here, living alone and loneliness – the further away an odds ratio is from 1, the stronger the relationship. Once we have obtained evidence for confirming the relationship, shown in Table 4.3, it would be more informative to know exactly how prevalent feeling lonely or frequently loneliness is among those living alone and those living with others, respectively. To show their relationship in this way, we need another table

(Table 4.4); here, it is sufficient to concentrate on frequent loneliness, as we shall do in the rest of the book.

The countries in Table 4.4 are rank-ordered by the last column, the difference between the percentage of frequent loneliness among one-person households (column 2) and the percentage of frequent loneliness among other households (column 3). It is very clear that living alone has the greatest impact on frequent loneliness in Poland, Hungary and Portugal – in these three countries, those living in one-person households have the highest rates of prevalence of frequent loneliness, more than one in three, and these rates have the biggest differences from those for households with two or more persons. In Switzerland, living alone has the smallest impact on frequently feeling lonely; the impact is actually ignorable if we recall the results in the previous table. In most other northern European countries, plus Austria, Germany, Ireland and the UK, living alone

Table 4.4 Percentage of frequent loneliness by number of inhabitants per household in Europe, 2014.

Country	Percentage 'frequently lonely'		Difference
	One-person households	Households of more than one person	
Poland	38.3	8.6	29.7
Hungary	33.9	5.5	28.4
Portugal	33.1	7.2	25.9
Slovenia	23.8	3.9	19.9
Spain	26.2	7.2	19.0
Lithuania	23.3	5.9	17.4
Belgium	20.3	4.2	16.1
Czech Republic	25.0	9.0	16.0
France	22.3	6.7	15.6
Israel	20.0	5.9	14.1
Estonia	16.0	5.9	10.1
Norway	9.8	1.5	8.3
UK	11.6	3.5	8.1
The Netherlands	9.6	1.9	7.7
Ireland	11.4	4.1	7.3
Germany	8.8	2.4	6.4
Sweden	9.4	3.6	5.8
Austria	9.8	4.2	5.6
Finland	7.1	1.8	5.3
Denmark	7.4	3.6	3.8
Switzerland	4.6	3.3	1.3

increases the chance of feeling lonely frequently only to a small degree; in these countries, *about 90% or more* of people living in one-person households were *not* frequently lonely.

An interesting connection has emerged if we examine these results with the numbers in Figure 4.3 – in countries having the highest percentages of one-person households, such as Austria, Germany and northern European countries, living alone has the smallest impacts on frequent loneliness, while countries with the lowest percentages of one-person households, such as Poland, Portugal and Spain, living alone has the largest impact on increasing the chance of feeling frequently lonely. In other words, the prevalence of one-person households and the effect of living alone on frequent loneliness are inversely correlated. Perhaps the connection is not as ironical as it sounds: it is exactly because living alone is not common in a country that it makes people lonely. Note that this is only a theory, and it may only apply to a special kind of people.

To sum up, regardless of the frequency of loneliness, living alone *does* increase the chance of feeling lonely. This is true everywhere in Europe, with the exception of Switzerland. The impact of living alone on loneliness, however, varies greatly from one country to another, indicating the importance of some factors at the societal or cultural level. We shall come back to the effects of these factors with further analyses in Chapter 8.

Why do more and more people live alone?

We now know that living alone does increase the chance of frequent loneliness, although the level of the risk varies from one country to another. Given this finding, if we want to stop people from becoming lonely, one thing we can do is to stop them from living alone. However, as we saw above, in most parts of Europe, North America and Asia, the prevalence of living alone has been on the rise. Figure 4.1 included only a small number of countries due to the lack of data, but it does show that except for Turkey and a few Near East countries, one-person households have become more prevalent across the world, even though the increase may not be as dramatic as we tend to think. Then Figure 4.2 confirmed the general trend of living alone in Europe. In China, the most populous country in the world at the moment, the percentage of one-person households increased from about 6% (or 19 million households) in 1995 to 14% (or 59 million households) in 2011.[17] In India, a country that is expected to overtake China in population size, the percent of one-person households increased slightly from 3.6% to 3.7%. The relative increase may appear to be very small, but the absolute number of households is very large (nearly 90,000).[18] The prevalence of one-person households in these countries remains much lower than those in Europe and North America, but the speed of increase and the total number of households have been remarkable.

Why do more and more people live alone across the world? It is not very difficult to think of some explanations for the increase of solo living at different stages of the life course. The most familiar situation would be that because of the physiological law that women usually outlive their male counterparts, women aged above the average male life expectancy very likely live alone after their spouses passed away. In this sense, living alone for older women is not their choice but what natural law has imposed on them, and such 'enforced' aloneness is particularly responsible for loneliness when the older women are not capable or resourceful enough to adapt themselves to the life without their spouses. This kind of loneliness could occur to a small minority of males, of course.

For the middle-aged and married adults, it is divorce rather than widowhood that will make some of them live alone: the dissolvent of a marriage is not only symbolically represented by the termination of the legal marriage certificate but more substantively by the physical separation of the couple. It is not news anymore that, similar to the trend of living alone, there has been an overall trend of increasing divorce rates along with economic development in Europe, North America, and east Asia, although for some countries the divorce rates may have fluctuated over a long period of time.[19] The end of one marriage will produce at least one solo-living adult, unless all divorcees will be able to remarry soon after their divorce or to live with other people, which at least in most Western countries are rare. To explain divorce properly is clearly beyond and not the concern of this study; there are a large number of various reasons and there is already a large literature on that topic. Living alone due to either widowhood or divorce means aloneness resulting from the loss of an intimate relationship, thus it is reasonable to expect a significant increase of the risk of loneliness, although the divorcees may have more control over the process than the widowers.

Moving down the age scale we come to the even younger group of adults, for whom marriage or civil partnership itself becomes a significant life event in living arrangement – when a large proportion of them prefer to stay alone, the overall prevalence of single-person households will move up, which we have seen Mark Easton's article and other reports mentioned at the beginning of the chapter. On the other hand, there is another group of young adults who want to marry or live with a partner but may not be able to do so for a variety of reasons: the difficulty of finding the right person, the struggle of supporting the shared life financially, and even the impossibility of keeping two jobs at the same time and place. While the first group's solo living is voluntary, the second group's is out of choice. Together, this may be the largest group of people responsible for the growing trend of living alone.

Regardless of specific life stage or group of population, here are a few key questions we should consider: Do people want to live alone? If so, why do they want to live alone? And if they want to live alone, can they live alone? If they do not want to live alone, do they have to live alone? Clearly, we will have a strong explanation for living alone if people want to live alone and they can do so, or when people do not want to live alone but they have to. We may need to examine these separate situations in order to understand living alone among different groups of people. For example, the high prevalence of single-person households in northern European countries could be explained as that a minority of older people do not want to live alone but they have to, while the large proportion (one-fourth to one-third) of adults across all ages want to live alone and they can. When I say 'they can', I mean all of the conditions are there that make living alone possible; more specifically, there are sufficient accommodations for one-person households, financially, those living alone do not have to rely on others, physically, nor do they have to depend on others for daily activities, and culturally, living alone is at least acceptable if not fashionable. When there is a will and all conditions for satisfying that will are available, the high prevalence of living alone should not surprise us anymore. This is clearly the case for residents of northern European countries, where they desire high autonomy of life, the culture is strongly oriented towards individualism, and living alone is highly affordable thanks to high income and generous welfare support. At the other end of the continuum, there are countries in which the culture, plus perhaps religious norms, discourages individual choices in life, making their residents losing the desire of living alone, and financially it is a struggle for anyone who wants to live alone. Many countries lie in between these two extreme situations, with moderate desire to live alone, less radical culture or religious environment, and mid-level economic and welfare supports.

It is my hope that what I have presented and discussed in this and the previous sections has made the following point clear: living alone is not a kind of living arrangement universally beneficial for all social groups, let alone all nations; it may be appealing to people with a certain set of attributes, particularly young adults with a professional job living in a metropolitan city, but the evidence for its association with loneliness and other health problems is indisputable and cross-national, and therefore living alone should not be promoted as a goal that all groups of people would want to achieve.

To readers who have read Eric Klinenberg's *Going Solo*, it is clear that I wrote the above words with his arguments in mind. Taking a position explicitly opposite to that of some other sociologists who worried about the weakening of social bonds and communities, Klinenberg is unreservedly excited and positive about the increasing prevalence of living alone. Although I would not say that I disagree with every point he made, I have found his general approach and overall argument far-fetched and worrying. Here I do not plan to launch a comprehensive critique of his work; I only aim to explain why I am worried about what he has been trying to promote.

To start with, Klinenberg was careful enough of establishing the phenomenon that his research targeted before asking and answering the why questions. With the statistics he presented and those I presented in a previous section of this chapter, there is no dispute over the increasing prevalence of single-person households in many parts of the world, particularly the economically advanced and fast growing countries. What I have found difficult to accept is that he appears to have taken *the increasing prevalence as necessarily a sign of its desirability*. After presenting some details of what happened in the Scandinavian countries (Sweden, Norway, Finland, and Denmark), he suggested that the

Scandinavian model would be the future of living arrangement for other countries, arguing that 'today more people throughout the world live alone than ever before' and 'even more will likely join them when they are affluent and secure enough to pull it off'.[20] Such assertion implies that living alone is appealing to people of all cultures in the world and the reason that not as many people in other countries as he has expected have lived alone is simply because they are not affluent enough. Consider Singapore, however, one of the richest countries in the world and a completely metropolitan city. Singaporeans enjoy the highest levels of income in the world and the government's support to housing, and few other people in the world are more affluent than the Singaporeans to find living alone affordable. Over the decade from 2007 to 2017, the percentage of single-person households did rise, but only from nearly 11% to 13%,[21] much lower than the percentages in the much less affluent countries in Europe. Consider also some other very affluent countries in the Middle East. It is true that economic prosperity makes living alone affordable, but it is only one condition. A more important condition is that people want to live alone. The question is: do people of all backgrounds all over the world find living alone appealing? I seriously doubt that the answer is a completely and unconditionally positive one. And it is not a job for academics to tell people how they should live.

This leads to the second characteristic of Klinenberg's work that I have found disagreeable. Reading his book, I couldn't help but observing that he tried his best to *promote the benefits of living alone while at the same time downplaying the potential difficulties or controversies*. It is understandable to do so as way of making an argument, but it would backfire when one goes too far in that direction. To avoid misrepresenting his views, please allow me to reproduce some of his paragraphs below:

> Freedom. Flexibility. Personal Choice. These rank among our most cherished modern virtues. Today, writes the demographer Andrew Cherlin, 'one's primary obligation is to oneself rather than to one's partner and children,' . . . Not long ago, someone who was dissatisfied with his or her spouse and wanted a divorce had to justify that decision. Today it's the opposite: If you're not fulfilled by your marriage, you have to justify staying in it, because of the tremendous cultural pressure to be good to one's self.[22]

> Living alone helps us pursue sacred modern values – individual freedom, personal control, and self-realization – whose significance endures from adolescence to our final days. It allows us to do what we want, when we want, on our own terms. It liberates us from the constraints of a domestic partner's needs and demands, and permits us to focus on ourselves. Today, in our age of digital media and ever expanding social networks, living alone can offer even greater benefits: the time and space for restorative solitude. This means that living alone helps us discover who we are, as well as what gives us meaning and purpose.[23]

> In recent decades a growing number of twenty- and thirtysomethings have come to the view living alone is a key part of the transition to adulthood. In

the large urban areas where it is most common, many young professionals see having one's own home as a mark of distinction and view living with roommates or partners as undesirable at best.

Living alone offers several advantages: It grants sexual freedom and facilitates experimentation. It gives time to mature, develop, and search for true romantic love. It liberates young adults from difficult roommates, including good friends who turn out to be better friends when they are not always in the next room. It enables them to socialize when and how they want to, and to focus on themselves as much as they need.[24]

According to Klinenberg, living alone, especially living alone among young metropolitan dwellers in the US, can be explained with a pulling factor and a pushing factor, which are clearly intertwined together. The pulling factor is the appeal of individual freedom and choice, which are essential for adulthood, experimentation, and restorative solitude. The pushing factor is the constraints of domestic and other social obligations. Klinenberg showed no sign of hesitance in promoting such a radically individualistic view of life. I have no intention of getting into any moral debates over whether such view of life is worth holding, but I do find the popularity of such view questionable. That the prevalence of living alone has increased over time is a fact; that most of those living alone are as individualistic as Klinenberg has described is far from being so certain. To take one step back, even if this highly narcissistic view is popular among young Americans and Scandinavians, I wonder whether other members of their society truly want to welcome such trend of living alone. Is it really desirable for other members of a society if its young and middle-aged generations see themselves as the centre of their world and find marriage and other social relations a set of burdens that they would not hesitate to abandon for the sake of their own freedom?

This question relates to a more general moral dilemma of individual freedom versus commitments to the collective good. However, rather than helping his readers to see the tension in this dilemma and to work towards a balanced solution, Klinenberg celebrated living alone as an ideal solution. Under his promotion of living alone, even divorce is not an issue anymore. He explained the 'divorce revolution' in the US as a result of not only 'women's increased participation in the labour market' but also 'an emerging moral code that placed one's obligation to care for the self on part with, if not above, one's commitment to family'.[25] Again, here is not the place for me to get into a debate of moral philosophy; nevertheless, I wonder how many sociologists would be happy to encourage members of any society to value their families less than their individual freedom. How many of the general public in the US would unhesitatingly put their own individual freedom above their families and friends? If the majority of American adults do think so, I think most people would agree with other sociologists that America is in some kind of trouble indeed.

All that said, I acknowledge an element of truth in Klinenberg's argument; that is, social commitments and relations could become obligations that people want to escape from, either because these relations demand a lot of effort and time from the individual, or in worse situations the relations could bring about troubles or even conflicts, or both. Some may be simply overwhelmed by intense interactions with other humans and thus would like to have some 'me-time' or a respite in one's own space.[26] From the individual's perspective, compared with coping with these obligations, troubles and conflicts, living alone – or being alone in general – is clearly more desirable. And being alone for a while may make one realize and appreciate the value of being with others. What Klinenberg has implicitly promoted is the ideal situation that people could get whatever they want, either being alone or being with others, whenever they want, and living alone would allow them to enjoy the benefits with others while also to be able to withdraw from the relations without consequences. I wish life could be so perfect, but I think it is not so easy to separate the benefits and the costs of social relations apart. If you do not invest in social relations, you will not enjoy their benefits; you must learn to compromise, to adapt, to give something you value away, in order to obtain something in return from others. The pros and the cons come hand in hand. As Klinenberg's respondents testified, living alone has its downsides as well, including loneliness and the lack of social support when it is needed. At best, it is an alternative to living with others, and it is not suitable to many people. Moreover, somehow sacrificing one's life may not be as bad as Klinenberg portrayed if you see your life as a meaningful component of a large community or even a mission. Some want to be alone so badly because they value so much everything of their own rather than their role in a family or community. In the end, it is down to the values that young people absorb in their socialization.

Klinenberg would probably defend himself by arguing that living alone does not mean that the singletons will not be involved in social relations anymore; in fact, he would argue that living alone would make people better prepared for social relations and communal life. And here some confusion arises. First of all, what does living alone mean? The kind of living alone that Klinenberg had in mind or at least he would like to promote is actually a kind of communal life, such as that in Sweden and other Scandinavian countries, not the case that the singleton lives alone without interacting with others. In such living arrangement, each adult lives alone in his or her apartment *but the apartments are in a communal environment.* 'By investing in each other's social welfare and affirming their bonds of mutual support, the Scandinavians have freed themselves to be on their own.'[27] Note that such style of living alone is not common in other metropolitan cities such as New York or Los Angeles. In this sense, it is misleading to talk about living alone in general as if it is the same across different areas. This brings us back to a point made above: what Klinenberg was trying to promote is an ideal situation where individuals live in their own personal space but are still able to enjoy the social life offered by a communal life at the same time. In Scandinavian countries, 'The idea that one could live quite socially while keeping a place of one's own shifts from being strange and unimaginable to being tantalizing and concrete.'[28] Similarly, older people have found ageing alone the best option as it gives them independence, self-respect, and dignity; it would be ideal for them to have 'intimacy at distance' with their family members, with the distance being kept by living alone, and the distance is necessary so as to 'avoid the kinds of emotional, financial, and physical entanglements . . . '.[29] He was also impressed with the Sweden's 'ongoing commitment to collectivism'.[30] The elderly in Sweden 'seek a more communal way to live alone'.[31] The ideal kind of housing would be 'where older people who live alone can come together and get support'.[32] If this kind of communal living alone is what Klinenberg was trying to promote and celebrate, he should have made it clearer.

Even so, there remains some confusion over how to square individual freedom into the circle of communal life of living. For example, he interviewed Lindh in Stockholm, who told him that once young people had the experience of living alone, 'they'll have a fuller life, a more social life, and they'll develop closer connections to friends'.[33] It remains unexplained why, compared with living with their families and roommates, young people's social life will become fuller, richer, and closer simply because they now live by themselves. Additionally, how would living alone let young people escape from obligations to their lovers and friends? I appreciate that living alone would reduce the number of daily encounters that young people dislike to have with their roommates, friends, and even lovers, and they have a space that they could withdraw to when such space is needed. However, if they do live a fuller and more social life, they are expected to have more interactions and commitments to others, at least some of which young people will perceive as constraining. I wonder how many social commitments, obligations, or even conflicts one could escape from by living alone if one still wants to live a rich and full social life.

To my concern, the most unacceptable is Klinenberg's attempt to downplay the potential risk of living alone to loneliness. As quoted above, he acknowledged the potential risk to loneliness, he interviewed several respondents who were very lonely when living alone, such as Kimberly[34] and Helen,[35] and he reported that 'Sometimes, indeed, they feel lonely, anxious, and uncertain about whether they would be happier in another arrangement'.[36] Unfortunately, he dismissed the association between living alone and loneliness as something 'worse than misleading' created by 'pop sociology'.[37] He made a few arguments to dismiss such connection. First, he argues that 'this [some people are lonely while living alone] does not mean living alone causes loneliness. It's possible, for example, that people feel lonely more often wind up living alone . . . '.[38] This is a fair point – indeed, we are not certain about the causal direction of relationship between living alone and loneliness. He should know, however, that social scientists can rarely prove or verify any causal relationship. This is why we have used the term 'risk' or 'risk factor' instead of cause. As shown previously, the association of living alone to loneliness has been found after controlling other factors, and it is almost universal in European countries. It is now extremely difficult for one to dismiss the risk of living alone to loneliness.

His second argument is that being in a relationship does not guarantee that one will not be lonely, which is indeed true; using his respondent's words, 'there's nothing more lonely than being with the wrong person'.[39] But again, it is logically in vain to dismiss a probabilistic relationship with such deterministic reasoning: while it is certainly possible that someone in relationship is lonelier than another person living alone, but there is abundant evidence showing that those living alone are more likely to be seriously or frequently lonely than those living alone. Moreover, following his logic, if living alone does not necessarily leads to loneliness, then being in marriage need not be constraining or miserable! That people in marriage, family or relationship could be lonely does not mean that to escape from those others or the relations with them is the solution. Why not improve the relations?

Finally, Klinenberg argues that being lonely might not be that bad anyway. After acknowledging that 'Men who live alone also have relatively high rates of loneliness', he said, 'Yet they are rarely miserable.'[40] I wonder how he could say that on behalf of the lonely.

Aloneness and solitude

As we saw in the previous section, aloneness is associated with a higher chance of feeling lonely. It is all too easy, however, to interpret such probabilistic statement as deterministic, that is, aloneness necessarily leads to loneliness. We saw the strongest evidence against such simplistic interpretation in the last few rows of Table 4.4: in Germany, Austria, Sweden, Denmark, Switzerland, and Finland, more than 90% of the people living alone were *not* lonely. Even for those at the top of the table, Poland, Hungary and Portugal, the majority (about two-thirds) of those living alone did not report being frequently lonely. In arguing for the benefits of living alone, Klinenberg has also found some support in the life philosophies of Ralph Waldo Emerson and Henry David Thoreau; that is, living alone provides the singleton with the opportunity to appreciate natural beauty, to nurture spiritual development, or to do anything that one enjoys without the distraction from others. Note, however, like the relationship between living alone and loneliness, living alone does not necessarily lead to the solitary joys. For the sake of strengthening his argument, Klinenberg downplays the uncertain association between living and loneliness while uplifting the uncertain relationship between living alone and enjoying being alone. A fairer point, at least to me, is that on the one hand we acknowledge the potential detrimental effect of solo living on an increased probability of frequent loneliness; on the other hand, we should not dismiss the possibility that one could live alone but does not feel lonely, perhaps even feels happy. In short, living alone could lead to either loneliness or solitary joy; both are possible outcomes of living alone. Which outcome living alone leads to is a rather complicated matter, as it depends on other factors. In this section, we shall explore further the relationship between being alone and solitude (the solitary joy).

It should become clear by now that it is necessary to clear up the possible confusion over the meaning of loneliness, aloneness, and solitude. I am not aware of any academics who would call the joys that one enjoys alone 'positive loneliness', although this term appears in some lay people's discussions. To me such term is an oxymoron – loneliness is necessarily a negative experience; otherwise, we are not talking about loneliness. To avoid confusion, I strongly suggest that we define loneliness as always a negative, undesirable, unpleasant, or even painful mental state, something we suffer from; therefore, it is something we all want to stay away from or get rid of. In contrast, I shall call the desirable and enjoyable state of being alone 'solitude'. Marina Keegan wanted 'the opposite of loneliness' in life,[41] and clearly she is not alone in having such a wish. Aloneness is a neutral description of the physical state, which is neither pleasant nor painful, because it is about a physical rather than a mental state. Sometimes the word 'alone' is used in daily language when in fact people mean 'lonely', as in 'I am so painfully alone'. Loneliness is when aloneness becomes painful. Solitude refers to a positive mental state while being alone; in solitude, people welcome, embrace, or even enjoy being alone, although such aloneness does not have to be a long-term living arrangement. I try to avoid the word 'solidary' as it could refer to either aloneness defined above or loneliness, similar to another word 'lonesome'.

Solitude does not necessarily require living alone – any form of chosen and enjoyable aloneness could be called solitude. It should be reasonable to hypothesize that on average, those living alone are less happy than those living with others, and I would also hypothesize that in northern European countries, the levels of happiness do not differ significantly between those living alone and those living with others, but the difference is significant in eastern and southern European countries. If these hypotheses turn out to be true, that does not mean solitude is impossible; it is only that solitude is an experience only for a minority. All I want to show is that one could be living alone and happy at the same time, and I want to demonstrate that solitude is possible not only for a small number of special people, such as monks, artists, and writers (see below), but there are evidence for its existence from large-scale sample surveys. That is, I would call those 'in solitude' if they live alone but are happy at the same time, and I would expect the percentages of people in solitude are the highest among northern European countries, lower in western European countries, and the lowest among eastern and southern European countries.

To discover how true these hypotheses are, here again I analyse the data collected from the seventh round of the European Social Survey. In this survey, happiness was measured by an eleven-point scale, from 0 to 10, with 0 meaning extremely unhappy and 10 extremely happy. To start with, let's compare the mean scores of the two groups, those living alone and those living with others, in each of the participating countries (Table 4.5).

Not surprisingly, in each and every country, the mean happiness score of those living alone is consistently lower than that of those living with others – living with others does make people happier. The last column shows the probability that the hypothesis 'the mean scores of happiness among the two groups are equal' is true; clearly, they are all very small, suggesting that the hypothesis has very slim chance to be true. If we follow the usual academic practice of using 0.05 as a cutting point, then all differences between those living alone and those living with

Table 4.5 Mean score of happiness by living arrangement in Europe, 2014.

Country	Living arrangement			p-value
	Living alone	Living with others	Difference	
Lithuania	5.42	6.53	1.11	<0.001
Slovenia	6.19	7.19	1.00	0.040
Estonia	6.22	7.15	0.93	0.041
Hungary	5.67	6.56	0.89	<0.001
Israel	6.85	7.72	0.87	<0.001
Sweden	7.24	8.10	0.86	<0.001
Germany	6.91	7.76	0.85	<0.001
Poland	6.50	7.34	0.84	<0.001
Portugal	6.21	7.02	0.81	<0.001
Spain	6.70	7.49	0.79	<0.001
Austria	6.81	7.56	0.75	<0.001
The Netherlands	7.25	7.96	0.71	<0.001
Denmark	7.68	8.38	0.70	<0.001
France	6.70	7.40	0.70	<0.001
Finland	7.60	8.19	0.59	<0.001
Ireland	6.75	7.34	0.59	0.012
Norway	7.52	8.10	0.58	0.002
Belgium	7.28	7.83	0.55	<0.001
UK	7.11	7.65	0.54	<0.001
Czech Republic	6.53	6.99	0.46	0.005
Switzerland	7.74	8.15	0.41	0.009

others in terms of mean happiness score are statistically significant. For Estonia and Slovenia, the *p*-values are 0.04, which is the closest to 0.05. Therefore, my previous hypothesis that the differences between the means scores of happiness in northern European countries are not significant could not hold anymore.

On the other hand and substantively, the absolute difference between the two happiness scores in each country does not appear to be shockingly high: the fourth column shows the differences, which range from the lowest 0.41 in Switzerland and 1.11 in Lithuania. This suggests that it is possible for those living alone to be happy, particularly for the countries where the difference of the scores is low. To confirm that, however, we will need statistics that describe the prevalence of happiness among those who live alone – as defined above, they are the ones in solitude. To produce the statistics, we also need to define 'happiness' in this dataset, because the happiness variable has eleven values, so the number of cases for each value could be very small, making the results less reliable. As the midpoint, value 5,

Table 4.6 Percentage of happy respondents among those living alone in Europe, 2014.

Country	% Happy	n living alone
Finland	89.6	512
Switzerland	89.1	239
Denmark	87.3	332
The Netherlands	87.0	276
Belgium	86.8	258
Norway	86.3	278
Sweden	85.1	389
UK	82.0	433
Spain	76.7	159
Austria	76.7	540
Germany	75.0	543
Israel	74.9	183
Ireland	73.9	257
France	72.5	258
Poland	66.3	160
Czech Republic	66.0	250
Estonia	63.8	428
Portugal	63.3	128
Slovenia	60.4	139
Hungary	49.7	314
Lithuania	48.2	276

indicates 'neither happy nor unhappy', all values from 6 to 10 indicate 'happy' rather than unhappy. In the following table I present, for each participating country, the percentage of those who were happy among all those who lived alone.

These results have confirmed one of my previous hypotheses: in northern European countries, the percentages of happy people among those living are the highest, while the lowest are seen in eastern and southern European countries. More specifically, in Finland, Switzerland, Denmark, The Netherlands, Belgium, Norway, Sweden, and the UK, about 80–90% of those living alone reported a happy score in the survey. In contrast, in Hungary and Lithuania, just under half of those living alone reported to be happy; in other eastern European countries such as Poland, Czech Republic, Estonia, Slovenia, and Portugal in southern Europe, the figures are in the 60s.

To sum up, collectively, those living with others do seem happier than those living alone; on the other hand, many among those living alone could be happy as well. These two are not necessarily in contradiction. And the national contexts make a considerable difference to the overall relationship between being alone and solitude.

Notes

1 M. Easton, 2018. 'How should we tackle the loneliness epidemic?', 11 February, available online at www.bbc.co.uk/news/uk-42887932 (accessed 12 February 2018).

2 E. Klinenberg. 2013. *Going Solo: The Extraordinary Rise and Surprising Appeal of Living Alone*. London: Duckworth Overlook.

3 Ibid., pp. 4–5.

4 I would not venture to review the debate over the evaluation of the trend of living alone here. Interested readers could consult the first and the concluding chapters of his book.

5 L. Jamieson and R. Simpson. 2013. *Living Alone: Globalization, Identity and Belonging*. Basingstoke: Palgrave Macmillan, p. 182.

6 Klinenberg, *Going Solo*, p. 26.

7 Ibid., p. 10.

8 See Jamieson and Simpson, *Living Alone*, table 2.1 (pp. 34–35).

9 The most important source of data is the UNECE website: see http://w3.unece.org/PXWeb/en.

10 However, according to the data published by Eurostat, more than 50% of households in Sweden in 2016 were occupied by only one person; see http://ec.europa.eu/eurostat/web/products-eurostat-news/-/DDN-20170905-1.

11 See fig. 3 in R. Ronald and Y. Hirayama. 2009. 'Home alone: the individualization of young urban Japanese singles', *Environment and Planning A*, 41: 2836–2854.

12 Four countries participated in the ESS for only once. Here is their percentage of single-person households: Albania (2012), 1.3%; Kosovo (2012), 0.6%; Latvia (2008), 21.1%; Romania (2008), 7.0%.

13 For example, J. Bennett and M. Dixon. 2006. *Single Person Households and Social Policy: Looking Forwards*. York: Joseph Rowntree Foundation, made the distinction between these two types of living alone.

14 Jamieson and Simpson, *Living Alone*, p. 181.

15 See, for example, C. R. Victor, S. J. Scambler, J. Bond, and A. Bowling. 2000. 'Being alone in later life: loneliness, isolation and living alone in later life', *Reviews in Clinical Gerontology*, 10(4): 407–417; K. Yang and C. Victor. 2011. 'Age and loneliness in 25 European nations', *Ageing and Society*, 31(8): 1368–1388.

16 J. Holt-Lunstad, T. B. Smith, M. Baker, T. Harris, and D. Stephenson. 2015. 'Loneliness and social isolation as risk factors for mortality: a meta-analytic review', *Perspectives on Psychological Science*, 10(2): 227–237.

17 National Bureau of Statistics of China. 2018. 'National economy maintained overall stability with momentum of progress in October', available online at www.stats.gov.cn/enGliSH (accessed 14 March 2018).

18 P. Dommaraju. 2015. 'One-person households in India', *Demographic Research*, 32: 1236–1266.

19 For example, see report created by the OECD at www.oecd.org/els/family/SF_3_1_Marriage_and_divorce_rates.pdf (accessed 2 April 2018).

20 Klinenberg, *Going Solo*, p. 212.

21 See official statistics published by Singapore Department of Statistics at www.singstat.gov.sg/modules/infographics/population (accessed 23 August 2018).

22 Klinenberg, *Going Solo*, p. 13.

23 Ibid., pp. 17–18.

24 Ibid., p. 31.

25 Ibid., p. 46.

26 For example, in their study of living alone, Lynn Jamieson and Roona Simpson found a number of their respondents who appreciated their time alone after considerable engagement with people during the day in their jobs. See Jamieson and Simpson, *Living Alone*, p. 178.

27 Klinenberg, *Going Solo*, p. 10.
28 Ibid., p. 41.
29 Ibid., pp. 161–163.
30 Ibid., p. 213.
31 Ibid., p. 218.
32 Ibid., p. 219.
33 Ibid., p. 218.
34 Ibid., pp. 76–77.
35 Ibid., pp. 86–87, 98–99.
36 Ibid., p. 230.
37 Ibid.
38 Ibid., p. 98.
39 Ibid., p. 99. See also ibid., pp. 64–65: 'To be sure, many occasionally struggle with loneliness . . . But so, too, do their married friends and family members . . . Finding a partner or a live-in companion is not enough to solve the social pain of loneliness, which is a fundamental part of human experience.'
40 Ibid., p. 100.
41 M. Keegan. 2014. *The Opposite of Loneliness: Essays and Stories*. New York: Simon & Schuster, p. 1.

Chapter 5

Lonely among others

After the death of her sisters Emily and Anne, Charlotte Brontë, according to Tim Dolin, was '[i]solated, lonely, and captive in the past'.[1] This may well explain how she could come up with descriptions of loneliness so precise and vivid that it is hard to believe that she herself had not experienced the pain. Having lost her mother and being separated from her beloved father, Paulina, the little girl character in the first three chapters of *Villette*, moved into a house where everybody was a stranger to her, although they were all friendly. Her father must have told her that she could trust everyone in the house; she was warmly welcomed by Mrs Bretton and Lucy Snowe, and later Graham, Mrs Bretton's son, became her close playmate. Nevertheless, living among these caring and friendly adults could not stop her from falling into loneliness – whenever she has to be alone, such as sleeping, or when Graham did not allow her to join him and his friends, she became lonely. The presence of her father was the only solution; she withdrew from others, or she must engross herself in some activities as a way of distracting herself from the pain of loneliness, and she would 'accept solace from none'.[2] Hers is a perfect illustrative case of John Bowlby's attachment theory of loneliness.

In dramatic contrast, in Charlotte Brontë's first novel, *Jane Eyre*, the household in which the young Jane grew up was much more hostile: she was repeatedly and intentionally excluded from the family life of her aunt, Mrs Reed, and her cousins, and she always had to take the blame when a conflict broke out between her and any of the other children. Like Paulina in *Villette*, Jane withdrew into her own world of picture books, but much more unlucky than Paulina, Jane had no parent to attach to, no friendly adult around (Bessie, a housemaid, showed signs of care on some occasions), and no playmate. The loneliest hours came when her aunt locked her up in the dark and desolated bedroom of the dead Mr Reed. The source of her loneliness was not the loss of an attached adult figure but the rejection from all those around her to taking her as an equal human being – in the minds of Mrs Reed and her children, there was a great albeit invisible wall of social status separating them from Jane.

Although both stories are cases of loneliness among others, they are different in an important way. Stemming from the absence of a very much desired relationship, Paulina's loneliness fits the existing definition of loneliness very well. But

Jane's does not: her loneliness comes from the presence of undesirable relation-ships and the exclusion of her from her immediate social circle.

We learnt from the previous chapter that living alone will increase the risk of feeling lonely although it does not mean that people will not be lonely anymore if they live with others. It depends on how they are related to the others. When people see one group versus another as categorically different, living together could become the very origin of loneliness. To me, this is the most saddening kind of loneliness: loneliness comes not because there is no one around but *exactly because some people are around* – these people are the source of loneliness. Some people may intentionally make others lonely; others simply do not care whether what they do will make others lonely or not. The commonly used definition of loneliness introduced in the first chapter is incomplete in the sense that it only draws on the absence of desired social relations as the source of loneliness; as a result, it misses the presence of undesirable social relations, such as discrimi-nation, stigma, bullying, ostracism, exclusion, and other forms of hostility. The definition needs to be expanded to include these situations in order to be complete.

My aim in this chapter is to shed some light on these forms of undesirable social relations that make people lonely. To do so, however, poses a challenge big-ger than what I did in the previous two chapters: first of all, the number of social hostilities as sources of loneliness is large, and most of them can only be vaguely defined and overlap onto one another; in addition, it has been very difficult for social scientists to collect reliable data about dark stories of social relations. The situations covered in this chapter are by no means comprehensive, let alone com-plete, but they should be sufficient to illustrate how loneliness arises as a result of bitter, hostile, or even malicious social relations.

Loneliness in the family

It may be unthinkable that one would fall into loneliness while living with a fam-ily. Take a minute and think about the following stories or any similar ones you already know, and it may not be that unthinkable anymore: as Tolstoy reminded us at the beginning of *Anna Karenina*, not all families are happy, and the unhappy families are unhappy for different reasons. Loneliness was also a recurring theme in his *Childhood, Boyhood, Youth*, all in the context of family life. Loneliness was portrayed more explicitly in *The Death of Ivan Ilyich*, in which the main character, living a decent life and surrounded by his wife and children, 'wept over his help-lessness, over his terrible loneliness, over the cruelty of people, over the cruelty of God, over the absence of God'.[3]

For a more recent and striking case, let's take a closer look at John Boyne's *A History of Loneliness*, in which almost all of the main characters were lonely, including the narrator, Odran Yates, and his sister Hannah. But it was the loneli-ness of the boys that is the consistent thread throughout the timeline. After years of bitter relations with Odran's mother, what his father did was much worse than filing a divorce – he literally broke the family by killing himself together with his own younger son. Once a family was broken like this, the hope of restoring life back to normal seems just too remote. Then Hannah's son, Jonas, lost his own father who died young of illness. It was not really living with his mother alone that was responsible for Jonas's loneliness; it was the unspeakable pain of feeling different from others. Jonas lived among others: his mother, occasionally his uncle Odran, his neighbours, and his schoolmates, but for him, the foundation of interacting with others was gone:

> He never spoke of friends. He had no girlfriend, had taken no one, not even himself, to his school's Christmas dance. He didn't join clubs or play sports. He went into school, he came home from school. He went to films alone on Sunday afternoons, foreign films usually. He helped out around the house. Was he a lonely boy, I wondered. I knew something of what it was to be a lonely boy.[4]

Why did he withdraw from others so completely? Why did he think he could not have a normal social life anymore? Yes, this is only a fiction, and I am speculating. It is extremely important, however, for us to get into the inner world of the lonely child's mind before we could offer any help with confidence. The loss of his father and brother separated him apart from other children – he was not like other children anymore, he was an unfortunate victim, someone to be pitied by others, and the sad psychological shock had sucked so much of his energy that to communicate with others was too much an effort to make. Even if he could make an effort, any communication would soon become a reminder of the tragic, so why bother?!

In the real world, such tragic events must be rare. Sadly, however, other tragic or at least unpleasant events would make children lonely. Divorce, or any parents' conflict visible to their children, is one of them. Two psychiatrists studied how the process of divorcing created loneliness among the children of the couple; although the study was reported nearly forty years ago, its findings are of general interest and therefore worth our attention.[5] The patients of these psychiatrists included '31 children from 28 families who were between nine and 10 years old', representing 'part of a cohort of 131 children from 60 divorcing families . . . '.[6] Children of divorcing parents felt 'left outside', powerless, and peripheral in major family decisions. For children at these ages, a sense of mutuality is already developed, so they expect to be involved but couldn't. The parents, in the middle of divorce, will withdraw their interests in their children, 'preoccupied with their own needs; their emotional availability, their attention span, and even the time spent with the children are often sharply reduced.' This is particularly so for children of nuclear families.

> Perhaps, however, the central ingredient in the loneliness and sense of isolation these children reported was related to their perception of the divorce as a battle between the parents, in which the child is called upon to take sides . . . By this logic, a step in the direction of the one parent was experienced by

the child (and, of course, sometimes by the parent) as a betrayal of the other parent, likely to evoke real anger and further rejection, in addition to the intrapsychic conflicts mobilized. Thus, paralyzed by their own conflicting loyalties and the severe psychic or real penalties which attach to choice, many children refrained from choice and felt alone and desolate, with no place to turn for comfort or parenting. In a true sense, their conflict placed them in a solitary position at midpoint in the marital struggle.[7]

Clearly, what the divorcing process alienates is not merely the relationship of the two adults but the relationship between them and their children as well. Caught in the middle of the fight, children suddenly find that it becomes increasingly difficult for them to attach to the two adults at the same time; rather, they have to attach either to one or none of the two parents. For the children involved, the process of distancing themselves from the arguments, the rows, the accusations, the smashing of wares, or even physical attacks is also a process of socially and psychologically isolating themselves from their attached figures. Loneliness is only one of the painful feelings arising throughout the whole process; for some, the lonely feeling may accompany them even long after the divorce was completed.

Expanding from the case of divorce to other conflicts and struggles within the context of family life, we may expect a similar albeit perhaps less dramatic effect on loneliness. And again, I am trying to go beyond studies conducted many years ago or based on a small number of cases. It is next to impossible, however, to obtain micro-level data on divorce and other related variables at a large scale, not simply because people tend to avoid talking about this extremely unpleasant topic but also because the difficulties in connecting the divorced parents with their biological children as they have already lived separately. Nevertheless, some data in the Millennium Cohort Study of the 14-year-olds describe situations that are similar to divorce. Perhaps the closest are the questions asking children whether they lived with their natural mother or father. Not living with their natural mother or father does not necessarily mean that their parents have divorced – it may well be that the separation was due to illness or employment, but it is common that children do not live with one of their biological parents anymore after the divorce; in other words, a large proportion of the children who did not live with their natural parents were those whose parents had divorced or at least separated. In this sense, it is worth inspecting the relationship between such living arrangements and loneliness. Of the 11,295 valid responses, 2.9% (or 331) did not live with their natural mother. In contrast, the percentage of 14-year-olds who did not live with their natural father was much higher, 27.8% (or 3051), out of 10,972 valid responses. Putting these together, nearly 30% (29.2%) did not live with either natural mother or natural father, while 0.8% did not live with any of their natural parents. It is reasonable to expect that loneliness is associated with these children, but let's see what the data tell us (Table 5.1).

The figures in this table show a very clear pattern: while the numbers in the first column decrease from the top to bottom, those in the second and the third

Table 5.1 Loneliness and living with natural parents among the 14-year-olds in the UK, 2014–2015.

| | *'I felt lonely'* | | |
	Not true	Sometimes true	True
Living with both natural parents	67.8	23.9	8.3
Living with natural mother but not natural father	63.2	26.4	10.4
Living with natural father but not natural mother	58.7	30.4	10.9
Not living with any natural parent	55.8	31.4	12.8

Table 5.2 Hurting or picking on among siblings among the 14-year-olds in the UK, 2014–2015.

| | | How often respondent hurt or pick on siblings | | |
		Rare and never	Sometimes	Often
How often siblings hurt or pick on respondent	Rare and never	55.2	2.9	3.4
	Sometimes	3.3	7.2	1.1
	Often	4.7	2.7	19.5

columns increase, although the rates of change in all columns are gentler than I expected. Perhaps unsurprisingly, loneliness is the most prevalent among those not living with any natural parent and least prevalent among those living both natural parents. Among those living with only one natural parent, living with their natural mother appears to offer better protection against loneliness than living with their natural father, although the difference could be contributed to the chance of sampling.

Besides their relationships with their natural parents, how happy the children were with their family in general and their relations with their siblings could also reveal the effects of these aspects of family life on loneliness among children. The study asked children how often their brothers or sisters 'hurt or pick on' them and conversely how often they hurt or pick on their siblings. The frequency was measured with six levels: 'most days', 'about once a week', 'about once a month', 'every few months', 'less often' and 'never'. To simplify the analysis and increase the number of cases for each specific type later, I have combined the first two into one category 'Often', the middle two into the category 'Sometimes', and the last two into the category 'Rare or never'. The number in each of the cells in the following table is the percentage of respondents for that particular cross-combined situation out of the total valid number of respondents (10,595); in other words, the sum of all of the numbers should be 100 (Table 5.2).

I have produced and calculated the total rather than marginal percentages because I want to show the prevalence of each cross-combination. Clearly, the relationship among siblings in this sample was highly reciprocal: if you don't hurt me, I won't hurt you, but if you pick on me, I will return the favour. As a measure of the strength of the relationship between the two variables, the value of Kendall's tau-b turns out to be very high, 0.69, and it is statistically significant. More specifically, we should be glad to see that the most popular type of relationship (more than 55%) is that the respondent and their siblings do not hurt each other. But on the other hand, of all the studied children who had at least one sibling, nearly one in five picked on each other. Most of the percentages of the other types of relations in this regard are almost all below 5%, except for the case when both sometimes pick on the other side, which, again, demonstrates the reciprocal nature of sibling relationship. We would expect that loneliness is a most common feeling among those who often had a mutual 'picking on' relationship with their siblings, but let's see if the data would bear this out (Table 5.3).

To show the effect of negative relationship between siblings on loneliness, the rows in Table 5.3 are ordered by the percentage of those answering 'True' to the statement 'I felt lonely'. The two letter code in the first column represents who hurt whom, with the first indicating the respondent picking on their siblings and the second the opposite. The letter then represents the frequency of conflict: R = 'Rare and never', S = 'Sometimes', and O = 'Often'; for example, the first row refers to the situation in which the respondent rarely hurt their siblings and their siblings rarely hurt them, too. The second row is for the respondent often picked on their siblings but their siblings rarely hurt them in return. We can see that the three rows, where the highest prevalence is found, are all of the situations in which the respondent's siblings often hurt them, regardless of how often they hurt their siblings. To put these percentages of loneliness (13–16%) in context, they

Table 5.3 Hurting or picking on and loneliness among siblings among the 14-year-olds in the UK, 2014–2015.

R hurting S	'I felt lonely'			Row total
	Not true	Sometimes	True	
RR	72.7	21.0	6.3	5828
OR	71.0	21.1	7.9	355
OS	69.6	20.9	9.6	115
SS	61.7	28.6	9.7	760
SR	65.2	24.9	9.8	305
RS	60.6	28.4	10.9	348
SO	55.0	32.1	12.9	280
OO	54.3	31.9	13.8	2061
RO	50.0	34.1	15.9	498

are much higher than those of frequent loneliness among older people in the UK, which usually stay below 10%.[8] To use a statistic that measures the overall association between loneliness and the frequency of being picked on by siblings, I can report that the Kendall's tau-b is 0.318, meaning the more frequent the respondent was picked on by their siblings, the more likely they would agree with the statement 'I felt lonely', and the statistic is statistically significant at the 0.001 level. Sibling hostility is certainly a source of loneliness.

Moving on from children to the adult populations, we could study the relationship between growing in a family with constant conflicts and feeling lonely by analysing some of the data collected from the seventh round of the European Social Survey (ESS). Perhaps the questionnaire designer intentionally did not ask the respondent to define the source or the nature of the conflicts in order to avoid embarrassing the respondent. But it should be reasonable to think that the most important and saddening conflicts are those between the parents, very likely including the conflicts that eventually led to a divorce; when divorce is sanctioned, there must be already a history of conflicts. As indicated previously, children caught in between such conflicts would become lonely as their parents were not only pushing each other away but also pushing their children away in the struggle. Even when the marriage survived, the damage was already done on themselves and their children. The relevant survey question is formulated as the following: 'please tell me how often there was serious conflict between the people living in your household when you were growing up?', with five options: 'always', 'often', 'sometimes', 'hardly ever', and 'never'. One could argue that not all 'serious conflicts' were necessarily between the respondent's parents, but it is reasonable to expect that a large proportion of them were. As there is no need to make so many distinctions on the one hand, and there is a need to increase the number of cases, I have combined the first two options into a new category of 'often and always', retained the middle category, and combined the last two into another new category of 'never or hardly ever'. And for each of the three new categories, I have produced the percentage of those who felt 'frequently lonely' (often, almost or all of the time) for each participating country (Table 5.4).

Reading through the numbers in the above table, we could make at least two important observations. First of all, for each country, the percentage of frequent loneliness increases from the second column ('never or hardly ever'), to the third ('sometimes') and then to the fourth ('often and always'); in other words, the frequencies of the two events (loneliness and serious conflicts in household) go in the same direction – the more serious conflicts, the more frequent loneliness. There is no need to present the Kendall's tau-b statistic anymore as they would simply confirm the same relationship in a different way. The second observation we can make is that most northern European countries plus the UK and Germany had the lowest rates of frequent loneliness even among those who grew up in households with constant serious conflicts; in contrast, southern and eastern European countries tend to have the highest percentages of frequent loneliness among those who grew up in the same kind of households. There are a few exceptions, of course, but the general connection is robust.

Table 5.4 Percentage of frequent loneliness by frequency of serious conflicts within household by country in Europe, 2014.

Country	Frequency of serious conflicts in household			n
	Never or hardly ever	*Sometimes*	*Often and always*	
Finland	2.8	2.7	5.4	2072
Denmark	2.2	4.6	6.0	1487
The Netherlands	1.7	3.2	7.0	1912
UK	3.7	6.6	7.5	2243
Germany	3.5	2.4	8.2	3016
Belgium	6.1	6.9	8.5	1765
Norway	3.1	4.0	9.2	1432
Sweden	4.1	4.3	9.9	1778
Israel	5.9	7.3	10.4	2439
Estonia	6.2	7.5	10.7	1998
Ireland	3.6	5.7	10.7	2343
Switzerland	1.6	5.0	10.9	1526
Slovenia	5.2	5.7	11.5	1207
Lithuania	6.0	7.9	13.5	2123
Austria	4.3	7.1	15.7	1772
Portugal	7.5	14.7	18.2	1258
France	8.0	8.5	18.3	1910
Czech Republic	8.9	15.4	18.8	2092
Spain	7.7	7.5	20.8	1912
Poland	9.1	14.3	21.2	1566
Hungary	7.5	12.2	24.7	1655

Given the connection found above, it will be more informative to examine the percentage of respondents who grew up in households where serious conflicts often or even always occurred in each country, because this percentage could be an important but so far neglected social source of loneliness. However, I was somehow surprised by the numbers shown in Figure 5.1.

A certain kind of paradox appears if we connect the numbers in this figure with those presented in the previous table, although the connection is not completely consistent. Other than France, the countries on the top of the figure (Denmark, Germany, UK, The Netherlands and Belgium) – that is, the countries having the highest percentages of those growing up in households with constant serious conflicts – are the countries that have the lowest percentages of frequent loneliness among such people. Conversely, the countries at the bottom of this figure (Spain, Czech Republic, Poland, Ireland) – those countries having the lowest

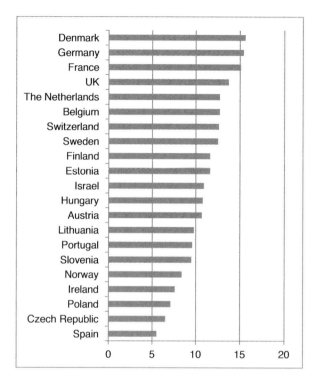

Figure 5.1 Percentage growing up in households of constant serious conflicts by country in Europe, 2014.

percentages of those growing up in households with constant serious conflicts – are among the countries that have the highest percentages of frequent loneliness in the above table. The only explanation that I could think of at the moment is the way in which people in each country interpret the conflicts will determine whether they feel lonely or not. In other words, my theory is that in Denmark, Germany, UK, The Netherlands and Belgium, serious conflicts within households are more common, but they are less likely to lead people to loneliness because the conflicts are interpreted as being part of their life or at least not making people feel alienated from each other; in contrast, in Spain, Czech Republic, Poland, and Ireland, although serious conflicts in households are less common, but once they occurred, they are more likely to make people feel lonely because the conflicts cause more fundamental damages to people's relations. In short, conflicts with the family in some national or cultural contexts are damaging than they are in other nations, which in turn push up the prevalence of loneliness. In Chapter 7 we shall examine more factors at the national and cultural levels in order to understand the national variation of frequent loneliness.

Bullying and loneliness among children

A History of Loneliness contains some of the saddest stories that I have ever read. Besides depicting vivid scenes of loneliness in family life in the context of Ireland, most parts of the novel present a few horrible cases of sexual abuse of children in the church and religious schools. The most tragic figure is Tom Cardle, the narrator Odran's roommate at Clonliffe, their religious school. As a young boy, he was repeatedly abused physically by his father. When Odran told him about how Odran's father drowned himself and his younger brother, Tom said, 'Lucky you. I wish my father had killed himself.'[9] Father, a figure to which a teenage boy is expected to be attached to in many ways, becomes a target of hatred. In this extraordinary case, loneliness appears pale in comparison with much stronger emotions, fear, hatred, and disgust. Staying away from his father did not help, because he was locked up in what the sociologist Erving Goffman calls 'a total institution',[10] the religious school, where the boys had to keep all their 'secrets and desires tightly within ourselves, furtive and clandestine'.[11] When it became clear that it was too painful to suppress the desires from puberty, they would solve the problem in their own ways. Tom did not explicitly admit that his past of being bullied and abused by his father and other adults led him to abuse other boys, such as Brian, a student of his who committed suicide, but the connection sounds highly sensible even without a psycho-analysis on the connection between being abused and abusing others. Here is his confession to Odran after being released from prison:

> 'Those people ruined my life,' he said, his voice deep and angry. 'They ruined it, Odran, can't you understand that? They took a poor, innocent seventeen-year-old boy who knew nothing of the world and locked him away in a prison for seven years. They told me that everything that made me human was shameful and dirty. They taught me to hate my body and to feel that I was a sinner if I looked at a woman's legs while she walked along the road in front of me. They threatened to expel me from Clonliffe if I so much as talked to a girl when we were out at UCD and my father threatened to kill me if they ever did . . . they made sure that I had no release for any of the natural desires that a human being has, and then they didn't give a damn if I didn't know how to live a decent life.'[12]

And this is why, in the end, he said that he had a long history of loneliness, a long history of supressing natural desires, a history of hiding what happened to him and what he did to others, a history of searching for someone to confide but repeatedly failing, and eventually a history of alienating from all humans around him.

Unfortunately, the reality could be much worse than fiction. Thanks to the sense of justice, courage, and hard work of many journalists such as those represented in the movies *The Magdalene Sisters*, *Spotlight*, and many others, many similar cases of sexual abuse on children by priests and other church officials have come to light. Obviously, it is next to impossible to obtain even an approximately accurate idea of the scale of the abuse – on the one hand, many victims would not report their experiences out of fear of repercussions or a strong sense of shame, and on the other hand, it is in the interests of church officials to suppress, hide, defuse or dilute the scale and the seriousness of the abuse. But the number of cases that have come to light is already staggering; for example, Wikipedia has compiled a long list by country and time under the heading 'Catholic Church sexual abuse cases'.[13] Note that the listed cases are only for the Catholic Church and collected from a limited number of countries where media agents have managed to investigate and report. We may never know exactly how many children have been sexually abused by adults in all sorts of institutions across the world even in a time period not too far back, but we shall definitely be shocked at the moment we become to know it. It is difficult to imagine that few of the sexually abused children did not experience the emotions of fear, loneliness and hatred, as Tom Cardle did. Being abused, sexually or not, must be more powerful than having no attached figure in terms of making the victim lonely: it signals to the victim that they are worth little in the eyes of some powerful adults. Isolation, or even rejection, would still leave some room for one to live on their own; there is still hope to wait for another chance or to connect to others. However, being abused, particularly systematically by a powerful institution and over a long period of time, shuts off all these hopes and opportunities. Perhaps such loneliness should be classified as a separate type of loneliness, 'loneliness from abuse'.

The data collected from the Millennium Cohort Study (MCS) in the UK, introduced initially in Chapter 3, have provided us with an opportunity to further examine the relationship between being abused and loneliness among children. Recall that this is a sample of children born in the year 2000 and interviewed when they reached the age of fourteen. The question about loneliness was how much they would agree with the statement 'I felt lonely', and they could choose one from the following three answers: 1 = not true; 2 = sometimes; 3 = true. The children were also asked whether they were 'sexually assaulted'. Of the 11,005 valid responses, 2.8% (or 313 children) returned a positive answer. At the moment it is difficult to assess the practical significance of this prevalence as other similar results are needed for meaningful comparison and contextualization. Now let's take a look at how such experience is related to loneliness (Table 5.5).

Table 5.5 Sexual assault and loneliness among the 14-year-olds in the UK, 2014–2015.

Sexually assaulted	'I felt lonely'			Row total
	Not true	Sometimes true	True	
Yes	27.2	39.3	33.5	313
No	66.9	24.6	8.4	10955

The numbers in the first three columns in each row add up to 100 as they are the percentages of children reporting each of the three loneliness categories among all children answering either Yes or No to the sexual assault question. These simple statistics demonstrate the powerful effect of sexual abuse on loneliness among children in the UK: although those children who were sexually abused were a small minority, once they were sexually abused, they were four times as likely to feel lonely as those who were not abused (33.5% is almost four times of 8.4%). Of the children who were sexually abused, 72.8% felt lonely at least sometimes, while the percentage was only 33% among those not sexually abused.

Furthermore, as in the MCS survey the experience of being sexually assaulted was included as one of the questions about victimization, it is useful and informative to examine whether the victims of sexual abuse were also abused in other ways. These include: the respondent was (1) 'insulted, threatened, shouted at', (2) 'physically violent against', (3) 'hit or used a weapon against', and (4) 'stolen from'. As all these variables are binary (having only two valid values), I have used the odds ratio as the statistic for measuring the relationship between being sexually assaulted and each of these four experiences. The odds ratio for sexual assault and verbal abuse is 4.99; for physical violence, 3.28; for weapon use, 5.45; and for being stolen, 4.56.[14] These numbers tell us that once children experienced one of these abuses or attacks, they were three to five times more likely than other children to suffer from other forms of abuse or attack as well. A very small number of children would actually be the victims of three to five types of abuse and attack, which might have occurred all at the same time. And the damages to their health will be multiple as well. What inflicted on the victim is not merely the abuse itself; it is also a chain of damages on the mind and the body over a long period of time.

So far our evidence shows that sexual abuse remains rare, at least among young adolescents in the UK. How about the other and relatively less serious forms of abuse among children? Are they more prevalent among children? And are they associated with loneliness as well? Previously, we produced some evidence on the effect of being bullied by siblings on loneliness. The MCS survey also included two questions about the young respondent's experiences of being bullied by other children and online: 'How often other children hurt or pick on the CM' and 'How often other children bullied the CM online', each having six options: 1 = most days, 2 = about once a week, 3 = about once a month, 4 = every few months, 5 = less often, 6 = never. The second question is particularly interesting and important as it could reveal a relatively new form of bullying.

As both the bullying and the loneliness variables are ordinal, the tau-b statistic formulated by Maurice Kendall is appropriate for measuring the strength of the correlation between loneliness and one of the three bullying variables (Table 5.6).

The signs of both statistics are negative, meaning when the value of each bullying variable goes down from 6 to 1 (i.e. when the frequency of bullying increases), the value of the loneliness variable goes up from 1 to 3 (i.e. the loneliness statement sounds more true to the young respondent). An intuitively accessible way of interpreting the statistics is that the more frequent a fourteen year was bullied, the

Table 5.6 Correlation between loneliness and bullying among the 14-year-olds in the UK, 2014–2015.

Statement	Kendall's tau-b with loneliness
How often other children hurt or pick on the respondent	−0.318***
How often other children bullied the respondent online	−0.298***

***: $p < 0.001$.

more likely they would become lonely. The data would not allow us to tell which of the two occurs first, bullying or loneliness, but it is clearly possible that being bullied is one of the factors responsible for loneliness among children. We may not confirm the applicability of such results in other national contexts either, but it would be surprising if what they describe is only confined in the UK.

While the results seem to show that the effect of bullying on loneliness remains the same regardless whether it occurred online or offline, online bullying deserves more serious attention due to the popularity of social media among children. As dramatized by the movie *Disconnect*, cyberbullying could lead to not merely loneliness but possibly a tragedy as well: Ben was shy and unpopular at school, and became the target of two boys in his school, Jason and Frye. Creating a fake account with the name Jessica, Jason and Frye tricked Ben to send a photo of himself naked. The photo was distributed as a laughing matter to other children in the school. Ben felt so humiliated that he attempted suicide by hanging himself. Although he was saved, he was in a coma.

Online bullying is potentially more powerful than bullying conducted face-to-face firstly because social media and other new technologies could be employed as an efficient tool of bullying. Moreover, the involvement of a large number of onlookers creates a shameful experience, which in turn creates a strong sense of loneliness as the victim is too ashamed to talk about the experience with anybody else. Accumulated over time, the combined sense of shame and loneliness could lead to desperate actions.

Exclusion, discrimination, and loneliness among adults

If all loneliness is caused by the lack of desired social relations, then it should be gone once the social relations are acquired or replaced with new ones. This, however, is not always the case. A person's loneliness may have multiple causes, so the removal of one cause cannot guarantee that the person is not lonely anymore. What happened in the movie *Fear Eats the Soul* comes as a powerful case, illustrating how the divide between 'they' and 'we' between social groups could entail so much loneliness. In the post-Second World War Germany, Emmi was a 60-year-old widow, working as a cleaning lady. She lived a lonely life despite the fact that she had a son, a daughter, and some grandchildren, because her children were busy and others gave her funny faces. Perhaps in searching for friendly human contacts, she ventured into a bar in a rainy evening where Arab music was played. After she entered, those already inside were not shy of staring at her, examining her, being amazed by her bravery of getting into a place to which she did not socially belong. Some of the customers were the migrant workers from Morocco, and Ali was one of them. Soon he developed a romantic relationship with Emmi after dancing together. Such relationship liberated Emmi from loneliness, but not for long, because it alienated Emmi from those around her, her children, her neighbours, her colleagues, even the owners of the shop she frequently visited. After learning her plan to marry Ali, her children became furious: their mother suddenly became a whore! Ali and Emmi did get married, but with nobody's blessing. Their persistence only proved that at that time and place, inter-racial marriage was a taboo, and everyone around you knew exactly how to punish you socially: leaving you alone at lunch, complaining to the police about trivial matters about you, refusing to sell you things in a shop, and collectively staring at you as if you belong to a different species. You simply cannot fail to realize that you were not one of them, you were separated apart from them no matter where you go, as all of the assumed principles previously regulating relations among these people do not apply anymore. The story is a powerful example of how social exclusion and ostracism could put the brave souls in an extremely lonely position in case they dare to violate social norms by crossing the boundaries of long-established social categories.

It is not easy, however, to study the connection between social exclusion or discrimination and loneliness. In the twenty-first century, after going through many waves of protests and struggles or learning about them, most people in most societies have developed a strong sense of justice, fairness, and equity. Except for a small minority of hardcore racists, most would try to be 'politically correct', at least in public places. As a result, forms of what may be called 'explicit discriminations or exclusions', such as separate seating areas on public places, have disappeared. Nevertheless, that does not mean discrimination or exclusion has disappeared; in many places, they simply have been replaced by more subtle forms that make it much more difficult to verify, that is, 'implicit discriminations or exclusions', such as 'diplomatic cold shoulders' that an immigrant from Trinidad warned his fellow immigrants in London. The nature of the damages thus caused has changed accordingly, from physical and institutional to psychological and personal; like the air, you feel it, but you don't see it. What matters now is how the victims feel. Fortunately, researchers have collected some data that allow us to explore whether the perception of being discriminated is associated with loneliness. Clearly, it is sensible to expect that loneliness is more prevalent among those who feel they have been discriminated in any society, although the strength of the connection may vary from one society to another. Now let's see how much support our data would lend to this hypothesis.

In the seventh round of the ESS in 2014, respondents were asked to report whether they would describe themselves 'as being a member of a group that is discriminated against in this country?' I have calculated the odds ratio of this variable and 'frequent loneliness' (most of the time, all or almost all of the time) for each participating country, alone with the corresponding confidence interval at the 95% level in Table 5.7.

As our interest here is in the relationship between loneliness and being discriminated, the figures in the above table are ranked by the odds ratios in the fourth column. The highlighted confidence intervals are those that do not contain the value of 1, which indicates that the value of odds ratio is very unlikely to be 1. Note that an odds ratio of 1 means no relationship.

Overall, the statistics present a rather complicated picture. First of all, notice that at the top of the table, the UK and Israel have the highest percentages of respondents who felt discriminated, 14.5% and 21.8%, respectively, but they have the lowest odds ratios, which are not statistically significant. This means that although these two countries have the highest percentages of people feeling

Table 5.7 Odds ratios of being discriminated and frequent loneliness by country in Europe, 2014.

Country	Percentage discriminated	n	Odds ratio with frequent loneliness	95% confidence interval
UK	14.5	2245	0.84	(0.59, 1.20)
Israel	21.8	2545	0.94	(0.45, 1.94)
Slovenia	3.5	1214	0.94	(0.90, 0.97)
Austria	4.8	1777	1.13	(0.26, 4.90)
Estonia	11.2	2008	1.27	(0.14, 11.42)
Belgium	7.0	1765	1.32	(0.51, 3.43)
Spain	6.9	1918	1.33	(0.89, 2.00)
Norway	5.8	1436	1.38	(0.17, 11.08)
Poland	4.3	1600	1.55	(1.00, 2.41)
Ireland	5.4	2356	1.73	(0.38, 7.97)
France	13.4	1908	1.87	(1.51, 2.32)
Hungary	6.6	1687	1.97	(0.92, 4.22)
Czech Republic	6.6	2131	2.11	(1.08, 4.14)
Portugal	4.0	1260	2.29	(0.89, 5.89)
Lithuania	10.3	2185	3.07	(1.02, 9.23)
Finland	8.8	2084	3.16	(0.84, 11.87)
Sweden	8.8	1768	3.18	(1.40, 7.26)
Germany	5.0	3040	3.39	(2.30, 5.01)
Denmark	5.3	1497	3.40	(0.71, 16.16)
Switzerland	5.6	1525	3.53	(1.15, 10.86)
The Netherlands	9.1	1910	3.83	(2.02, 7.25)

discriminated, such feeling does not seem to be a source of loneliness. In contrast, at the bottom of the table, the prevalence of feeling discriminated is quite low in Sweden, Germany, Switzerland and The Netherlands, but such feeling is a significant source of loneliness. Poland and Czech Republic have even lower rates of feeling discriminated but such feeling is a significant risk factor for frequent loneliness. The most worrying cases are France and Lithuania, where the percentages of respondents feeling discriminated are more than 10% and it is significantly associated with frequent loneliness. In this sense, we need to worry the least about the other countries, where discrimination is not widely felt and even if it is felt, it is not significant related to frequent loneliness. Overall, these statistics demonstrate the importance of national context in specifying the association between the experience of being discriminated and feeling frequently lonely. To explain these various connections between feeling discriminated and frequent loneliness is much more difficult; at the moment, we could only hypothesize that they might come from how liberal a country's political and social environments are, as we shall explore in Chapter 8.

Trust and loneliness

One social origin of loneliness that has been rarely captured by psychological and health studies is the difficulty for the lonely in establishing trustworthy relations with people around them. Hamlet felt lonely because he couldn't trust anybody around him. He knew a secret of grave importance, to himself personally and to the whole kingdom, but he couldn't share it even with his mother, his lover, or his friends. Winston Smith, a clandestine rebel to the totalitarian regime in George Orwell's *1984*, lived an extremely lonely life until he could have a secret love affair with Julia. In the totalitarian regime, everyone is under constant surveillance, everyone could be spying on anyone else; as a result, everyone can trust no one. The loneliness in this situation is perhaps the scariest – everyone could harm you but you don't know who they are and when they will attack, and you have nowhere to hide.

In even the most supressing contemporary society, things are clearly not so dramatic. Nevertheless, the relationship between trust and loneliness should be the same. In contemporary societies, it should be safe to assume that most people have at least one or two others that they can trust, although as we shall see below that the actual percentage of people in such position may vary quite widely from one country to another. Moreover, it is reasonable to hypothesize that in societies that have experienced recent and major social, economic, or political transformations, the level of trust is expected to be low, the prevalence of loneliness therefore high, and the association between the two stronger than societies that have been relatively peaceful and stable. This is particularly the case for trust of strangers and institutions, which is sometimes referred to as 'generalized trust'.[15] In societies where frauds, corruptions, and crimes occur regularly, attachments and trusts among family members may not be sufficient for keeping one away from loneliness. This kind of loneliness refers to the feeling of estrangement or alienation from the wider and impersonal social environments or systems.

To study these issues empirically, the ESS does contain some relevant data that allow us to find out how true these hypotheses may be. Although data collected from social surveys cannot pinpoint the specific events and persons that make people diligent and lonely, they can show us notable connections between the two kinds of feelings. Drawing on the designs of survey instruments, we could examine the relationship between loneliness and each of the three types of trust: interpersonal, social, and political.

Data that would allow us to analyse the relationship between loneliness and trust among children are very rare. Luckily, I have found some useful data about the relationship between interpersonal trust and loneliness among the 14-year-olds in the UK's MCS mentioned above. As one of the three questions regarding social support, these young participants were asked to consider how true the statement 'there is someone I trust whom I would turn to if I had problems'. Of the 11,313 valid answers, 78.7% reported 'very true', 18.7% 'partly true', and 2.6% 'not true at all'. Figures in Table 5.8 show a clear correlation between having a trusted person and loneliness.

The Kendall's tau-b could capture the strength of the correlation, which is 0.156 and statistically significant at the 0.001 level. While the magnitude of this statistic is not high, the correlation is very clear: if a 14-year-old did not have someone they could trust, the chance that they would feel lonely ('true' to the loneliness question) would double the percentage of each of the other two categories each time. The percentage of children who were both lonely and had no person that they could trust was very low, constituting only 0.8% of more than eleven thousand valid responses, but they were much more likely to be lonely and therefore are the ones that deserve serious attention.

For the adult populations, we need to turn to the seventh round of the ESS. Here, 'interpersonal trust' is represented by the question 'How many people, if any, are there with whom you can discuss intimate and personal matters?', with the following options: 0, 1, 2, 3, 4–6, 7–9, and 10 or more. Although the question does not directly ask about trust, there should be no doubt that trust is a precondition of discussing intimate and personal matters. Furthermore, it should be reasonable to expect that the more people the respondent can trust, the less likely the

Table 5.8 Having trusted person and loneliness among 14-year-olds, UK, 2014–2015.

Having someone I trust and would turn to if having problems	'I felt lonely'			Row total
	Not true	Sometimes	True	
Very true	69.4	23.6	7.0	8866
Partly true	53.4	31.5	15.1	2104
Not true at all	45.1	25.0	29.9	288

respondent will be lonely. For loneliness, the respondents were asked how often they felt lonely during last week and to choose one of the following four options: 1 = 'none or almost none of the time', 2 = 'some of the time', 3 = 'most of the time', and 4 = 'all or almost all of the time'. Again, because both variables are ordinal, we could compute Kendall's tau-b to measure their relationship, as we did in a previous section. Table 5.9 shows the statistics by the participating country of the seventh round of the ESS.

In several ways, the figures presented in the table are highly consistent. First of all, the signs of the Kendall's tau-b statistics are negative in all countries; that is, in every country the more people with whom the respondents could discuss intimate and personal matters, the less frequently that they would feel lonely. This may not be surprising but reassuring – it has confirmed the value of a confidant in preventing people from becoming lonely. Next, the values of the statistics are very close – if we round up the decimals into one significant number, all will become –0.1, with only those for Hungary and Lithuania being –0.2. This may indicate a weak relationship between the two variables, but given small number of

Table 5.9 Correlation between number of confidants and loneliness in Europe, 2014.

Country	Kendall's tau-b	Valid sample size (n)
Austria	−0.130***	1779
Belgium	−0.132***	1767
Switzerland	−0.125***	1528
Czech Republic	−0.078***	2108
Germany	−0.096***	3037
Denmark	−0.119***	1488
Estonia	−0.102***	2018
Spain	−0.113***	1905
Finland	−0.103***	2078
France	−0.095***	1910
UK	−0.118***	2245
Hungary	−0.195***	1662
Ireland	−0.089***	2363
Israel	−0.083***	2475
Lithuania	−0.213***	2088
The Netherlands	−0.170***	1918
Norway	−0.031	1433
Poland	−0.097***	1573
Portugal	−0.121***	1253
Sweden	−0.079***	1784
Slovenia	−0.081***	1209

Note: ***: $p \leq 0.001$.

values for each variable, this is not surprising. Finally, the three stars indicate that all statistics are statistically significant with the exception of Norway. This means that except for Norway, the probability that the Kendall's tau-b in the population equals to zero is extremely low, thus showing stronger evidence that we should take the relationship between the two variables seriously.

Once the general relationship of loneliness and having a confidant is confirmed, it is useful to study some intuitively more interesting statistics. Here, we are more interested, as we always are in this book, in 'frequent loneliness' (lonely most of the time, or almost all of the time, or all of the time) as this type of loneliness is the most worrying. We are also more interested in those who have no one to discuss intimate or personal matters at all rather than the exact number of confidants. The percentage of those who were frequently lonely among those with no confidant and those with at least one confidant, respectively, will give us more specific information about the relationship between the two attributes. The percentages in these countries are shown in Table 5.10.

Table 5.10 Frequent loneliness and having at least one confidant in Europe, 2014.

Country	Percentage feeling frequently lonely		Odds ratio and 95% confidence interval
	No confidant	At least one confidant	
Norway	9.1	3.0	0.31 (0.04, 2.57)
Finland	10.0	2.9	0.27 (0.03, 2.30)
Germany	13.3	3.4	0.23 (0.12, 0.43)
Ireland	14.3	5.3	0.33 (0.07, 1.61)
Poland	16.1	11.2	0.65 (0.47, 0.91)
Spain	16.9	8.4	0.45 (0.27, 0.74)
Belgium	20.0	6.0	0.26 (0.10, 0.65)
UK	20.1	5.5	0.23 (0.16, 0.33)
Israel	20.4	7.2	0.30 (0.14, 0.63)
Czech Republic	22.1	11.5	0.46 (0.26, 0.82)
Switzerland	23.1	3.2	0.11 (0.03, 0.44)
Lithuania	23.5	7.5	0.26, (0.10, 0.69)
Portugal	24.1	11.4	0.40 (0.21, 0.77)
Slovenia	25.0	5.4	0.17 (0.03, 0.98)
Estonia	25.0	6.9	0.22 (0.04, 1.32)
France	25.1	10.4	0.35 (0.27, 0.45)
Sweden	27.3	4.6	0.13 (0.03, 0.50)
The Netherlands	28.6	3.4	0.09 (0.04, 0.21)
Denmark	30.0	2.4	0.06 (0.01, 0.26)
Austria	30.4	5.3	0.12 (0.05, 0.33)
Hungary	31.4	9.8	0.24 (0.13, 0.45)

The countries in this table have been ordered by the numbers in the second column (the percentage of respondents who were frequently lonely among those who had no one with whom they could discuss intimate matters). Clearly, there is a considerable variation in the effect of having no confidant on the chance of feeling frequently lonely: at the lower end are Norway, Finland, Germany and Ireland (less than 15%), and at the higher end are Denmark, Austria and Hungary (about 30%). To measure the association between the two variables more rigorously, I have also produced and presented the odds ratios and their corresponding 95% confidence intervals in the last column. For four countries, the confidence intervals contain the value of 1 (highlighted), meaning that the probability that this confidence interval contains 1 is higher than what we could usually accept (5%). Note that for odds ratios, the value of 1 indicates no relationship between the two variables, so we need to refrain from making any claim about the relationship for these three countries. Overall, there does not appear to be any clear pattern in terms of the variation of the relationship across the studied European countries.

'Social trust' refers to trust of people in society at large. In MCS, there is a question about how much the 14-year-old respondent trusted others, measured by an eleven-point scale (0 to 10, with 0 meaning no trust at all). While the meaning of 'others' is not specific enough for us, they should refer to people that the 14 year-old respondent knew either personally and strangers. Here are the mean scores in relation to the three levels of loneliness: regarding the statement 'I felt lonely', for those who did not think it was true to their situation, the mean of their trust of others is 4.54, followed by 5.60 for those who thought it was sometimes true, and finally 6.59 for those who thought the statement was true. That is, the level of trusting others is in reverse relationship with loneliness: the more they trusted others, the less likely they would be lonely. These statistics would not help us establish the causal direction between the two kinds of feelings; it is likely that the relationship moves in both directions, although there should be a time point at which one emotion triggered the chain of mutual reactions.

In the ESS, 'social trust' is measured more specifically and comprehensively with the following three questions:

- 'Generally speaking, would you say that most people can be trusted, or that you can't be too careful in dealing with people?'
- 'Do you think that most people would try to take advantage of you if they got the chance, or would they try to be fair?'
- 'Would you say that most of the time people try to be helpful or that they are mostly looking out for themselves?'

For each question, respondents were asked to choose a score of 0 to 10, where 0 means absolutely no trust and 10 highest trust; for example, for the first question, 0 means that you can't be too careful and 10 means that most people can be trusted. The first question relates to trust directly. The second is about perception of fairness and the third relates to perceived helpfulness of other people; these two questions relate to social trust in an indirect manner: we would trust other people if we find them generally fair and helpful. As the response to these three questions are highly correlated, it is statistically appropriate to put them into a single scale,[16] whose values are in the range of 0–30. Connecting this newly created score with the four values of the loneliness variable, we would expect an inverse relationship between the two; that is, the more frequently the respondents in a particular country feel lonely, the lower the average of their social trust score will be. The results are shown in Table 5.11.

The countries in this table are ranked by the mean score of social trust among the most frequently lonely ('all or almost all of the time). What these mean

Table 5.11 Means of social trust by levels of loneliness and country in Europe, 2014.

Country	Frequency of loneliness				F-statistic and p-value
	None or almost none of the time	Some of the time	Most of the time	All or almost all of the time	
Hungary	13.8	12.4	11.8	10.6	13.3***
Poland	12.6	12.3	10.9	10.8	5.0**
Portugal	13.6	12.2	11.3	11.1	12.1***
Slovenia	14.0	14.1	11.9	11.2	4.2**
Israel	16.0	14.8	14.0	11.8	18.4***
Czech Republic	14.3	14.0	13.2	12.4	4.5**
Estonia	17.0	15.9	14.6	12.5	19.5***
Spain	14.9	14.1	12.3	12.5	13.8***
Lithuania	15.5	14.0	12.6	12.6	19.6***
Belgium	15.9	14.4	13.8	13.8	14.4***
Germany	16.6	15.6	14.8	13.9	10.4***
Ireland	17.5	15.7	15.3	14.0	24.8***
France	15.7	15.0	14.0	14.3	7.9***
Switzerland	18.0	16.7	15.6	14.5	10.5***
The Netherlands	18.4	16.9	15.3	14.7	27.2***
Austria	16.2	15.1	13.4	14.8	10.0***
Denmark	20.5	19.7	15.5	14.9	23.0***
UK	17.5	16.5	15.3	15.6	9.4***
Sweden	19.5	18.5	17.8	16.9	9.9***
Finland	19.8	18.8	16.7	17.5	11.8***
Norway	19.9	18.5	17.1	18.2	12.7***

Note: ***: $p \leq 0.001$; **: $p \leq 0.01$.

scores reveal is that in terms of social trust, the distinction is more between the first two categories ('none' or 'almost none of the time' and 'some of the time') than between the latter two ('most' or 'all or almost all of the time'). On average, people in the two lower categories of loneliness are clearly more trusting than those in the two more lonely categories, and the difference is statistically confirmed with the F statistic and the corresponding p-value presented in the last column. The difference between the more lonely categories is less distinctive because for some countries (Spain, France, Austria, UK, Finland and Norway), the mean score of social trust among the 'some of the time lonely' is actually lower than that among the 'all or almost all of the time lonely', and for two countries (Lithuania and Belgium) the mean scores are the same. All in all, we can say that people who felt 'frequently lonely' had lower levels of trust than those who were not frequently lonely.

Finally, 'political trust' refers to the respondent's trust of political institutions of the country that they live in. The suppressing environment described by George Orwell's *1984* comes to mind: the Big Brother was watching everything and everybody, every room had a camera, and everybody could report on anybody else, even among family members, making trust, either interpersonal or institutional, an unaffordable luxury. What portrayed here is not purely fictional; rather, the story is dramatized reality, which can gain much support from realistic memoirs such as collected in *The Whisperers*[17] or studies of everyday life in the former USSR.[18] This does not necessarily mean that political trust of the residents of the national members of the USSR will increase years after the collapse of the USSR. Given the economic and other difficulties that these nations have gone through since the fall of the Berlin Wall, one would not expect to see a high level of political trust within any of these nations. More relevant to our concern in this book is the potentially tenuousness of the connection between political trust and loneliness: for most people and most of the time loneliness is an emotion predominantly influenced by inter-personal relations, while political trust pertains to institutions that few have personal relations, even in small and highly democratic societies. In today's Europe, the kind of loneliness induced by a strong sense of alienation from the political system is most likely reserved for a minority of residents who have had some very unpleasant experiences with the political system or hold some very strong political ideology against the existing political system. Even for these people, the loneliness translated from 'political distrust' is different from the loneliness usually emerging at the personal level.

In the ESS, the questions are formulated as the following: 'please tell me on a score of 0–10 how much you personally trust each of the institutions I read out. 0 means you do not trust an institution at all, and 10 means you have complete trust': the country's parliament, the legal system, the police, politicians, and political parties.[19] For each participating country in the seventh round of the ESS, the statistical consistency of the responses to these five items is very high,[20] meaning that if people have high political trust, they would trust the politicians and the political institutions in their country. This lends great legitimacy of creating a summed score of 'political trust' by summing up the responses to the five questions, whose values will range from 0 to 50. As we have found that the major difference lies between those frequently lonely and those not, here we make comparison between these two categories rather than the original four categories of loneliness in terms of the mean of the political trust summed score.

The countries in this table are rank ordered by the difference between the mean of political trust among those not frequently and that among those frequently lonely (the penultimate column). It is very interesting and somehow surprising to note that the biggest differences (above the value of 3) are found among most northern European countries, plus Austria, Germany and the UK, and the differences are all statistically significant. That is, in these countries, those frequently lonely had significantly lower levels of political trust than those not frequently lonely. Furthermore, except for Switzerland, the levels of political trust tend to

Table 5.12 Means of political trust and frequent loneliness by country in Europe, 2014.

Country	Not frequently lonely	Frequently lonely	Difference	F-statistic and significance
Switzerland	30.3	29.6	0.7	0.32
Israel	20.7	20.0	0.7	0.98
Hungary	19.8	19.0	0.8	1.0
Slovenia	15.3	14.5	0.8	0.6
Estonia	22.9	21.5	1.4	2.6
Czech Republic	21.1	19.4	1.7	5.7*
France	20.9	19.2	1.7	6.3*
Poland	15.7	13.9	1.8	5.7*
Belgium	24.3	22.2	2.1	4.7*
Ireland	22.0	19.7	2.3	8.3**
Spain	18.5	16.1	2.4	7.9**
Lithuania	19.2	16.6	2.6	11.7***
Portugal	17.1	14.3	2.8	11.8***
Austria	23.8	20.7	3.1	9.4**
The Netherlands	27.3	24.2	3.1	9.6**
Sweden	29.8	26.5	3.3	10.5***
Germany	25.3	21.9	3.4	13.4***
UK	23.3	19.7	3.6	15.7***
Norway	32.0	27.9	4.1	11.8***
Finland	29.6	25.4	4.2	14.4***
Denmark	31.2	25.9	5.3	14.9***

Note: ***: $p \leq 0.001$; **: $p \leq 0.01$; *: $p \leq 0.05$.

be higher in these countries as well. In contrast and surprisingly, in nations that were members of the former USSR, including Hungary, Slovenia, Estonia, Czech Republic and Poland, the differences in political trust between the frequently lonely and those not are either not only among the smallest but also statistically insignificant or only marginally significant. How do we explain these differences? Here is my theory, although I cannot provide further supporting evidence at the moment: in eastern European countries the lower levels of political trust mean that the residents in these countries politically tend to be more apathetic than the other group of countries (northern Europe plus UK, Germany, Austria), and one consequence of their political apathy is that there is not much connection between their political views and their personal feelings; that is, loneliness remains an almost exclusively personal matter that has little to do with politics. Conversely, it is in countries where people take politics seriously that the connection between political trust and loneliness is much likely to be stronger and significant.

Notes

1 T. Dolin. 2000. 'Introduction', in C. Brontë, *Villette*. Oxford: Oxford University Press, p. x.
2 Ibid., p. 22.
3 L. Tolstoy. 2010. *The Death of Ivan Ilyich and Other Stories*, trans. R. Pevear and L. Volokhonsky. New York: Vintage Books, p. 83.
4 J. Boyne. 2014. *A History of Loneliness*. London: Transworld Publishers, p. 14.
5 J. S. Wallerstein and J. B. Kelly. 1980. 'The effects of parental divorce: experiences of the child in later latency', in J. Hartog, J. R. Audy, and Y. A. Cohen (eds), *The Anatomy of Loneliness*. New York: International Universities Press, pp. 148–169.
6 Ibid., p. 149.
7 Ibid., p. 161.
8 See, for example, the two papers that Christina Victor and I have produced: C. Victor and K. Yang. 2012. 'The prevalence of loneliness among adults: a case study of the United Kingdom', *The Journal of Psychology: Interdisciplinary and Applied*, 146(1–2): 85–104; K. Yang and C. Victor. 2011. 'Age and loneliness in 25 European nations', *Ageing and Society*, 31(8): 1368–1388.
9 Boyne, *A History of Loneliness*, p. 248.
10 E. Goffman. 1991. *Asylums: Essays on the Social Situation of Mental Patients and Other Inmates*. London: Penguin.
11 Boyne, *A History of Loneliness*, p. 260.
12 Ibid., p. 463.
13 See https://en.wikipedia.org/wiki/Catholic_Church_sexual_abuse_cases (accessed 24 April 2018).
14 All these odds ratios are statistically significant at the 0.05 level.
15 The literature on the concept of generalized trust is large. Readers interested in this concept could consult the following publications: D. Gambetta. 1988. *Trust: Making and Breaking Cooperative Relations*. New York: Wiley-Blackwell; T. Yamagishi. 2001. 'Trust as a form of social intelligence', in K. Cook (ed.), *Trust in Society*. New York: Russell Sage Foundation, pp. 121–147; and R. Hardin. 2002. *Trust and Trustworthiness*. New York: The Russell Sage Foundation.
16 More precisely, for all participating countries of the seventh round of the ESS, the Cronbach's alpha is between 0.6 and 0.8.

17 O. Figes. 2008. *The Whisperers: Private Life in Stalin's Russia*. London: Penguin.
18 For example, see the following two studies: S. Fitzpatrick. 1999. *Everyday Stalinism: Ordinary Life in Extraordinary Times; Soviet Russia in the 1930s*. New York: Oxford University Press; C. Chatterjee, D. L. Ransel, M. Cavender, and K. Petrone (eds). 2015. *Everyday Life in Russia Past and Present*. Bloomington, IN: Indiana University Press.
19 The European Parliament and the United Nations are also included in the list, but they are not included in the analysis here as they are not the political institutions of the country in which the respondent lives.
20 For all participating countries, the Cronbach's alphas are above 0.8, and some are even above 0.9.

Chapter 6

Loneliness across social groups

One thing that separates sociologists apart from other social scientists is that they take differences across social groups and contexts very seriously. Groups and contexts are closely related: either consciously or inadvertently, a social group creates a social context for each of its individual members. Here, social groups are defined very broadly as any large number of human beings belonging to any categories deemed important in a given society, which include age, gender, marriage, ethnicity, race, immigration, religion, socio-economic status (or class) and related attributes such as being in poverty or unemployment. We studied how age, gender, marital status and other attributes are related to loneliness in the previous chapters. In this chapter we examine how the experience of loneliness varies across other social groups. Clearly, my list of social groups is by no means exhaustive,[1] but it should include most of the important ones covered in sociological textbooks. More importantly, my purpose here is not to conduct a survey of the relationships between loneliness with all social groups but to demonstrate why loneliness is a social rather than merely a psychological or individual problem. Obviously, before answering this why question, the connection between loneliness and each grouping factor must be established. Sociologists care about such relations because of their ultimate concern with social justice; it is a sign of injustice when one social group suffers from a painful condition due to some institutional or structural factors. Sociologists of medicine, health and illness have studied forms of inequality for a long time, but almost few among them have attempted to discover how loneliness is distributed across social groups. If we accept that loneliness is a painful feeling that has serious medical consequences, as I showed in the first chapter, and that it is a form of inequality if one social group suffers significantly more from loneliness than another, then we must start to learn about how loneliness exists in different social groups. My analyses in this chapter may appear preliminary in statistical terms and my observations restricted to the countries under study, but given the shortage of research on this topic, there should be no doubt that the analyses conducted in this chapter are a worthwhile endeavour.

Living in other people's country: loneliness among immigrants

I start this chapter by examining the loneliness among immigrants as it well connects this chapter and the previous one. More precisely, the immigrants under study here refer to 'international immigrants', that is, those who have moved from one country to another without a pre-determined time point of leaving the new country. On the one hand, the loneliness among such immigrants could be classified as 'loneliness among others', with the others being the local or the long-term residents (or the natives, or any other acceptable label). Here, I would choose 'the natives' purely as a descriptive term. On the other hand, this kind of loneliness could be seen as stemming from the divide between the immigrants and the natives as two distinctive social groups.

Immigrants thus defined can become lonely for at least two reasons: missing their country of origin, and finding it difficult to integrate themselves into the new country. In most cases, it is the combination of these two struggles that makes immigrants lonely, although the relative weight of each may vary from one immigrant to another. Eilis in Colm Tóibín's *Brooklyn* provides a good example. As a young Irish lady, she was both pushed and pulled to move to New York City in the early 1950s. The push was the hardship of life and the lack of employment opportunities in Ireland. The pull was an opportunity to work in a major department store in New York, offered by an Irish priest of her acquaintance in Brooklyn. While it was psychologically hard for anybody who moved to a very different environment, she was actually very lucky as an immigrant: everything was arranged for her, she lived in a decent house with several other ladies, a job in a large department store was waiting for her, the priest later paid for her classes in accounting, and an Italian young man became her boyfriend. All of these would be a dream for many other immigrants to the US in those years and even long after. But these events couldn't stop her from falling into loneliness, however: she couldn't fit into the circle of her housemates, the job was stressful, and it was terrifying for her to stay in her room during the night. 'She was nobody here. It was not just that she had no friends and family; it was rather that she was a ghost in this room, in the streets on the way to work, on the shop floor. Nothing meant anything.'[2] It would be too disheartening and shameful for her to tell her true feelings to her mother, sister and friends in her letters. Is this simply homesickness, as the priest claimed? If it is, we can say that homesickness is a specific form of loneliness; that is, homesickness is loneliness as longing for getting back to home where everything is familiar (psychologically easy) if not necessarily desirable. When one is lifted out of that familiar context and planted into a new environment, unless the new environment is very welcoming, the person will have the desire of going back to the original context. The aloneness in the new environment becomes painful as everything is either strange or even hostile, so the mind suffers from taking in so many unfamiliar and unfriendly signals. The capacity of most human minds to take in unpleasant information has long proved to be very limited; over the limit, the mind would soon suffer or even break down.

Many immigrants were not as lucky as Eilis – few arrangements were made before they arrived at the hosting country, and few natives would be ready to help them. Besides the inconveniences and even hardships, immigrants came to a new country usually with the high hope of starting a new and richer life but soon became disappointed to find out that they did not seem to belong to the new country, a problem easily overwhelmed by the positive prospects of a new life. This bitter feeling of not fitting in is well described by Sam Selvon in his *The Lonely Londoners*. Moses was an immigrant from Trinidad in London. A strong sense of loneliness suddenly came to him when he was arriving at the Waterloo station to pick up his fellow countryman Galahad. Along with loneliness he also felt homesick and miserable – again, loneliness rarely comes alone. Although he had already lived in London for several years, he did not feel belonging to the UK. His loneliness came at personal (lack of families and friends) as well as societal and cultural levels (most people around him belong to a different culture). Immigrants may not be aware of their loneliness if they are constantly occupied with work or other activities, but the sense of loneliness will come to their mind whenever places, particularly public places such as train stations, airports or busy streets, remind them of their relationship with the hosting country. The train station reminded Moses that he could leave the hosting country, and he could go back to his original country that he was familiar with and felt belonging to. In these places, you are among a large crowd of strangers; they are humans, like you, but they do not relate to you in any meaningful way except that you and they are all human beings. But that may make you even lonelier, because at the bottom of your heart you expect them to relate to you, to be nice to you, to share a good life with you, but they don't. Even more frustrating, there are very few ways, all implicit and subtle, in which you could initiate any relationship with the natives around you, and as you are new, you are in a clearly disadvantageous position of being ignorant of those implicit and subtle rules that regulate how social relations are constructed and maintained in this particular context. If you break any of these rules, the natives would see you as a threat or at least a source of trouble. A norm followed widely in almost all societies in the West, particularly in large cities, is 'do not talk to strangers'. If you talk to strangers, you take the risk of being ignored, rejected, ridiculed, humiliated, or even attacked. If a stranger talks to you and you accept, you may risk being deceived into a vicious plot. Therefore, when Galahad went out to look for work on his own,

> and he stand up there on Queensway watching everybody going about their business, and a feeling of loneliness and fright come to him all of a sudden. He forget all the brave words he was talking to Moses, and he realise that

here he is, in London, and he ain't have money or work or place to sleep or any friend or anything, and he standing up here by the tube station watching people, and everybody look so busy he frighten to ask questions from any of them. You think any of them bothering with what going on in his mind? Or in anybody else mind but their own?[3]

Later, he was smiling to a little child on the street, but the child's mother became very suspicious, which made him even more puzzled by the divide between the white natives and the darker-skinned immigrants:

Lord, what it is we people do in this world that we have to suffer so? What it is we want that the white people and them find it so hard to give? A little work, a little food, a little place to sleep. We not asking for the sun, or the moon. We only want to get by, we don't even want to get on.[4]

Thus, it should not come as a surprise when loneliness was found more prevalent among immigrants than the natives. Several academic studies have found that immigrants to Britain and North America seemed to share a very strong sense of isolation and sorrow due to the loss of their family and social relations back in their original countries.[5] Migrant women were particularly likely to feel the absence of family and close local community at times of childbirth, but some-times men spoke of similar feelings of loss as well, when the immigrants were of an advanced age, unemployed, or did not speak the language of the hosting country well, although this does not mean that immigrants are not able to adjust themselves psychologically over time.[6]

The relationship between immigration and loneliness is actually a complicated one, very much due to the multiple aspects of the immigration and the immigrants; it is certainly impossible for me to present a comprehensive analysis on this topic in this section. For example, the answer to the question who is qualified to be an immigrant is not always clear, particularly when we want to distinguish the first, the second and later generations of immigrants. Immigration and ethnicity could be strongly associated, but it could be very difficult to disentangle the effects of one from the other. Also, the country of origin may play a role as well; that is, in the same hosting country, immigrants from some different original countries may feel lonelier than those from other countries. Without going into these complicated details, I would concentrate on two simple questions, again by analysing the data collected from the European Social Survey. I shall start by discover whether immigrants are lonelier than the natives in some participating countries of the ESS, which will establish the phenomenon firstly and demonstrate the effect of national context. Then I shall study whether the natives' attitudes towards immigrants are associated with the immigrants' loneliness; my main aim is to show that if a welcoming attitude is less popular among the natives, then loneliness is expected to be more prevalent among the immigrants.

Before studying the relationship between immigration and loneliness, we need to make two important decisions on the subjects of our subsequent analyses. First, studies on immigrants and minority ethnicities usually encounter the difficulty that unless in surveys that purposefully designed for studying them, the percentages of these people in a general survey are usually very low. A related issue is the distinction between the hosting nations and the sending nations of immigrants. In general, the nations that are economically more prosperous and liberal in welcoming immigrants are mostly likely to have the highest proportions of immigrants. That is, we have to exclude the nations in which the percentage of non-citizens or those born in other countries is very low; here, I have excluded the following nations as their percentages of non-citizens are below 5% and their percentages of those not born in the country are under 10%: Poland, Hungary, Czech Republic, Lithuania, Finland, Portugal, Denmark, Slovenia, and The Netherlands. Israel will not be included either because although its percentage of those not born in Israel is the highest among all these nations (28.3%) but it has a very low percentage of non-citizens; this is so clearly because many Israelites went to Israel to become its citizens although they were born in other countries. As a result, the following ten countries are included for analysis in this section: Germany, Norway, Austria, France, Belgium, Ireland, Sweden, UK, Estonia, and Switzerland. Finally, even in these countries, the sample size of immigrants tends to be very small. Fortunately, the fifth, the sixth and the seventh rounds of the ESS include the same variables of our interest, which allows me to combine the data from these three rounds for a particular country in order to maximize the sample size of the immigrants. The only loss is Austria, who missed the sixth round. Therefore, nine countries will be studied here.

The other important question we need to consider is who qualify as an immigrant. This is an issue more complicated than you might have thought because it involves several dimensions, including citizenship, country of birth, length of stay in the hosting nation, parents' country of birth, and speaking the official language of the hosting nation. There is no consensus among immigration specialists on how these dimensions should be used in determining a person's identity as an immigrant,[7] because on the one hand it is not reasonable to use any one of these criteria alone, but on the other hand it would soon become too complicated if two or more criteria are combined. In practice, what matters is that researchers make clear how they have defined the concept in a particular study.

My approach here aims to strike a balance between sensibility and simplicity. First, I would not use citizenship as a criterion not merely because the percentages of non-citizens in the national samples of the ESS are usually very low but more importantly because not being born in the hosting nation is a much more effective indicator. In at least two situations non-citizens are not necessarily immigrants: some non-citizens do not intend to become immigrants in the sense of settling in the hosting nation in the long run, or some are long-term residents in the hosting nation but have not become citizens for a variety of reasons. Not being born in the hosting nation is a stronger necessary condition for being an immigrant, but it is not sufficient – a baby coming to the hosting nation with parents and growing up in it is no less a native than those who were born there, which is why we need a second condition: the length of stay in the hosting nation. Researchers of immigration usually draw a line at the age of thirteen: only those who were born outside the hosting nation and came to the hosting nation aged thirteen or above qualify as immigrants.[8] Their reasoning is that socialization is basically completed by the time a person reaches thirteen years of age (or the starting point of adolescence). Clearly, socialization never stops but varies from person to person, but if we must draw a line in order to proceed to the next step thirteen seems to be the most reasonable. In short, here a respondent is classified as an immigrant if he or she was not born in the country under study and came to live in this country before reaching the age of thirteen.

After many hours of preparing the data, I am now ready to present the results showing the relationship between being an immigrant and feeling frequently lonely (Table 6.1). Reading through the percentages of frequent loneliness among the immigrants and the natives, respectively, we can see that for each and every country, frequent loneliness is more prevalent among the immigrants than among the natives. To measure the association and its statistical significance, the nine countries in this table are ordered by the values of odds ratios. The UK, France, and Ireland are at the top of the table as their odds ratios are the smallest. Note that their corresponding confidence intervals at the 95% level do include the value of 1, meaning that the odds ratio for the population to be 1 is smaller than 5%. As

Table 6.1 Frequent loneliness by immigrant status in nine European countries, 2010–2014.

Country	% frequently lonely		Odds ratio	95% CI
	Natives	Immigrants		
UK	6.7	7.1	1.1	(0.8, 1.5)
France	12.1	14.3	1.2	(0.9, 1.6)
Ireland	6.2	7.3	1.2	(0.9, 1.6)
Belgium	6.4	9.2	1.5	(1.1, 2.1)
Estonia	8.1	11.8	1.5	(1.2, 1.9)
Germany	4.1	8.4	2.2	(1.6, 2.9)
Switzerland	2.8	6.5	2.5	(1.8, 3.5)
Sweden	4.5	10.6	2.5	(1.8, 3.5)
Norway	2.1	7.2	3.6	(2.4, 5.6)

the value of 1 indicates no relationship between the two variables, these figures provide some support to the observation that in these three countries there is no significant difference in terms of frequent loneliness between the immigrants and the natives.

The reader may have noticed that France is somehow different from the UK and Ireland as the prevalence of frequent loneliness is high in both groups; it is just that the two groups are not sufficiently different in statistical terms. In all other six countries, the difference is statistically significant. For example, in Norway, the chance of feeling lonely frequently among the immigrants is 3.6 times of the chance among the native Norwegians, even though only 7.2% of the immigrants felt lonely frequently.

Why are the immigrants more likely to feel frequently lonely than the natives? As suggested at the beginning of this chapter, there could be several reasons, including homesickness, difficulty of finding employment, difficulty of making friends, feeling isolated from the majority of the population, etc. Here I want to explore the effect of another factor, the natives' attitudes towards immigrants; all other factors have been mentioned from the perspective of the immigrants, while this one comes from the opposite direction. Clearly, the expected connection is that immigrants in a more welcoming nation are expected to be less lonely than those in a less welcoming one. It is important to point out that when studying this connection, we must move the unit of our analysis up from the individual to the nation. More precisely, we would expect a negative relationship between how welcoming a nation is and the prevalence of frequent loneliness among immigrants in that nation. As we have already produced the latter in the above table, we need statistics that indicate how welcoming the natives of a receiving country are to immigrants. I shall produce a mean score by drawing on the natives' responses to the following questions included in the fifth, the sixth and the seventh rounds of the ESS that tap into the effects of the immigrants on the hosting country:

- 'Would you say it is generally bad or good for [country]'s economy that people come to live here from other countries?'
- 'Would you say that [country]'s cultural life is generally undermined or enriched by people coming to live here from other countries?'
- 'Is [country] made a worse or a better place to live by people coming to live here from other countries?'

Responses to each of these questions consist of an 11-point scale, and, unsurprisingly, they are highly correlated,[9] thus lending support to the creation of a summed score. Figure 6.1 maps out the relationship between the mean of this summed score and the prevalence of frequently loneliness among immigrants in the corresponding country:

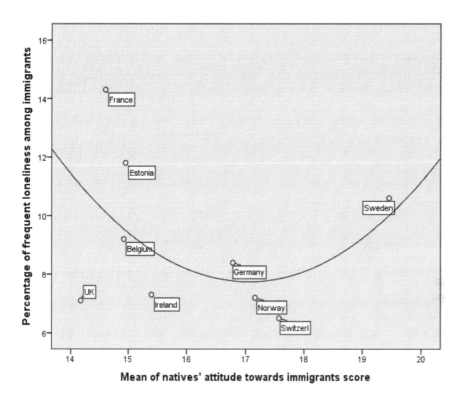

Figure 6.1 Prevalence of frequent loneliness among immigrants and mean of attitudes towards immigrants among natives in nine European countries, 2010–2014.

The expected negative relationship turns out to be confirmed by this graph, except for Sweden, which is the most welcoming to immigrants (measured by the mean of the summed score) but unfortunately has a higher than expected percentage of frequent loneliness among its immigrants. This may not be so puzzling – it is not reasonable to hope that a welcoming attitude of the natives will be sufficient to stop the immigrants from becoming lonely. The case of the UK is intriguing as it is the opposite of Sweden: while the UK is the least welcoming to immigrants, immigrants there have the lowest percentage of frequent loneliness. Further research is needed for finding out what conditions would be sufficient for immigrants not to feel lonely in a particular hosting country.

Race, ethnicity, and loneliness

In understanding the experience of loneliness, race and ethnicity are related to immigration but should not be seen as equivalent. It is intuitively sensible to expect immigrants to be lonelier than the natives, but it is not equally straightforward to expect people of a particular, usually minority, race or ethnicity to be lonelier than those of another, usually majority, race or ethnicity, because immigration usually means the loss of social relations established in the original country but a person's race or ethnicity does not have clear logical implications for social relations. However, in two ways a minority race or ethnicity could become sensible risk factors for loneliness. The first is through its connection with immigration; that is, a large number, if not all, of immigrants are of a race or ethnicity that is different from that of the natives. If immigrants tend to be lonelier than the natives, as shown above in most economically prosperous European countries, people of a particular minority race or ethnicity are subject to a higher chance of frequent loneliness not necessarily because of their race or ethnicity but because of their immigration status.

Secondly, race or ethnicity may be responsible for loneliness on its own account; that is, we are considering the situation in which people of a particular race or ethnicity *who are not immigrants* are found to be lonelier than people of another race or ethnicity. In the previous chapter, I used the story of the movie *Fear Eats the Soul* to illustrate how racial prejudices could make those who dared to ignore the social taboo literally isolated and lonely. Inter-racial hostilities could go very far, of course, if we simply remind ourselves of what happened to the Jews in Nazi Germany and to the black people in the US. They would be very lucky if loneliness was the only pain they had to bear with. When one human group's hatred of another is legitimized by an ideology and supported by the collective will, the people of the majority race or ethnicity, no matter how civilized they have been so far, would not mind inflicting an enormous amount psychological or even physical pain on the human beings of a minority group.

But isolation and loneliness could become the major and constant pain in relatively less violent times. In the movie *Suburbicon*, a black family moved into a white-dominant neighbourhood. Nowhere in the movie did they say they were lonely, but how couldn't they?! The black boy was fortunate to have a white playmate, but the supermarket manager forced his mother to leave by raising the prices of the groceries that she would like to purchase on the spot. Later, the hostility of their white neighbours towards the black family escalated to such a high level that they started to physically attack the family's house. Ironically, all these are only the sideline of the story; the main story is about something much more vicious and vile within a white family! Perhaps this is partly why people of ethnic minorities and immigrants would like to live together: it is simply so hard for some human beings to perceive categorical differences as assets rather than liabilities. Some differences of human categories, no matter how natural and innocuous they should be, become sources of collective enmity, which in turn becomes a source of loneliness of a collective scale.

In other words, once a physiological attribute takes on some kind of social meaning, its potential capacity of becoming a source of loneliness increases dramatically. Unfortunately, no human physiological attribute has been immune from turning into a social attribute, and in most cases, the newly established social attribute is a negative, unwelcomed one, or in another word, a stigma in the eyes of the majority group. The classification of human beings based on a categorical attribute ultimately becomes a process of putting human groups in a ranking order, drawing a line between 'we' and 'they', and determining who could enjoy a certain kind of benefits. It is this process of identifying who belong to which category and which category is 'better' than another, in short a process of discriminating for and against that makes those in the less desirable category lonely. In the previous chapters, we saw some evidence of how bullying and abuse increased the chance of frequent loneliness among both adults and children. Discrimination based on race or ethnicity is another form of abuse or bullying at a much larger scale. As a couple of psychiatrists pointed out many years ago, 'When racism is a prime factor in human interaction, barriers are constructed that foster alienation and loneliness.'[10]

The above analysis leads to the following hypothesis: frequent loneliness is more prevalent among those who have experienced discriminations against their race or ethnicity than among those who have no such experience. Unfortunately, to test this hypothesis empirically is a great challenge. The reason is well-known among researchers on race and ethnicity: the number of studies that were designed for collecting specific information about the respondents' race or ethnicity is very small in the first place, and those including information about race or ethnicity and loneliness are close to none. General social surveys such as the ESS are not of much help as they usually target the general population and therefore the number of respondents of minority races or ethnicities is so small that researchers would refrain from drawing any conclusions from them. No survey of the ESS included any question with the aim of soliciting the respondent's race. The only question related to race asks the respondent whether they belonged to any group that was discriminated against in that country, and if they did whether the discrimination was based on their race or skin colour. After examining the data I have decided not to present the results because nine of the twenty-one participating countries had fewer than ten people who responded to that question, and except for Israel all other countries had fewer than fifty respondents, which are simply too small a size to be reliable given the sample size for most countries is in the range of 1500 to 3000.

For ethnicity, there is a question asking the respondents whether they belong to any group of ethnic minority, with the binary options of yes or no. So let's examine the relationship between belonging to any minority ethnic group and frequent loneliness in each participating country of the seventh round of the ESS. Table 6.2 contains the results (with the application of design weight) for the countries whose sample size of ethnic minority respondents is above 50.

Compare the percentages of frequent loneliness between the minority ethnic group and the ethnic majority group in columns three and four, we can see that, except for Belgium and Estonia, the percentage of frequent loneliness among the ethnic minority group is always higher than that among ethnic majority group, which is consistent with what we have expected. But we should not draw any conclusion yet purely based on the difference between the two percentages. The odds ratio in the next column reflects the relative size of the two percentages (i.e. the ratio of column four to column three); for example, in Norway, the odds

Table 6.2 Membership of ethnic minority and frequent loneliness by country in Europe, 2014.

Country	n of ethnic minority	Frequently lonely			
		Percentage among ethnic minority	Percentage among ethnic majority	Odds ratio	95% CI
Norway	70	8.6	2.9	0.3	(0.1, 0.7)
Netherlands	156	7.7	2.2	0.3	(0.1, 0.5)
Germany	160	8.8	3.0	0.3	(0.2, 0.6)
Switzerland	122	7.4	3.2	0.4	(0.2, 0.9)
Sweden	73	8.2	4.6	0.5	(0.2, 1.3)
Hungary	91	18.7	10.8	0.5	(0.3, 0.9)
France	90	13.3	8.0	0.6	(0.3, 1.1)
Ireland	93	6.5	4.7	0.7	(0.3, 1.7)
UK	212	6.6	5.0	0.7	(0.4, 1.3)
Austria	103	7.8	5.9	0.7	(0.3, 1.6)
Lithuania	169	9.5	7.3	0.8	(0.4, 1.3)
Israel	398	7.3	7.0	0.9	(0.6, 1.4)
Denmark	58	3.4	3.0	0.9	(0.2, 3.7)
Belgium	88	5.7	6.4	1.1	(0.5, 2.9)
Estonia	498	6.6	8.2	1.3	(0.8, 1.9)

of feeling frequently lonely among the ethnic majority group is about 30% of the odds among the ethnic minority group. As such results could be due to sampling fluctuations, the last column shows the confidence interval at the 95% level. Therefore, the difference between the two groups in terms of frequent loneliness is statistically significant (the confidence interval does not include the value of 1) only for the following countries: Norway, The Netherlands, Germany, Switzerland, and Hungary. These results show that whether people of ethnic minority feel frequently lonely depends on the national context in which they live.

Unfortunately, we are short of information for explaining the national variation at the moment. For example, the 'ethnic density effect' theory suggests that 'the enhanced mutual social support and stronger sense of community and belongingness offered by living in close proximity to others with the same ethnic background can buffer, or protect against, the direct and indirect health consequences of experienced racist victimisation'.[11] If this theory is correct, we could hypothesize that ethnic groups that have high 'ethnic density' should be subjective to less risk of feeling lonely, but note that this is true with a strong condition, 'the enhanced mutual social support', which is hard to come by and difficult to maintain. In addition, any tradition of high 'ethnic density' would raise its members' expectation of social support, which is more difficult to be disappointed or even betrayed, which in turn would raise the likelihood of feeling lonely.

The shortage of large-scale, reliable and relevant data has prevented researchers on loneliness from being able to tackle two important issues. The first is the connection between frequent (or severe) loneliness with each specific ethnic group. Obviously, the distinction between ethnic minority and majority is very crude, glossing over the differences between minority ethnic groups. Differences between these groups in terms of cultural values, living arrangements, and expectations of social relations make it highly probable that some ethnic groups may be less subjective to loneliness than others, but we know little about such differences. Only a few small scale studies have managed to cover several ethnic groups and loneliness. In one such study, Christina Victor and her colleagues conducted a survey on 300 people aged 65 and above, which purposefully targeted 'the key minority groups in Britain', with a secondary analysis on an even smaller sample in Birmingham.[12] Frequent loneliness was found much less prevalent among older people originally from India (around 10%) than it was among those from China, Africa, the Caribbean, Pakistan and Bangladesh (at least 40%). In a longitudinal study conducted in the US, the researchers found that the Hispanics appeared to be very good at protecting themselves from becoming lonely, although the authors could only speculate that this is because the Hispanics have strong social networks.[13]

The other important and related issue is the entanglement of race or ethnicity with other risk factors, particularly immigration. In the above study by Victor and colleagues, all subjects of ethnic minority groups were immigrants as well. And for the Hispanics in the US, a small study found that loneliness was much more prevalent among young immigrants (11–15-year-olds) than among the US-born or Mexican Americans,[14] which is at odds with the finding of the above study, therefore suggesting that it was immigration rather than ethnicity that was responsible for loneliness. In contrast, two immigrant groups in the same hosting nation may have very different rates of loneliness, such as the Turkish and the Moroccan in The Netherlands,[15] indicating that ethnicity, very likely in connection with cultural backgrounds, plays a bigger role than the status of being an immigrant. All in all, these studies point to the complicated connections between race, ethnicity, immigration, via cultural values and practices, to the experience of loneliness. Research on these issues is highly significant because we could gain much deeper understanding of why some socio-demographic groups suffer so much more from loneliness than others.

Religion, religiousness, and loneliness

The relationship between religion and loneliness can be approached from two perspectives: the discursive or the empirical. The former considers and reflects on the experience of loneliness from a religious perspective. Religion has its own unique relevance to loneliness: to the seriously religious, loneliness carries a special meaning. In contrast, academics and particularly social scientists follow the empirical approach, who study the actual connection between religion and loneliness by examining empirical evidence. In this section I shall briefly discuss some religious understandings of loneliness before moving on to the empirical investigations.

The number of texts on loneliness by religious scholars – at least those available to me – is rather small, and I do not plan to do full justice to the field. My reading of the limited discourses suggests, however, that it is difficult to find a coherent and consistent message in such wrings. The first tension lies in the nature of loneliness: is it a spiritual or secular experience? Keith Clark, a Capuchin, claimed firstly that 'Loneliness and intimacy are spiritual experiences',[16] but soon he acknowledged that 'Loneliness and intimacy seem like unavoidable moments of life for normal people'.[17] Similarly, some religious scholars attribute loneliness to the first sin committed by Adam and Eve; since then, loneliness becomes an inherent aspect of humanity, dubbed as 'godforsakenness'.[18] Loneliness is a product of sin; or, 'sin always and necessarily makes for loneliness'.[19] However, such spiritual interpretation of loneliness is later mixed up with estrangements between humans: abandonment by either God, or other individual, or communities is a source of loneliness. Perhaps these could be reconciled by defining the loneliness from God being the most profound, but one cannot help noticing the struggle to characterize loneliness as a spiritual experience on the one hand and to describe the human feeling on the other.

Religious scholars seem to be ambivalent about loneliness's desirability as well. At the beginning, Keith Clark portrayed loneliness as something neutral: 'No alienation, no paranoia, no hostility, no self-doubt; just loneliness'; 'in and of itself, loneliness is simply one of life's moments';[20] even when he ate alone in a pancake house before Christmas while his father was sick far away. To him, loneliness was just one of the moments of life that naturally occurred, such as a young father coming home alone after a party of celebrating the birth of his baby, a women waking up after sex with her lover, etc. Later, he started to distinguish 'good' and 'bad' loneliness. Loneliness is particularly bad when it comes with other undesirable emotions, such as 'self-doubt, depression, sadness, a sense of alienation or hostility, fear and anxiety'. As some other religious scholars, he is not interested in what we may call 'the secular version of loneliness'; rather, they emphasize the benefit of 'the spiritual version of loneliness'. There are two spiritual benefits of loneliness: the privacy of praying and the reflection on one's humanity, particularly the desire of being with others, and the relationship with God, with the second being obviously more important. Essentially, spiritual loneliness is a process of realizing one's relationship with other human beings, the universe, and the God. Such awaking awareness is the benefit that only loneliness can bring to the human mind. It may be painful when loneliness is felt initially, but the subsequent realization is far more valuable. Loneliness is not only unpainful; it is 'one of God's best gifts for our lives'[21] or even '*is* God's presence'.[22] To the religiously devoted, it is no doubt worthwhile to bear with the secular version of loneliness in order to accomplish the spiritual one. Seen in this light, loneliness is not a problem, let alone an illness; it is actually an opportunity that we all should appreciate and embrace. This is why a religious scholar criticized the early loneliness scholars (Peplau, Perlman and Weiss) for their inability of going beyond the secular understanding of loneliness and seeing the spiritual gain.[23]

By now you may have already had a strong feeling for the need of making a sharp distinction between the two general types of loneliness. Enough religious understandings of loneliness. We now turn to the secular or academic understanding of loneliness and examine its relationship with religion and religiousness.

Religion and ethnicity are closely related, although there is no one-to-one correspondence between the two. As shown above, the connection between belonging to ethnic minority or majority groups and frequent loneliness varies across national contexts. The picture is already considerably complicated even before we could look at specific ethnic groups and their relations with immigration status. Similarly, the relationship between religion and loneliness is expected to be no less complicated as several issues are involved, including the prevalence of frequent loneliness across major religions in a particular country, whether a particular religion is the majority or a minority, and how religious members of a particular religion are.

Some researchers have derived from Sigmund Freud's writing that he attributed religious belief as a way of buffering the pain from social isolation.[24] Here is their reasoning: first, Freud claimed that religion 'is born from man's need to make his helplessness tolerable';[25] second, the suffering from social relations, particularly the loss of the loved ones, 'is perhaps the more painful to us than any other'.[26] It should be sensible to count loneliness as a form of suffering from the loss of social relations. Then, 'the Freudian theory of loneliness and religion' is that people join a religion *after they feel lonely*. It will be difficult to test such theory empirically, however, because the mechanisms are not certain. One possible situation we should observe is that those not belonging to any religion are much less lonely than the members of a religion; this assumes that being lonely is the sole reason for joining a religion, which, obviously, is not the case.[27] Therefore, we cannot test the theory by comparing the two groups in terms of loneliness. We may still try to find out which group is lonelier, but we will not be able to determine the cause behind the observed difference, although some have argued that humanizing the divine entity could be the mechanism.[28] Another possible situation is that religion members have become less lonely after joining the religion for some time if their religion, as expected, has relieved them from loneliness. However, they may not have become less lonely than the non-believers if the latter are not lonely in the first place. In short, the most convincing way of testing the effect of believing in a religion on loneliness is to analyse a longitudinal dataset with relevant variables. Unfortunately, I do not have access to such dataset at the moment. The statistics presented below can only describe the associations and serve as a springboard for suggesting potential explanations.

In the seventh round of the European Social Survey, respondents were first asked 'Do you consider yourself as belonging to any particular religion or denomination?', with the binary options 'yes' or 'no'. In Table 6.3 I present, for each participating country, the percentage of the frequently lonely (with design weight) among those belonging to a religion and those not belonging, respectively, and the corresponding odds ratio measuring the strength of the relationship.

Statistics presented above depict a highly diverse relationship between belonging to a religion and feeling frequently lonely. First of all, for the majority (fifteen)

Table 6.3 Association between frequent loneliness and belonging to religion in Europe, 2014.

Country	Percentage frequently lonely			Valid n
	Belong to a religion	Do not belong to a religion	Odds ratio with 95% CI	
Austria	5.9	6.2	1.05 (0.68, 1.61)	1783
Belgium	7.3	5.8	0.77 (0.53, 1.13)	1765
Switzerland	2.8	5.1	1.86 (1.08, 3.19)	1523
Czech Republic	13.3	10.1	0.74 (0.52, 1.05)	2126
Germany	3.4	3.2	0.94 (0.63, 1.42)	3030
Denmark	2.3	4.1	1.85 (1.02, 3.36)	1493
Estonia	8.9	7.3	0.81 (0.58, 1.12)	2026
Spain	9.7	6.8	0.68 (0.47, 0.97)	1922
Finland	3.7	2.3	0.62 (0.37, 1.04)	2078
France	9.0	7.8	0.86 (0.62, 1.19)	1910
UK	4.6	5.6	1.23 (0.84, 1.79)	2249
Hungary	12.9	9.4	0.70 (0.52, 0.96)	1617
Ireland	4.8	4.6	0.95 (0.61, 1.49)	2350
Israel	7.1	0.0	NA	2488
Lithuania	7.3	8.2	1.12 (0.74, 1.72)	2185
Netherlands	3.6	2.2	0.60 (0.34, 1.04)	1918
Norway	3.4	2.8	0.82 (0.45, 1.49)	1433
Poland	11.6	15.0	1.35 (0.83, 2.18)	1592
Portugal	12.4	5.0	0.37 (0.21, 0.65)	1260
Sweden	5.4	4.7	0.87 (0.55, 1.38)	1783
Slovenia	7.5	5.3	0.69 (0.43, 1.11)	1208

of the (twenty-one) participating countries of the ESS, the relationship between believing in a religion and frequent loneliness, here measured by the odds ratio, is statistically not significant; that is, we do not have sufficient evidence for such relationship. This is the big picture. The relationship is significant only for the following five countries: Switzerland, Denmark, Spain, Hungary, and Portugal. Furthermore, even for these five countries, whether belonging to a religion makes people more or less likely to feel frequently lonely depends on the country they live in: those belonging to a religion were less likely to be frequently lonely in Switzerland and Denmark, but the opposite is true for Spain, Hungary and Portugal. It is beyond this study to offer a well-researched explanation for such diversity. One cannot help but noticing, however, that the majority of the population in the latter three countries are followers of Catholic, while those in Switzerland and Denmark follow other sects of Christianity (Reformed and Evangelical Lutheran, respectively). Whether this is the reason behind their differentials of frequent loneliness remains an open-ended question.

This observation leads to the conjecture that it may not be belief in *any* religion but the *particular* religion that matters to loneliness. Fortunately, the ESS contains some information to allow us to explore such connection. For those who answered 'Yes' to the above question, they were then asked to report the specific religion that they belonged to; here are the eight categories of religion: Roman Catholic (RC), Protestant (P), Eastern Orthodox (EO), Other Christian denomination (OC), Jewish (J), Islamic (I), Eastern religions (E), and Other non-Christian religions (ONC). I was planning to present the percentage of respondents who were frequently lonely for each particular religion in each country; however, I encountered a practical issue: for some religions, the number of respondents in a particular country could be very small, making the percentage of frequent loneliness very unstable. For example, there were only three non-Christian respondents in Belgium, and with one of them frequently lonely, the percentage is 33.3%, which is deceptively high. To avoid such potentially misleading results, I have

Table 6.4 Prevalence of frequent loneliness for each religion by country in Europe, 2014.

Country	RC	P	EO	OC	I
Austria	6.1	3.3	3.0	–	1.3
Belgium	7.5	–	–	–	7.8
Switzerland	2.1	3.1	–	–	5.0
Czech Republic	12.1	–	–	–	–
Germany	2.5	4.1	–	0.0	3.2
Denmark	4.8	2.0	–	–	6.5
Estonia	–	9.4	7.5	–	–
Spain	9.4	–	–	13.3	18.9
Finland	–	3.8	–	–	–
France	8.4	6.3	–	–	15.9
UK	5.4	4.1	–	5.3	7.9
Hungary	12.4	15.5	–	–	–
Ireland	4.9	4.7	–	–	–
Israel	–	–	–	–	7.9
Lithuania	6.8	–	10.7	–	–
Netherlands	2.8	3.3	–	0.0	10.0
Norway	–	2.5	–	–	–
Poland	11.4	–	–	–	–
Portugal	11.9	–	–	28.1	–
Sweden	–	4.2	–	–	15.0
Slovenia	7.5	–	–	–	–

included the percentage of frequent loneliness only if the total number of respondents of that religion in a country was 30 or more (Table 6.4). It turns out that in none of these countries, the number of 'Other non-Christian religions' was above 30, so this category is not included. Similarly, only in Israel the 'Jewish' religion and only in the UK 'Eastern religions' had more than 30 respondents; for the former, 7.0% were frequently lonely and for the latter, 4.4% were frequently lonely.

This table clearly demonstrates why it would not be wise to present the prevalence of frequent loneliness only by religion without considering the national context: for followers of the same religion, the prevalence of frequent loneliness varies considerably from country to country; for example, less than 3% of Roman Catholics felt frequent lonely in Sweden, Germany, and The Netherlands, in remarkable contrast to the corresponding rates in Czech Republic, Hungary, Poland, and Portugal, which are higher than 10%. The contrast applies to Islamism as well: in Austria, only 1.3% of Islamic believers were frequently lonely, but in Spain, France, The Netherlands, and Sweden, the rates are above 10%. The country of residence appears to exercise more influence than religion on frequent loneliness.

Finally, let's move one step further by examining, in addition to belief in religion and specific religion, whether religiousness (how religious people are) increases or reduces the chance of feeling frequently lonely. As discussed above, it is rather difficult for us to detect a clear direction for this relationship, and the national context may make it even more complicated. In the seventh round of the ESS, religiousness was measured with the following three questions:

- 'Regardless of whether you belong to a particular religion, how religious would you say you are?' Respondents were asked to choose a number on an 11-point scale, with 0 being 'not at all religious' and 10 'very religious'.
- 'Apart from special occasions such as weddings and funerals, about how often do you attend religious services nowadays?', with seven options: 1 = 'every day', 2 = 'more than once a week', 3 = 'once a week', 4 = 'at least once a month', 5 = 'only on special holidays', 6 = 'less often', and 7 = 'never'. The coding has been reversed so as to make the value of the number and the frequency consistent.
- 'Apart from when you are at religious services, how often, if at all, do you pray?' The options are the same as the previous and the coding has been reversed as well.

As the three questions were designed to measure the same concept (religiousness), a reliability test was conducted to confirm whether it is appropriate to combine them into a single scale. The Cronbach's alpha is 0.812, lending support to the creation of the scale, whose values range from 2 to 24. Taking this new scale as the predictor and the binary frequent loneliness as the response variable, I present the results of a binary logistic regression model for each country Table 6.5.

For eight countries (Belgium, Czech Republic, Spain, France, Hungary, Lithuania, Norway, and Portugal), religiousness shows statistically significant effect on the probability of feeling frequently lonely: with one point increase of religiousness,

Table 6.5 Religiousness and frequent loneliness by country in Europe, 2014.

Country	Religiousness coefficient	95% CI of exponential	p-value
Austria	0.008	(0.975, 1.043)	0.626
Belgium	0.036	(1.006, 1.070)	0.021
Switzerland	−0.002	(0.953, 1.046)	0.945
Czech Republic	0.036	(1.011, 1.062)	0.004
Germany	0.023	(0.989, 1.058)	0.186
Denmark	−0.002	(0.940, 1.059)	0.940
Estonia	0.020	(0.990, 1.051)	0.190
Spain	0.038	(1.013, 1.065)	0.003
Finland	0.015	(0.970, 1.063)	0.509
France	0.029	(1.003, 1.056)	0.028
UK	0.011	(0.982, 1.042)	0.459
Hungary	0.045	(1.019, 1.074)	0.001
Ireland	−0.004	(0.965, 1.028)	0.799
Israel	0.001	(0.980, 1.023)	0.937
Lithuania	0.075	(1.045, 1.112)	<0.001
Netherlands	0.029	(0.986, 1.074)	0.187
Norway	0.076	(1.027, 1.134)	0.003
Poland	0.018	(0.988, 1.050)	0.244
Portugal	0.066	(1.034, 1.104)	<0.001
Sweden	0.041	(1.001, 1.084)	0.046
Slovenia	0.039	(0.999, 1.081)	0.054

the odds of frequent loneliness will increase multiplicatively by a small amount; or in more accessible but technically less accurate words, the more religious, the higher the risk to frequent loneliness. For Sweden and Slovenia, the effect is on the borderline of statistical significance if we follow the usual practice of taking 0.05 as the significance level. For the remaining eleven countries, the effect of religiousness is clearly not statistically significant. At the moment, I cannot come up with a sensible conjecture, let alone a convincing explanation, for such national differences in terms of the effect of religiousness on frequent loneliness. What all these results could tell us with certainty is that the relationship between religion and loneliness is complicated and varies considerably across different national contexts in Europe.

Who are lonelier: urban or rural residents?

Following immigration, race and ethnicity, the rural and urban divide is another line along which social groups are classified, and such classification is relevant to our concern with loneliness. These factors are closely associated with each other – many residents of cities, particularly big and metropolitan areas, are migrants or children of migrants from rural areas, and usually they are ethnically more diverse than those still living in rural areas. Migration from rural to urban areas could be a source of loneliness; similar to international migration, migration within the same country also means putting existing social relations in jeopardy – it is difficult to keep social relations close when the people involved in these social relations are geographically separated apart with long distance. What we need to keep in mind is that those staying in rural areas may not be less lonely than those moving to cities. China's rapid process of urbanization after decades of imposed separation of rural and urban areas comes as a powerful case. Researchers have only started to pay attention to the mental wellbeing of migrant workers and the loneliness that their parents and children have suffered.[29] This section is not about the specific loneliness among migrant workers as a result of China's urbanization; rather, my interest here is in two more general and interrelated questions: (1) Who are lonelier, urban or rural residents? (2) If there is any significant difference, how could we explain it? These questions are important because they will help us not only identify a potentially special social group who suffers from loneliness but more importantly point to different social environments that may be responsible for loneliness.

Yet again, although urbanization is a huge area in sociology and human geography, few academics have conducted serious research on how urbanization or city life has made people lonely. As far back as 1903, the German sociologist Georg Simmel wrote on the effect of the metropolis on mental wellbeing.[30] In this seminal albeit rather abstract piece, Simmel made some observations on the contrasting effects of the metropolitan versus rural life on their respective residents' mental states. It is worth quoting his words as they are strikingly relevant to our interest here:

> so today metropolitan man is 'free' in a spiritualized and refined sense, in contrast to the pettiness and prejudices which hem in the small-town man. For the reciprocal reserve and indifference and the intellectual life conditions of large circles are never felt more strongly by the individual in their impact upon his independence than in the thickest crowd of the big city. This is because the bodily proximity and narrowness of space makes the mental distance only the more visible. It is obviously only the obverse of this freedom if, under certain circumstances, one nowhere feels as lonely and lost as in the metropolitan crowd. For here as elsewhere it is by no means necessary that the freedom of man be reflected in his emotional life as comfort.[31]

The philosophical flavour of Simmel's observations should not be surprising as sociology at that time was barely out of the womb of philosophy, and he noted at the end of this article that his arguments were more fully represented in his monography *The Philosophy of Money*. This means that Simmel was not much interested in making an empirical statement that urban residents are lonelier than those in small towns or rural areas, but he did imply that this could be the case when social relations in large cities became so impersonal due to increased 'mental distances'. In the earlier parts of the article, he explained why urban life had become so impersonal: the dominance of money in people's mind and all of the mental and behavioural consequences of such dominance. Trapped in the density and richness of urban life and the pursuit of money, people become myopic of what is happening to their psyche. This special kind of loneliness experienced by residents of metropolitan cities is vividly and acutely described from the perspective of an immigrant:

> [London is] powerfully lonely when you on your own.[32]

> It have people living in London who don't know what happening in the room next to them, far more the street, or how other people living. London is a place like that. It divide up in little worlds, and you stay in the world you belong to and you don't know anything about what happening in the other ones except what you read in the papers.[33]

> People in this world don't know how other people does affect their lives.[34]

Today, sociology has become a highly empirical discipline, but no sociologist has tried to test the above statement with any data.[35] This seems particularly important as John Cacioppo, the influential researcher on loneliness mentioned many times previously, would not accept this hypothesis while acknowledging the absence of data for testing it.[36] Similarly, after telling many sad stories of loneliness among some artists in the City of New York, Olivia Liang, the author of *The Lonely City*, is ambivalent about whether residents of cities like New York are necessarily lonelier than those in small cities and rural areas, suggesting that loneliness in the metropolis has a unique tang, which however could be transient. Luckily, the data collected from the ESS would allow me to examine the hypothesis with more systematic and rigorous evidence.

Rounds 5, 6, and 7 of the ESS contain the question on loneliness and ask the respondent to describe the area where they live with one of the following categories: 'a big city', 'the suburbs or outskirts of a big city', 'a town or a small city', 'a country village', or 'a farm or home in the countryside'. The last two categories have been combined to represent 'countryside' or 'rural areas'. As the sample of each participating country was drawn independently, I shall present the results by country, which will also demonstrate the potential effect of national context. Initially I produced the results with the data collected in Round 7 (2014). If a country participated in Round 6 but not 7, the data from Round 6 (2012) was used. Croatia and Greece participated in only Round 5 but not 6 or 7, so results for these two countries came from the data collected in Round 5 (2010). All results were produced with design weight (Table 6.6).

As our interest here is especially in the effect of living in big cities on loneliness, the countries in the table are rank ordered by those in the third column (i.e. the percentage of frequent loneliness in big cities in each country). To measure the association between types of living area and frequent loneliness, I have

Table 6.6 Living area and loneliness by country in Europe.

Country	Valid n	Percentage frequently lonely				Kendall's tau-b
		Big city	Suburb	Small city	Countryside	
Norway	1433	2.3	3.6	3.0	3.4	0.011
Denmark	1496	2.8	3.0	3.7	2.6	−0.002
Finland	2082	3.1	3.9	2.4	3.0	−0.006
Netherlands	1918	4.0	3.2	3.2	1.9	−0.047*
Germany	3037	4.1	3.3	3.6	2.7	−0.023
Iceland	745	5.3	3.4	2.6	2.8	−0.039
Sweden	1788	5.7	5.0	5.0	4.3	−0.016
Slovenia	1217	5.8	9.9	4.2	7.3	0.022
Austria	1787	5.9	5.2	6.7	5.9	0.004
Switzerland	1530	6.1	6.0	3.1	3.0	−0.045
Lithuania	2213	6.5	8.8	8.4	7.9	0.025
Ireland	2374	6.7	4.1	4.9	4.8	0.000
Slovakia	1834	6.8	5.8	8.1	8.5	0.03
Estonia	2037	7.1	5.7	9.0	7.9	0.024
Israel	2490	7.3	6.5	6.7	7.7	0.000
Cyprus	1113	7.8	12.8	6.6	9.0	0.001
Greece	2701	8.5	10.4	10.2	10.7	0.029
UK	2250	8.9	5.6	4.6	4.4	−0.04
Croatia	1597	9.1	9.4	7.1	6.5	−0.039
Belgium	1768	9.1	6.9	7.2	5.2	−0.05*
Hungary	1695	9.7	14.0	10.1	13.3	0.041
Albania	1181	10.0	14.3	11.0	11.2	0.011
Czech Republic	2073	10.1	15.0	10.4	10.8	0.003
Spain	1924	10.2	7.6	7.0	9.3	0.004
Italy	945	11.0	9.6	10.0	9.9	−0.007
France	1915	11.0	7.6	10.4	5.9	−0.062**
Russia	2427	11.1	27.2	15.7	16.6	0.053**
Poland	1589	12.7	7.1	9.0	14.0	0.039
Ukraine	2112	22.3	14.3	18.9	20.9	−0.01

Note: *: $p < 0.05$, **: $p < 0.01$.

produced the Kendall's tau-b statistics and presented them in the last column. Type of living area is treated as an ordinal variable in the sense of how urban or rural a place is. It is clear that the relationship between the two variables is very weak – none of the absolute values of the tau-b statistics is bigger than 0.02. Moreover, it is only for four countries (The Netherlands, Belgium, France, and

Russia) that the tau-b is statistically significant, meaning that the likelihood that its value is not zero is lower than the threshold set before the test (5%). Overall, the type of living area in terms of how urban or rural it is does not seem to make much difference to the prevalence of frequent loneliness. The reader could see this by reading the numbers through each row, which tend to be much more similar than those across the countries (columns). In other words, which country the respondents live appears to be much more important than whether they live in a city or countryside in terms of becoming frequently lonely. Although the prevalence of frequent loneliness is relatively higher in big cities than in other areas for each country, the differences are mild and could be down to sampling variations. In the end, all we can say about this relationship is that in most countries of Europe, whether people live in big cities or other types of areas makes little difference to the prevalence of frequent loneliness in that area; four countries seem to be exceptional, and even in these countries, the effect is very weak. Researchers should look for the sources of loneliness at the national level rather than in the area of residence.

Notes

1 For example, there is sporadic evidence showing that sexuality appears to be an important factor for loneliness; that is, the homosexuals and those of other non-heterosexual orientations tend to suffer from severe loneliness as until recently these people were not accepted by those around them nor by the society at large. In *The Lonely City*, Olivia Liang described such experiences of some artists in the city of New York. Unfortunately, the lack of systematic data and expertise does not allow me to do justice to this important topic in this chapter.
2 C. Tóibín. 2009. *Brooklyn*. London: Penguin Books, p. 67.
3 Sam Selvon. 2006. *The Lonely Londoners*. London: Penguin Books, p. 23.
4 Ibid., pp. 76–77.
5 E.Bauer and P. Thompson. 2006. *Jamaican Hands Across the Atlantic*. Kingston: Ian Randle; K. Gardner. 2002. *Age, Narrative and Migration*. Oxford: Berg; J. Nazroo, M. Bajekal, D. Blane, I. Grewal, and J. Lewis. 2003. *Ethnic Inequalities in Quality of Life at Older Ages: Subjective and Objective Components. Research Findings: 11 from the Growing Older Programme*. Available online at www.growingolder.group.shef.ac.uk/ Nazroo_Findings_11.pdf (accessed 15 May 2016); C. Phillipson, N. Ahmed, and J. Latimer. 2003. *Women in Transition: First Generation Migrant Women from Bangladesh*. Bristol: Policy Press, pp. 95–112.
6 A recent study that compared the local residents and immigrants from former Soviet Russia in Israel has found that over the period 2009–2013, while the Russian immigrants were significantly lonelier than the Israelites at the beginning, the discrepancy disappeared four years later, very likely due to psychological adjustments over time. See P. Dolberg, S. Shiovitz-Ezra and L. Ayalon. 2016. 'Migration and changes in loneliness over a 4-year period: the case of older former Soviet Union immigrants in Israel', *European Journal of Ageing*, 13(4): 287–297.
7 Interested readers could consult the brief introduction to this issue created by the Migration Observatory at University of Oxford: www.migrationobservatory.ox.ac.uk/ resources/briefings/who-counts-as-a-migrant-definitions-and-their-consequences/#kp1 (accessed 5 May 2018).

8 See A. Portes and M. Zhou. 1993. 'The new second generation: segmented assimilation and its variants', *Annals of the American Academy of Political and Social Sciences*, 530(1): 74–96; A. Portes and R. G. Rumbaut. 2001. *Legacies: The Story of the Immigrant Second Generation*. Berkeley, CA: University of California Press.

9 For each of the nine countries, the Cronbach's alpha is above 0.8.

10 E. F. Dunn and P. C. Dunn. 1980. 'Loneliness and the black experience', in J. Hartog, J. R. Audy, and Y. A. Cohen (eds), *The Anatomy of Loneliness*. New York: International University Press, pp. 284–304.

11 S. Karlsen, L. Becares, and M. Roth. 2012. 'Understanding the influence of ethnicity on health', in G. Craig, K. Atkin, S. Chattoo, and R. Flynn (eds), *Understanding 'Race' and Ethnicity: Theory, History, Policy, Practice*. Bristol: Policy Press, pp. 115–132.

12 C. R. Victor, V. Burholt, and W. Martin. 2012. 'Loneliness and ethnic minority elders in Great Britain: an exploratory study', *Journal of Cross Cultural Gerontology*, 27(1): 65–78.

13 K. G. Emerson and J. Jayawardhana. 2016. 'Risk factors for loneliness in elderly adults', *Journal of the American Geriatrics Society*, 64(4): 886–887.

14 A. J. Polo and S. R. Lopez. 2009. 'Culture, context, and the internalizing distress of Mexican American youth', *Journal of Clinical Child and Adolescent Psychology*, 38(2): 273–285.

15 D. D. van Bergen, J. H. Smit, A. J. L. M. van Balkom, E. van Ameijden, and S. Saharso. 2008. 'Suicidal ideation in ethnic minority and majority adolescents in Utrecht, The Netherlands', *Crisis: The Journal of Crisis Intervention and Suicide Prevention*, 29(4): 202–208.

16 K. Clark. 1982. *An Experience of Celibacy: A Creative Reflection on Intimacy, Loneliness, Sexuality and Commitment*. Notre Dame, IN: Ave Maria Press, p. 19.

17 Ibid., p. 20.

18 P.C. Zylla. 2012. *The Roots of Sorrow: A Pastoral Theology of Suffering*. Waco, TX: Baylor University Press, p. 11.

19 Piet Schoonenberg, SJ. 1965. *Man and Sin: A Theological View*, trans. J. Donceel. Melbourne: Sheed and Ward, p. 91.

20 Clark, *An Experience of Celibacy*, pp. 26, 27.

21 P. Ripple, FSPA. 1982. *Walking with Loneliness*. Notre Dame, IN: Ave Maria Press, p. 25.

22 Ibid., p. 18, emphasis original.

23 Ibid., pp. 13–14.

24 Burris, Batson, Altstaedten and Stephens (1994).

25 S. Freud. 1927. *The Future of an Illusion*, trans. W. D. Robson-Scott. New York: Doubleday.

26 S. Freud. 1930. *Civilization and its Discontents*, trans. J. Strachey. New York: W. W. Norton.

27 A small number of studies have tried to examine the relationship empirically and found that turning to God was a consequence of being rejected socially or feeling lonely. See, for example, J. E. Gebauer and G. R. Maio. 2012. 'The need to belong can motivate belief in God', *Journal of Personality*, 80(2): 465–501; N. Aydin, P. Fischer, and D. Frey. 2010. 'Turning to God in the face of ostracism: effects of social exclusion on religiousness', *Personality and Social Psychology Bulletin*, 36(6): 742–753.

28 See, for example, N. Epley, S. Akalis, A. Waytz, and J. T. Cacioppo. 2008. 'Creating social connection through inferential reproduction', *Psychological Science*, 19(2): 114–120.

29 N. Argent, M. Tonts, A. Stockdale, Y. He, and J. Ye. 2014. 'Lonely sunsets: impacts of rural-urban migration on the left-behind elderly in rural China', *Population, Space and Place*, 20(4): 352–370.

30 G. Simmel. [1903] 1950. 'The metropolis and mental life', in his *The Sociology of Georg Simmel*, trans., ed., and introduced by K. H. Wolff. New York: The Free Press, pp. 409–424.

31 Ibid., p. 418.

32 Selvon, *The Lonely Londoners*, p. 29.

33 Ibid., p. 60.

34 Ibid., p. 62.

35 An exception is a study by Barry Wellman of the network of primary ties among some 800 respondents in Toronto, in which he 'found little to substantiate the "myth of the lonely urbanites"'. B. Wellman. 1973. 'The Network Nature of Future Communities: a Predictive Synthesis', presented at 23rd Annual Meeting of the Society for the Study of Social Problems, New York.

36 See C. M. Gillies. 2016. 'What's the world's loneliest city?', *The Guardian*, 7 April, available online at www.theguardian.com/cities/2016/apr/07/loneliest-city-in-world (accessed 11 May 2018).

Chapter 7

Loneliness and class

This chapter is a sequel of the previous one; clearly, we can classify social groups by class in addition to all other dimensions discussed in the previous chapter. I present this as a separate chapter firstly because the previous chapter would have been too long had this chapter remained part of it, and secondly because as an important concept in social science research, class deserves a concentrated treatment. Here, I use 'class', 'social class', and 'socio-economic status' (SES) interchangeably, and the reader can find an explanation for its specific meaning and measurement in the following statistical analyses.

Social class and loneliness

There is no need to review the large literature or present many details about the general relationship between class and health – with many years of research, social scientists have well established it as common sense by now that the level of health and the position of social class are persistently associated with each other in a positive manner: the higher one's social class, the better one's health, either physically or mentally.[1] Summarizing the findings of academic research on the class and mental disorder relationship, William Cockerham observed:

> The pattern is clear: Although there are some differences between the classes, in general there is more mental disorder among the lower class and more schizophrenia in general; anxiety and depression are more common among the middle and upper classes, but the lower class does not entirely escape these problems – especially if they live in poverty and have lives that are anxious or depressing . . .[2]

Taking loneliness as a special problem of mental health, we may expect to observe a relationship between loneliness and social class similar to the one described by Cockerham above. To facilitate the subsequent exploration on the relationship between class and loneliness, it is necessary to have some brief discussion about the concept of class.

Essentially, a social class refers to a group of people in a society based on how much a certain kind of resources is at their disposal relative to other groups. As there are multiple kinds of resources, there are several ways of grouping people into different social classes. Since the establishment of sociology as an academic discipline at the end of the nineteenth century, sociologists have kept expanding the meaning of social class while focusing on different resources. For Karl Marx, the most important resource was the means of production; therefore, he derived a polarized social structure in which the capitalists, who possessed the means of production, were the upper class, while the proletariats, who possessed nothing but their own labour, were the lower class; the middle class, according to Marx, was not of much historical significance. Max Weber thought such classification was too restricted and thus included status in social hierarchy and political power in addition to wealth as the resources; clearly, the three kinds of resources must not have direct correspondence – possession of one resource such as economic assets does not necessarily lead to the possession of social status or political power; otherwise, it would be unnecessary to treat the three as distinctive types of resources. In the 1960s, economists started to pay serious attention to 'human capital', which became a key resource and criterion of social class.[3] In the mid-1980s, the French sociologist Pierre Bourdieu, the American sociologist James Coleman and others started to treat 'social capital' as a new kind of resource, which has been highly influential but caused some confusion and controversy at the same time.[4] More recently, again inspired by Bourdieu's work, some sociologists have argued for 'cultural capital' as a new kind of resource as well. The meaning, the definition, and the measurement of social class thus keep changing according to the nature of resources under study, which in turn determines which class a member of a society belongs to.

In my view, it is not necessarily a merit for any particular study to cover all these types of capitals or resources at the same time or to create a single scheme of class by integrating a variety of indicators. Many prominent sociologists have invested an enormous amount of effort in developing a single class scheme so that every member of the particular society could be classified as a member of a particular class in that hierarchy.[5] For example, as I produce most of the statistics in this book by analysing the data collected from the European Social Survey, I should mention 'the ESeC', 'a common socio-economic classification for all EU Member States based on the concept of employment relations',[6] developed by David Rose and his associates. And 'employment relations' in this scheme are consisted of three elements that could be directly measured with the ESS data: employment status (employed, self-employed, and unemployed, with the unemployed being at the bottom of the hierarchy), establishment size (in terms of number of people), and supervisory status (the number of people under the respondent's supervision).[7] Restricted only to employment attributes, this scheme does not include most of the other indicators of class, such as income, wealth, education, and social status that are widely used in other schemes of class. However, if we include different indicators of class that are not expected to correspond to each other in a fixed matter unless for the very top or bottom groups, which is why they are included in the first place, wouldn't it be clearer and more informative to examine the effect of each indicator separately? The most important principle we need to follow is to be clear about what we are referring to.

In this chapter, I shall examine economic resources, represented as employment (or the lack of it), household income, and people's feeling about it, education as an indicator of human capital, and social capital (to be defined later), as the indicators of social class. I look at income because, as observed above by Cockerham, being in lower class (or poverty) is tightly connected to mental disorders, and education is expected to be strongly associated with income. Similarly, the possession of a large amount of social capital is expected to be the antidote of loneliness. Note that these indicators have been believed to be tightly connected, although it would be naïve to directly translate the value of one indicator into another's; for example, Iain Duncan Smith, the UK's former secretary of state for work and pensions, believed that poor social networks were both a contributor and a sign of poverty, as it damaged people's prospects of employment and health.[8]

How should we explain such connections? The connection between low SES and loneliness is not obvious, not even intuitively sensible; that is, it requires the identification of further mechanisms that make sense of the connection. Some researchers attribute the increased risk of loneliness with low socioeconomic resources to fewer opportunities of social participation and a smaller and less supportive social network,[9] or conversely, those of higher SES are financially more capable to establish and maintain a larger network of friendship and support.[10] Such explanation assumes that the costs of participating social activities and maintaining supportive social networks are so high that they prevent those in the lower class from possessing the social capital that is essential for staying from loneliness. In this sense, *social capital becomes an intermediary factor in between economic capital and loneliness*. As some researchers have argued,

> Socioeconomic status may be considered an 'upstream' or distal factor affecting the more proximate or predisposing conditions for social contact and loneliness. For example, socioeconomic status may relate to self-esteem and social skills, making people more confident and uninhibited in social interactions and more attractive to others. Greater educational attainment also enables persons to demonstrate greater competence and mastery over their lives, which in turn allows individuals to shape behaviour in a way that increases social integration, promotes healthy psychological states, and reduces risk of loneliness in old age . . .[11]

While this may sound logical in relative terms – that is, in comparing the rich and the poor, many important questions remain unanswered: *how rich* do people have to be in order to stay away from loneliness? Couldn't people of the lower class be social among themselves and provide psychological and social, if not financial, support to each other? Does it truly require a large amount of economic capital to stay out of loneliness? It would sound more sensible to expect the effect of income or education on loneliness to level off once it reaches a certain point. Another explanation for the expected higher prevalence of loneliness among the lower classes is that a painful sense of being excluded from a better life that their coun-terparts of the relatively higher classes are enjoying. Relative deprivation and stark inequalities between social classes have long been demonstrated to cause financial as well as mental stresses.[12] Regardless of the kind of resources used for classifying people into different classes – be it means of production, accumulated wealth, power, reputation, cultural taste, or social capital, the perception of such social divides by the relatively disadvantaged will almost certainly induce what we may call 'collective loneliness', *a sense of loneliness collectively experienced by a large social group of people.* Karl Marx's well-known notion of 'class con-sciousness' refers only to a sense of belonging to a class whose members are aware of their shared position and fate in society. It is highly likely, however, that at least some members of a lower social class share a sense of self-pity, a sense of loneliness as unfulfilled longing to join a 'better' social group, or even the hope-lessness of achieving that. Those members of the same lower class with a stronger sense of pride and dignity may be determined to overturn the social structure, an enormous challenge that will take a very long time; until then, the existing social class structure remains a fundamental source of a special version of loneliness.

We may not be able to answer these questions or verify these theories in the rest of this chapter, but they would be the ultimate puzzles that guide the subsequent analyses and integrate the statistics into a logical narrative. Given the existing def-initions and measurements of class, let's examine the relationship between each of the following components of class and loneliness by analysing the data collected from the seventh round of the ESS.

Employment and frequent loneliness

To analyse the relationship between class and loneliness, I start with the attributes of employment, including unemployment, size of establishment and supervisory role, which are used as the elements of the ESeC class scheme mentioned above. Frequent loneliness is expected to be significantly higher among the unemployed because of both the loss of the financial gain from employment but also the loss of the social connections brought with employment. Conversely, employment is important for reducing one's vulnerability to loneliness firstly because establishing or maintaining social relations requires financial resources. Employment provides an opportunity not merely to earn an income but also to interact with people, to make friends or at least people you can talk to; employment offers a social life, and unemployment means a deprivation of social relations. As an employed man confessed, 'I've only seen her [his daughter] twice this year, because I can't afford it, it costs a fortune.'[13]

The ESS contains several measures of unemployment, each referring to a dif-ferent time frame. The first two ask the respondent whether they were unem-ployed during the past seven days, differentiating further whether the respondent was actively looking for jobs or not. In two ways these two questions are very informative. First, referring to the same time period (past week) as the question on loneliness, the two questions allow us to learn about whether the respondent felt lonely frequently while they were unemployed. Second, whether the respondent was actively searching for jobs or not *per se* could be interpreted as a state of mind, which could in turn relate to the sense of loneliness. More specifically, actively searching for jobs indicates hope, resilience, and interactions with others; therefore, frequent loneliness is expected to be much less prevalent among this group of unemployed people than among the group who were not actively searching for jobs. There is a practical difficulty in making use of the activeness of searching for jobs, however; that is, the number of respondents in this category may be very small – in some countries, fewer than five respondents reported to be frequently lonely and actively searching for jobs. As a result, this distinction has to be ignored; that is, the two groups of unemployed respondents have been merged into one, making their number in most countries above one hundred. Overall, we would expect the unemployed to be subject to a higher risk of frequent loneliness than the employed, although again this may vary from one country to another. Such variation is measured and presented in Table 7.1.

Table 7.1 Unemployment and frequent loneliness during past week in Europe, 2014.

Country	Percentage frequently lonely		
	Unemployed: past 7 days	Paid work: past 7 days	Ratio
Czech Republic	9.7	9.9	1.0
Israel	6.5	5.7	1.1
Sweden	5.6	3.6	1.6
Ireland	5.8	3.4	1.7
Poland	13.9	8.4	1.7
UK	8.0	3.9	2.1
Austria	9.6	4.4	2.2
Spain	13.2	5.8	2.3
Netherlands	3.1	1.2	2.6
Finland	3.4	1.3	2.6
Hungary	17.3	6.3	2.7
Slovenia	5.9	2.1	2.8
Switzerland	8.9	2.8	3.2
Estonia	15.5	4.8	3.2
France	17.9	5.4	3.3
Belgium	13.2	3.9	3.4
Lithuania	18.5	5.0	3.7
Portugal	20.4	5.5	3.7
Germany	9.5	2.5	3.8
Denmark	8.0	1.8	4.4
Norway	11.4	2.2	5.2

As our concern here is with the effect of unemployment on frequent loneliness, I have ranked the countries in Table 7.1 according to the values in the last column for each country, which is the ratio of column 2 to column 3. The numbers in column 2 are the country-specific percentages of frequent loneliness among the unemployed, and those in column 3 the percentages among those who did paid work (a separate question in the ESS), all referring to the past seven days at the time of the survey. Czech Republic comes at the top as the difference between the unemployed and the employed in paid work with regard to frequent loneliness is ignorable; in fact, frequent loneliness is surprisingly a little bit more prevalent among the employed respondents. The contrast is the biggest in Norway: the unemployed were more than five times more likely to be frequently lonely than those in paid work, followed by Denmark and Germany. Portugal deserves some attention as well because not only its ratio is among the highest, the absolute percentage of frequent loneliness among the unemployed, 20.4%, is the highest as well, meaning one in five unemployed people were frequently lonely. In this sense, Lithuania, France, and Hungary are not far behind. It is however difficult to detect any regularity in terms of the national attributes in the distribution of the countries across the ranking order. One possible explanation is that unemployment has different meanings across national contexts, with these meanings to be discovered.

Moreover, the ESS contains three questions that could shed some light on the question whether frequent loneliness becomes more prevalent with the increasing length of unemployment. We need to apply some caution here, however, as the questions have not been formulated in a way that the length of unemployment was measured accurately. The first question is: 'Have you ever been unemployed and seeking work for a period of more than three months?', followed by two sequels: 'Have any of these periods lasted for 12 months or more?' and 'Have any of these periods been within the past 5 years?', each having two valid options: 'yes' and 'no'. While it is impossible to know the exact temporal length of unemployment, positive answers to these three questions should indicate a respectively longer period of unemployment. The first two questions' meaning is much clearer than that of the third, so our analysis below will concentrate on comparing the prevalence of frequent loneliness between these two groups of people. In addition, it is worth pointing out that some respondents who answered 'Yes' to the first question gave a positive answer to the second as well. In other words, respondents to these questions are not completely two different groups of people. With these cautions in mind, let's take a look at the results (Table 7.2).

In Table 7.2, the countries have been rank-ordered by the prevalence of frequent loneliness among those unemployed for more than three months (second column); the fourth column then reports the corresponding prevalence for those unemployed for more than a year. The percentages in these two columns follow a broadly positive but not perfect association. If we then read across the numbers

Table 7.2 Length of unemployment and frequent loneliness by country in Europe, 2014.

Country	Percentage frequently lonely: unemployed			
	3 months+	Odds ratio with 95% CI	12 months+	Odds ratio with 95% CI
Finland	3.9	0.6 (0.4, 1.1)	5.1	0.6 (0.3, 1.3)
Netherlands	4.3	0.5 (0.3, 0.9)	6.4	0.4 (0.2, 1.1)
Norway	4.8	0.5 (0.3, 1.0)	6.9	0.6 (0.2, 1.6)
Denmark	4.9	0.5 (0.3, 0.8)	8.4	0.3 (0.1, 0.7)
Germany	5.4	0.5 (0.3, 0.7)	7.1	0.6 (0.3, 1.0)
Ireland	6.1	0.6 (0.4, 1.0)	6.1	1.0 (0.5, 2.0)
Sweden	6.4	0.7 (0.4, 1.1)	10.1	0.4 (0.2, 0.9)
Slovenia	6.5	1.0 (0.6, 1.7)	8.9	0.4 (0.1, 1.0)
UK	7.3	0.6 (0.4, 0.8)	9.0	0.7 (0.4, 1.2)
Israel	7.9	0.9 (0.6, 1.2)	9.1	0.8 (0.4, 1.4)
Austria	8.0	0.7 (0.4, 1.0)	9.5	0.7 (0.4, 1.5)
Belgium	8.9	0.6 (0.4, 0.9)	12.6	0.4 (0.2, 0.8)
Switzerland	9.1	0.2 (0.1, 0.4)	11.5	0.7 (0.3, 1.5)
Estonia	9.1	0.8 (0.6, 1.1)	13.4	0.4 (0.2, 0.7)
Spain	9.4	0.8 (06, 1.2)	10.4	0.8 (0.5, 1.2)
France	11.1	0.6 (0.4, 0.8)	14.9	0.5 (0.3, 0.8)
Czech Republic	11.2	0.9 (0.7, 1.2)	15.4	0.5 (0.3, 0.9)
Poland	11.9	1.0 (0.7, 1.4)	14.5	0.6 (0.4, 1.1)
Lithuania	12.0	0.5 (0.3, 0.6)	16.8	0.5 (0.3, 0.8)
Hungary	14.4	0.7 (0.5, 1.0)	15.5	0.9 (0.5, 1.6)
Portugal	15.2	0.5 (0.4, 0.8)	15.6	0.9 (0.5, 1.6)

for each country, we can see that except for Ireland, where there is no change, the prevalence of frequent loneliness increases when the length of unemployment increases from 'more than three months' to 'more than twelve months'. The change remains small, mostly in the range of about 1% to 3%, with that for Lithuania the largest (4.8%). Overall, the general pattern of association is not surprising: the longer the time period of unemployment, the more prevalent the frequent loneliness. Instead of unemployment at a particular time point (past seven days), *the length of unemployment over time* is clearly associated with a higher risk of loneliness.

To explore the variation of such relationship across national contexts, for each of the above sets of percentages, I have added a corresponding column of odds ratios with the corresponding confidence interval at the 95% level for each country. They enable us to study the effect of unemployment on loneliness from a different perspective; that is, they tell us the relative risk of feeling frequently lonely by comparing those unemployed for more than three (or twelve) months with those who responded otherwise. While the two sets of percentages compare the unemployed in two different lengths of unemployment, the odds ratios compare the unemployed with the employed. Here, the results appear consistent as well: almost all odds ratios are smaller than 1 (the three 1.0s are actually rounded up numbers that were originally smaller than 1), meaning that in each and every country, those choosing the negative answer to the unemployment question were subject to smaller risk of feeling frequently lonely than those giving a positive answer. To give an indication of the possible sampling fluctuation of these odds ratios, a 95% confidence interval is attached, and those do not include the value of 1 have been highlighted. Nevertheless, as the sample size of these respondents is much smaller than the original one, it is wise to take these figures with caution.

To summarize, being unemployed does not necessarily make people vulnerable to a higher risk of feeling lonely frequently; what matter to loneliness is the length of unemployment, the longer the unemployment, the higher the risk.

Next, we move on to the size of the establishment and any supervisory role. Obviously, these two attributes are valid only for those who are employed. Although David Rose and others have taken these two employment attributes as key components of class and as shown before, others have argued that those of lower class tended to be lonelier, I find it difficult to draw a sensible connection between these two attributes and loneliness. Do we expect those in a large organization to be more or less likely to be lonely? There is simply no intuitively straightforward answer. Similarly, should we expect those supervising other employees to be more or less likely to feel frequently lonely? Some have demonstrated that top leaders, such as a nation's president or a military general, tend to feel lonely as they could not rely on anybody else to make decisions of grave consequences.[14] But it does not make much sense, at least not to me, to put supervisors in most organizations on par with these top leaders. Let's see which direction the statistics would point to.

In the seventh round of the ESS, respondents were firstly asked, 'Including yourself, about how many people are/were employed at the place where you usually work/worked', and the size of the establishment is categorized into five groups: 'under 10', '10–24', '25–99', '100–499', and '500 and above'. The following question asks, 'In your main job, do/did you have any responsibility for supervising the work of other employees?', which has two dichotomous options ('yes' or 'no'). As establishment size and the original loneliness variable both are ordinal with several categories, their relationship is measured with Kendall's tau-b. I have then calculated an odds ratio for measuring the relationship between whether being a supervisor and frequent loneliness as both have binary values. These statistics, all produced with the application of design weight, are presented for each country in Table 7.3.

Table 7.3 Establishment size, supervisory role, and loneliness in Europe, 2014.

Country	Kendall's tau-b of size and loneliness	Odds ratio of supervisor and frequent loneliness	Valid n
Austria	−0.013	2.02 (1.04, 3.93)	1639
Belgium	−0.008	1.81 (1.12, 2.93)	1553
Switzerland	−0.042	2.01 (1.04, 3.93)	1415
Czech Republic	−0.050*	1.22 (0.81, 1.85)	1754
Germany	−0.036*	2.04 (1.27, 3.28)	2841
Denmark	−0.060**	2.05 (0.94, 4.47)	1428
Estonia	0.014	1.31 (0.90, 1.91)	1897
Spain	−0.029	1.23 (0.84, 1.81)	1630
Finland	−0.054**	1.23 (0.66, 2.30)	2008
France	−0.029	1.08 (0.75, 1.56)	1708
UK	−0.003	1.16 (0.76, 1.77)	2091
Hungary	0.052*	1.53 (0.91, 2.58)	1446
Ireland	−0.057**	1.04 (0.64, 1.69)	1922
Israel	0.002	1.14 (0.79, 1.63)	2167
Lithuania	0.020	2.21 (1.18, 4.15)	1772
Netherlands	−0.028	1.66 (0.89, 3.09)	1767
Norway	−0.048*	3.59 (1.51, 8.55)	1366
Poland	−0.025	1.76 (1.07, 2.90)	1359
Portugal	−0.041	1.60 (1.00, 2.55)	1074
Sweden	0.011	1.91 (1.15, 3.15)	1707
Slovenia	0.054	2.98 (1.50, 5.92)	1019

*: $p < 0.05$, **: $p < 0.01$, ***: $p < 0.001$.

It turns out to be rather difficult to detect any meaningful regularity in the statistics presented in this table. For relationship between the size of the organization and the level of loneliness (from 'not at all' to 'almost always'), six of the twenty-one countries (Czech Republic, Germany, Denmark, Finland, Hungary, and Ireland) show statistical significance, meaning that the association statistics are very unlikely to be nil. The negative value of the statistic means that the bigger the employing organization, the less likely the respondent will feel frequently lonely; in other words, in these six countries, those working in a larger organization are subject to a lower risk of loneliness, while in all other fifteen countries, the size of organization does not matter. It is difficult to propose any sensible explanation for why such relationship exists in these six countries and not others – they are from different regions of Europe and have different economic, political and social backgrounds. The relationship between being in a supervisory role and frequent loneliness poses a similar puzzle: all the odds ratios are above 1, meaning that those in a supervisory role are less likely to feel frequently lonely than those not supervising others. Note, however, that such relationship is statistically significant only in ten countries which, again, show little regularity in terms of their social, economic or political attributes. All in all, none of the three components used in this class scheme seems to be informative in their relationship with loneliness; instead, the temporal length of unemployment – of all unemployed, of course – has a certain regular connection with loneliness.

Income, satisfaction with financial situation, and frequent loneliness

Income, particularly income from employment, is a key component of economic capital and social class. A relatively lower income has been found to be associated with a higher risk of feeling lonely across all adult age groups.[15] For at least two reasons, however, a low income is not necessarily a cause of mental stress such as loneliness. Firstly, income from employment is important only when it is the major or even sole source of financial capital for a person or a family. While this is true for most ordinary people, some could rely on other sources, such as inheritance, income from renting out properties or trading stock shares. This means that those with a low income are not necessarily under financial constraints or in poverty, a caveat that we must keep in mind when analysing the relationship between income and loneliness here. This leads to the other important point: a low income does not necessarily induce psychological stress, as some factors may ameliorate the expected strain of a low income on mental state, such as a thrifty lifestyle or participation in low-budget activities. For our purposes, the level of income or wealth is important *only when it is translated into a certain kind of unpleasant mental state*, particularly when it brings about a sense of desperation of making ends meet. As early as the early 1960s, Michael Harrington pointed out how poverty made the Americans lonely:

> Psychological deprivation is one of the chief components of poverty . . . And the terrible thing that is happening to these people [the poor] is that they feel themselves to be rejects, outcasts . . . They tend to be hopeless and passive, yet prone to bursts of violence; they are lonely and isolated, often rigid and hostile. To be poor is not simply to be deprived of the material things of this world. It is to enter a fatal, futile universe, an America within America with a twisted spirit.[16]

In such a situation, a low income or even no income is expected to come with a higher risk for loneliness because, as pointed above, it becomes a severe constraint on establishing and maintaining social support networks. In almost all cultures it is highly embarrassing to talk about one's financial difficulties and to seek for help, which in turn makes one feel lonely in the sense of being unable to share one's feelings with others and to obtain effective support.

As it is the perception of financial situation, not necessarily the level of income *per se*, that we suspect is a trigger for loneliness, let's analyse this relationship first. The ESS team designed a question asking the respondents which of the following 'comes closest to how you feel about your household's income nowadays?': 1 = 'living comfortably on present income', 2 = 'coping on present income', 3 = 'finding it difficult on present income', and 4 = 'finding it very difficult on present income'. Table 7.4 presents, for each participating country, the percentage of respondents who were frequently lonely in each of these four groups, and a statistic (Kendall's tau-b) that measures the strength of the relationship between the two variables.

The numbers in this table send us several interesting and important messages. As our concern here is with the effect of experiencing financial difficulty on

Table 7.4 Feeling about household income and frequent loneliness in Europe, 2014.

Country	Percentage frequently lonely				Kendall's tau-b
	Comfortable	Coping	Difficult	Very difficult	
Sweden	3.5	6.5	11.2	8.8	0.09***
Denmark	1.5	4.9	12.7	9.5	0.14***
Finland	1.7	2.9	5.3	10.4	0.07**
Netherlands	1.5	2.0	9.5	10.8	0.11***
Israel	6.1	5.5	8.8	11.6	0.06**
Ireland	2.6	4.3	6.2	15.4	0.10***
UK	2.3	4.4	12.9	15.9	0.15***
Switzerland	1.8	4.6	8.5	17.1	0.13***
Germany	1.7	3.2	9.1	17.1	0.11***
Belgium	2.0	5.6	14.4	17.5	0.18***
Austria	4.8	5.7	7.7	18.8	0.06**
Estonia	5.3	5.8	9.9	21.6	0.12***
Spain	5.4	6.9	13.3	22.2	0.13***
Portugal	7.8	6.6	14.8	22.8	0.15***
Norway	1.6	3.8	11.3	25.0	0.13***
Slovenia	4.4	4.4	13.2	25.4	0.13***
Czech Republic	6.9	8.9	12.4	25.8	0.11***
Hungary	1.9	6.3	16.8	26.3	0.21***
Lithuania	1.5	5.0	10.4	31.3	0.21***
France	5.6	6.7	14.9	41.0	0.13***
Poland	5.3	8.2	21.6	48.6	0.21***

**: $p < 0.05$; ***: $p < 0.001$; all numbers were produced with design weight.

frequent loneliness, the countries have been ranked by the prevalence of frequent loneliness among those who reported their financial situation 'very difficult' (the penultimate column). First of all, a positive relationship between feeling financial difficulty and frequent loneliness comes up consistently: the Kendall's tau-b statistic is positive and statistically significant across all participating countries – although their absolute values are not very high, they follow a generally increasing pattern and all of them are statistically significant (that is, their chance of being 0 is very low). For each country, it is almost always the case that the more difficult people felt about their financial situation, the more prevalent frequent loneliness. There are a few exceptions though: for Sweden and Denmark, the percentages of frequent loneliness have declined from the 'difficult' group to the 'very difficult' group, so do those from 'comfortable' to 'coping' for Israel and Portugal, but these are a small minority. Second, the major divide lies between the first two groups ('comfortable' and 'coping'), where most of the percentages are below 6%, and the latter two groups ('difficult' and 'very difficult'), where most percentages are in the range of 10% to 26%. The worst case is clearly in Poland, where nearly half of those who reported their financial situations 'very difficult' felt frequently lonely at the same time. Among western European countries, France fared the worst with the second highest rate of frequent loneliness among those suffering from a very difficult financial situation. While most northern European countries plus Ireland, Israel, UK, and Germany are at the top of table, perhaps there is no room for complacency as about 20% (or one in five) of those in difficult or very difficult positions were frequently lonely.

Drawing on these findings, we could attempt to answer other important questions such as which country has the highest percentages of people in financial difficulties and who these people are; answers to these questions will help us identify the class of people who are the most vulnerable to loneliness. To make my analysis concise in order to save space, I will focus on the following question: in each country, at what income level do people start to feel that they are in financial difficulties? Clearly, we can only study this relationship at the country rather than the individual level. In the ESS, respondents were asked to report the decile in which their household total income belonged to in their country. There is a dilemma in using this variable though. On the one hand, as there are ten deciles, the number of respondents in some income deciles, most likely the highest ones, may be very small. On the other hand, if we reduce the number of income deciles by collapsing two or three into one, it will become difficult for us to see a more refined picture of the relationship. In the end, I have decided to keep the original ten deciles of income as the importance of the latter outweighs the former (Figure 7.1).

Each graph in the above figure depicts the relationship between income level and feeling of financial situation in a particular country; the vertical axis represents the ten income deciles, and the horizontal axis the percentage of respondents, of all those in the corresponding income decile, who reported that their financial situation was either difficult or very difficult. Unsurprisingly, for every country the dots show a downward or negative relationship – respondents of lower income

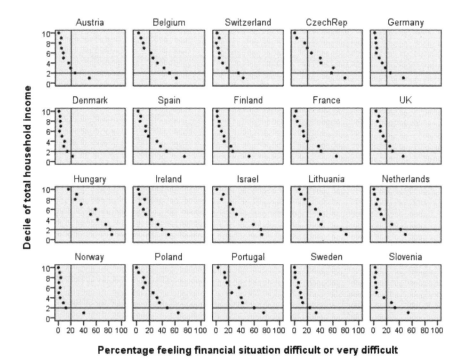

Figure 7.1 Level of household income and feeling financial difficulties in Europe, 2014.

levels are more likely to report financial difficulties. Of these twenty countries,[17] half of them (Austria, Switzerland, Germany, Denmark, Finland, UK, Netherlands, Norway, Sweden, and Slovenia) share about the same pattern: when the income decile is above 20%, less than 20% of the respondents reported themselves being in financial difficulties; it is only when the income level is in the lowest two deciles that the percentages of respondents in financial difficulties go above 20% but no more than 40%, except the lowest one in Slovenia. It is clear that in this group of countries, the relative level of income has the smallest impact on people's feeling about their financial difficulties.

The next group of five countries share a more worrying picture, including: Belgium, Spain, France, Ireland, and Poland, where residents have to be in the fourth or even the sixth decile of income in order to reach a rate of reporting financial difficulties below 20%. Among those in the third and the fourth deciles of income, 20% to 50% of the corresponding respondents reported financial difficulties. For those in the first and second deciles, more than 50% reported financial difficulties.

The remaining five countries (Czech Republic, Hungary, Israel, Poland, and Portugal) are in the worst situation, with Hungary being the extreme case. Even among the middle-level income groups, the percentage of reporting financial difficulties could reach 40–60%. For those in the lowest two deciles, the percentages could be as high as 60–80%.

To summarize, it is definitely the case in every country that income level and the chance of feeling financial difficulties are associated negatively; nevertheless, the exact form of relationship varies noticeably across the national contexts.

Education and loneliness

In comparison with employment and income, education is expected to have a weaker association with loneliness. First of all, part of the effect that education has on loneliness may go through employment and income, and such indirect route may dilute the education's effect. One would be naïve to believe that income will increase linearly with the level of education. However, it is reasonable to expect a higher level of education to increase one's chance of getting employed, and as we saw in a previous section, in some countries being employed is indeed an antidote of loneliness. In addition to that indirect effect, a higher level of education is expected to lower the chance of feeling lonely by providing one with the skills for expanding one's social horizons as well as the confidence of establishing social connections with others. The better educated have been found to have larger and more diverse social networks than the less educated and therefore are expected to be less lonely.[18] I would add that a better education could increase one's abilities to live alone or even to enjoy being alone, for example, a more educated person is better prepared to enjoy creative hobbies such as writing, painting, playing music instrument, etc., which reduce the chance of feeling lonely when being alone.

Keeping the above mechanisms in mind, let's examine the relationship between education and loneliness empirically. Measuring the respondents' education, however, turns out to be a challenge in analysing the ESS data. As the ESS is designed as a cross-national survey, comparability is a key objective. The challenge is that the participating countries have considerably different education systems and have classified the levels of education in different ways. To reflect the diverse national schemes, the researchers designing the ESS have created 27 valid levels of education (besides 'other' and 'don't know'). The pros and cons of such schemes are very clear: the large number of levels is so comprehensive that it is difficult for the survey respondents not to find their education level on the list, but few analysts of the data would need so many levels. I have found these 27 levels unnecessarily detailed and thus have collapsed them into four categories: primary, secondary, university undergraduate, and university postgraduate. Table 7.5 shows the prevalence of frequently lonely respondents within each of these four groups in each country.

Unlike what we did in the previous table, here the countries are ranked with their values of Kendall's tau-b in the last column, as our interest here is more in the overall connection between educational levels and the prevalence of frequent loneliness than in any particular category of education. For the three

Table 7.5 Level of education and frequent loneliness in Europe, 2014.

Country	Percentage frequent loneliness in level of education				Kendall's tau-b
	Primary	*Secondary*	*Undergraduate*	*Postgraduate*	
Czech Republic	0.0	10.6	8.7	10.7	−0.01
Sweden	9.1	4.6	3.9	4.1	−0.02
Spain	12.5	7.1	5.4	5.5	−0.04
Austria	8.7	4.9	7.5	1.3	−0.05**
Denmark	6.5	3.5	1.0	4.3	−0.05**
Norway	6.1	3.2	1.6	1.4	−0.07**
Switzerland	10.9	3.3	1.2	2.6	−0.08**
Netherlands	3.9	2.0	1.8	0.9	−0.08**
Slovenia	25.7	5.6	3.0	0.0	−0.08**
Belgium	12.8	6.7	4.4	2.4	−0.08***
Finland	6.4	3.0	1.8	1.1	−0.08***
Lithuania	12.0	8.7	6.3	4.8	−0.09***
Estonia	18.0	8.1	7.8	4.1	−0.10***
France	14.0	9.1	3.7	2.9	−0.10***
UK	8.6	4.1	4.0	2.1	−0.10***
Ireland	10.4	3.9	2.9	3.4	−0.10***
Israel	16.4	5.9	6.8	3.9	−0.10***
Germany	4.8	3.7	1.6	1.7	−0.11***
Poland	31.6	10.4	13.1	6.2	−0.11***
Hungary	38.3	10.1	3.7	7.4	−0.12***
Portugal	15.8	7.7	7.8	1.0	−0.17***

**: $p < 0.05$;   ***: $p < 0.001$; all numbers were produced with design weight.

countries at the top, the Kendall's tau-b statistics are not statistically significant, meaning that the chance for them to be 0 is above what we have set up (usually 5%); in other words, there seems to be little support for the relationship between levels of education and frequent loneliness in these countries, which has confirmed the expectation presented at the beginning of this chapter. Most of such weak or even nil relationship comes from the small differences between the last three levels of education; for example, in Czech Republic, there were only fourteen respondents with primary education, and none of them happened to be frequently lonely.

For the remaining nineteen countries, overall there appears to be a negative, weak, but statistically significant association between the two variables: the higher the level of education, the lower the prevalence of frequent loneliness, which is in line with our expectation. Taking a closer look at the percentages, we can see that these countries fall into three groups. For countries in the first and the largest group (Belgium, Germany, Estonia, Finland, France, UK, Lithuania, Netherlands, Norway, Portugal, and Slovenia), the relationship is consistently linear; that is, a higher level of education always comes with a lower rate of frequent loneliness. For four countries (Austria, Ireland, Israel, and Poland), the overall shape of association is negative but not completely linear: the prevalence of frequent loneliness among those with an undergraduate university education is actually higher than among those with a secondary school education. There is a similar pattern for those with a postgraduate university education for the following three countries: Switzerland, Denmark, and Hungary. Without further evidence and research for explaining the relatively higher prevalence of frequent loneliness among the more educated, I could only offer an unconfirmed theory: in these countries, there is a higher proportion of people among the more educated who live a socially more isolated life, either because they choose to live such a life or because they find it more difficult to keep stable social relations with others.

In case the recoded educational levels are too crude to capture the relationship between education and loneliness, I have found it necessary to verify the overall association found above with another measure of education (i.e. the total number of years of full-time education, a metrical and therefore more refined measurement of educational level). It is worth keeping in mind that although the two may not correspond to each other in all cases – one could spend many more years than others to obtain a certain level of education, there should be a general positive relationship between years of education and level of education. The metrical nature of the years of full-time education means, however, that we need to reverse the direction of our comparison in order to make our analysis more meaningful; more specifically, rather than comparing the prevalence of frequent loneliness at a particular number of years of education – there will be very few people for each number of years, we will compare the mean number of years of education between those frequently lonely and those not so lonely. The reader can find the relevant statistics in Table 7.6.

In this table, countries are ranked with the values in the fourth column, which represent the respective difference in the mean years of full-time education between the frequently lonely and those not so lonely. As most of the corresponding p-values in the last column are statistically significant (below the usual threshold of 0.05), except for Denmark, Sweden, and Switzerland, we arrive at the same observation that in most European countries, less educated people are more vulnerable to the risk of frequent loneliness. Again, Portugal is the country where the difference in education has the largest effect on frequent loneliness. For other countries, the two different ways of measuring education make a difference to the effect, which is represented in the different positions a country takes in the two tables.

Table 7.6 Years of education and frequent loneliness in Europe, 2014.

Country	Mean number of years of education		Difference	p-value for difference
	Frequently lonely	Not frequent lonely		
Portugal	6.14	8.90	−2.76	<0.001
Finland	10.93	13.50	−2.57	<0.001
Norway	11.58	13.93	−2.35	<0.001
Slovenia	10.10	12.33	−2.23	<0.001
France	11.17	12.96	−1.79	<0.001
Netherlands	12.09	13.78	−1.69	0.002
Ireland	12.36	14.04	−1.68	<0.001
Spain	11.21	12.88	−1.67	<0.001
Poland	10.81	12.40	−1.59	<0.001
Hungary	10.79	12.36	−1.57	<0.001
Israel	12.02	13.35	−1.33	<0.001
Lithuania	11.65	12.86	−1.21	<0.001
Belgium	12.19	13.33	−1.14	0.002
UK	12.73	13.78	−1.05	0.003
Estonia	12.21	13.25	−1.04	<0.001
Austria	11.59	12.62	−1.03	0.002
Denmark	12.18	13.12	−0.94	0.205
Germany	13.41	14.15	−0.74	0.031
Sweden	12.48	13.19	−0.71	0.072
Czech Republic	12.49	12.89	−0.40	0.021
Switzerland	10.91	11.06	−0.15	0.731

Social capital and frequent loneliness

'Social capital' has become one of the most influential concepts created by social scientists – it has been promoted as a powerful remedy for many social ills, including poverty, poor health, inequality, underdevelopment, crimes, conflicts, etc. There is neither space nor need to review the academic literature on social capital here. Suffice it to raise two important points. The first relates to the units that possess social capital; that is, whether social capital is an asset of a community, an individual, or both. Originally, social capital was defined as an asset of a community that could not be attributed to an individual person, something the members of a community contribute to and have the right to share its benefits. If so, it is not meaningful to talk about a person's social capital. However, the individual is a natural unit of data collection in social surveys, so to study social capital empirically, social scientists have no choice but to measure and study social capital as an individual asset, which could easily cause some confusion.[19] The second important point is that social capital is not necessarily positive or desirable, at least not necessarily to all people under study, as it could be inclusive to some while exclusive to others at the same time. If social capital can only be possessed and used within a certain social circle with clearly defined boundaries, those outside the circle are deprived of such privilege.

Considering our interest in loneliness, we must be clear about what we mean by social capital when studying its relationship with loneliness. If social capital means participation in social activities and social support gained from membership of a community, the possession of social capital is expected to be an anecdote of loneliness. We need to confirm whether such expectation holds firstly, and if it is confirmed, the next important task is to find out how social capital is associated with other indicators of class.

Like other 'umbrella concepts', social capital has several components. To popularize its use, it is highly effective for researchers to promote the overarching nature of the concept. However, if we are looking for clarity, it is wiser to study its components. While what constitutes social capital remains a controversy, here are the usual suspects that researchers commonly include: general trust (i.e. trust of people one does not know personally), memberships of civil organizations and social networks (clubs, associations, charities, etc.), and social (informal) relations. As we already studied trust in relation to loneliness in the previous chapter and questions about civic engagement were not included in the ESS anymore when the loneliness question was included, here we carry out a simple analysis on the relationship between social relations, or more precisely, sociality and loneliness. In the ESS, sociality is measured with the following three questions:

- 'How often do you meet socially with friends, relatives or work colleagues?' 1 = never, 2 = less than once a month, 3 = once a month, 4 = several times a month, 5 = once a week, 6 = several times a week, 7 = every day.
- 'How many people, if any, are there with whom you can discuss intimate and personal matters?' 0 = none, 1 = 1, 2 = 2, 3 = 3, 4 = 4–6, 5 = 7–9, 6 = 10 or more.
- 'Compared to other people of your age, how often would you say you take part in social activities?' 1 = much less than most, 2 = less than most, 3 = about the same, 4 = more than most, 5 = much more than most.

As these variables have a very limited number of values and are not highly correlated between each pair of them, I have refrained from creating a score by summing up the responses to them. Rather, I present the Kendall's tau-b for measuring the association between each of these three variables and loneliness (weighted by design weight) for each participating country of the seventh round of the ESS (Table 7.7).

Table 7.7 Sociality and loneliness in Europe, 2014.

Country	Valid n	Meet socially	Discuss intimate matters	Take part in social activities
Belgium	1768	−0.018	−0.132***	−0.090***
Germany	3039	−0.018	−0.103***	−0.108***
Denmark	1496	−0.029	−0.119***	−0.144***
Sweden	1786	−0.034	−0.079***	−0.114***
France	1917	−0.040	−0.058**	−0.148***
Norway	1423	−0.047	−0.031	−0.133***
Spain	1924	−0.049*	−0.114***	−0.087***
Israel	1992	−0.049*	−0.063***	−0.153***
Poland	1580	−0.049*	−0.099***	−0.128***
Finland	2082	−0.053**	−0.103***	−0.119***
UK	2250	−0.063**	−0.100***	−0.105***
Switzerland	1530	−0.069**	−0.125***	−0.128***
Estonia	2036	−0.077***	−0.102***	−0.106***
Slovenia	1216	−0.078**	−0.081**	−0.175***
Lithuania	2179	−0.097***	−0.184***	−0.131***
Austria	1789	−0.104***	−0.126***	−0.152***
Netherlands	1926	−0.108***	−0.159***	−0.187***
Ireland	2370	−0.110***	−0.081***	−0.156***
Portugal	1264	−0.120***	−0.095***	−0.154***
Hungary	1693	−0.124***	−0.195***	−0.193***
Czech Republic	2113	−0.142***	−0.074***	−0.118***

***: $p < 0.001$; **: $p < 0.01$; *: $p < 0.05$.

In this table, the countries have been rank ordered with the values in the third column, i.e. the strength of the relationship between the frequency of loneliness and the frequency of meeting with others socially. Clearly, the strength of the relationship, represented by the value of this statistic, goes in tandem with its statistical significance; for the first six countries (Belgium, Germany, Denmark, Sweden, France, and Norway), the relationship is both weak and insignificant, that is, there is no evidence that meeting others socially made a difference to loneliness in these countries. Then the relationship increases with statistical significance for the rest of the countries, becoming the strongest for Portugal, Hungary, and Czech Republic.

Such a pattern does not apply to the relationship between the other two variables of social capital and loneliness. Except for having a confidante in Norway, both having someone to discuss intimate matters and taking part in social activities are strongly, negatively, and significantly associated with loneliness; the exact strength of the relationship between each of these variables and loneliness varies from country to country, but the variation is quite mild. In other words, those having a confidante and participating in social activities more than peers are less likely to feel lonely frequently, and such effect appears almost universal across European countries. While the overall ameliorating effect of social capital on loneliness is not surprising,[20] the above analyses have demonstrated that, first, not all components of social capital are equally important to loneliness, and second, the national variation of social capital's effect on loneliness remains.

After studying the relationship between each of the social class factors and frequent loneliness, finally we need to examine the relationship between these factors in each national context in order to see whether the single factor that we could call 'social class' exists. To simplify and save space, I shall focus on only three variables: feeling about household income representing economic capital, the highest level of education representing human capital, and participation in social activities representing social capital. There are three non-redundant pairs of relationship between these three variables, and each is measured with a Kendall's tau-b statistic in Table 7.8 (with design weight).

Table 7.8 Correlation of pairwise relationships between three forms of capital in Europe, 2014.

Country	Income–education	Income–SC	Education–SC
Austria	−0.204***	−0.156***	0.076**
Belgium	−0.225***	−0.109***	0.165***
Switzerland	−0.189***	−0.074**	0.051*
Czech Republic	−0.241***	−0.119***	0.064**
Germany	−0.207***	−0.150***	0.057***
Denmark	−0.132***	−0.119***	0.065**
Estonia	−0.193***	−0.180***	0.178***
Spain	−0.256***	−0.084***	0.197***
Finland	−0.192***	−0.131***	0.155***
France	−0.264***	−0.170***	0.118***
UK	−0.171***	−0.157***	0.054**
Hungary	−0.316***	−0.195***	0.112***
Ireland	−0.170***	−0.164***	0.070**
Israel	−0.201***	−0.146***	0.137***
Lithuania	−0.192***	−0.175***	0.005
Netherlands	−0.229***	−0.103***	0.103***
Norway	−0.138***	−0.114***	0.051*
Poland	−0.236***	−0.119***	0.059*
Portugal	−0.297***	−0.153***	0.224***
Sweden	−0.137***	−0.062**	0.079***
Slovenia	−0.266***	−0.086**	0.108***

***: $p < 0.001$; **: $p < 0.01$; *: $p < 0.05$.

Reading through the numbers across the countries in each column, we can see that most statistics are statistically significant (the more stars attached to each correlation statistic, the more significant), which lends some support to the practice of taking income, education, and sociality as key components of social class. This is somehow different from a point made earlier as different variables and statistics have been used. However, note that the magnitude of each statistic remains quite small, usually between 0.05 and 0.3, indicating weak albeit significant relationship.

Of the three pairs, the relationship between the feeling of financial difficulties and education is the strongest: everywhere it is the case that people with a higher level of education are less likely to feel difficult in their economic situations. In comparison, the relationship between feeling about income and social capital is slightly weaker in terms of both the size and the statistical significance of the association. The weakest connection lies in education and participation in social activities. In Lithuania, the relationship is extremely weak, and it is not statistically significant (that is, the likelihood of no relationship is higher than expected). In about half of these countries (Austria, Switzerland, Czech Republic, Germany, Denmark, UK, Ireland, Norway, Poland, and Sweden), the magnitude of the association is less than 0.1, indicating considerably weak albeit statistically significant relationship. In other words, people with higher education enjoy only a little bit higher level of participation in social activities (a form of social capital).

All in all, income and the feeling about one's financial situation appears to be the most useful indicator of social capital and ultimately of social class as well. Other factors are strongly related to the feeling but not always among themselves. It is wise to be specific about which component of social class we are referring to when attempting to examine the relationship between social class and loneliness.

Notes

1 I would not list the large number of publications on this topic as they will take a lot of space. Interested readers could consult the following two chapters that summarize the relevant academic research very well: G. Scambler (ed.). 2018. *Sociology as Applied to Health and Medicine*, 7th edition. Basingstoke: Palgrave, ch. 8; W. C. Cockerham. 2017. *Medical Sociology*, 14th edition. New York: Routledge, ch. 3.
2 W. C. Cockerham. 2017. *Sociology of Mental Disorder*, 10th edition. New York: Routledge.
3 See the seminal study by Gary Becker. 1964. *Human Capital: A Theoretical and Empirical Analysis, with Special Reference to Education*. New York: National Bureau of Economic Research. Pedro Teixeira edited a three-volume set on the subject, *Human Capital*, published by Routledge in 2014.
4 The literature of social capital has become so large that it is perhaps impossible to provide a comprehensive list; even the number of publications on the controversy over the concept's meaning is enormous. Interested readers could go to the Social Capital Gateway website at www.socialcapitalgateway.org for further information. An old paper of mine might still serve as a useful introduction to the concept and the related debates: K. Yang. 2007. 'Individual social capital and its measurement in social surveys', *Survey Research Methods*, 1(1): 19–27.

5 For the UK, a well-known class scheme was developed by John Goldthorpe and his colleagues in the 1990s; see R. Erikson and J. H. Goldthorpe. 1992. *The Constant Flux: A Study of Class Mobility in Industrial Societies*. Oxford: Clarendon Press. More recently, Mike Savage and his colleagues have created a new and more comprehensive one: M. Savage, F. Devine, N. Cunningham, M. Taylor, Y. Li, J. Hjellbrekke, B.Le Roux, S. Friedman, and A. Miles. 2013. 'A new model of social class? Findings from the BBC's Great British Class Survey experiment', *Sociology*, 47(2): 219–250.

6 D. Rose, E. Harrison, and D. Pevalin. 2010. 'The European Socio-economic Classification: a prolegomenon', in D. Rose and E. Harrison (eds), *Social Class in Europe: An Introduction to the European Socio-economic Classification*. New York: Routledge, p. 3.

7 See R. Davies and P. Elias. 2010. 'The application of ESeC to three sources of comparative European data' by in the above monograph', in D. Rose and E. Harrison (eds), *Social Class in Europe: An Introduction to the European Socio-economic Classification*. New York: Routledge, ch. 3.

8 See R. Shorthouse. 2014. 'Loneliness should be recognized as a signal of poverty in today's Britain', *The Guardian*, 26 February, available online at www.theguardian. com/commentisfree/2014/feb/26/loneliness-signal-poverty-britain-iain-duncan-smith (accessed 15 May 2018).

9 M. Pinquart and S. Sörensen. 2001. 'Influences on loneliness in older adults: a meta-analysis', *Basic and Applied Social Psychology*, 23(4): 245–266.

10 S. E. Taylor and T. E. Seeman. 1999. 'Psychosocial resources and the SES – health relationship', *Annals of the New York Academy of Science*, 896: 210–225; J. S. House, K. R. Landis, and D. Umberson. 1988. 'Social relationships and health', *Science*, 241(4865): 540–545.

11 T. Hansen and B. Slagsvold. 2016. 'Late-life loneliness in 11 European countries: results from the generations and gender survey', *Social Indicator Research*, 129: 445–464.

12 See the relevant parts of two classic studies: R. Sennett and J. Cobb. 1977. *The Hidden Injuries of Class*. Cambridge: Cambridge University Press; R. Wilkinson and K. Pickett. 2010. *The Spirit Level: Why Equality is Better for Everyone*. London: Penguin Books.

13 L. Jamieson and R. Simpson. 2013. *Living Alone: Globalization, Identity and Belonging*. Basingstoke: Palgrave Macmillan, p. 182.

14 For example, see Horne's biography of David Montgomery: A. Horne. 1994. *The Lonely Leader: Monty, 1944–1945*. London: Macmillan.

15 For example, see the study on a large German dataset by M. Luhmann and L. C. Hawkley. 2016. 'Age differences in loneliness from late adolescence to oldest old age', *Developmental Psychology*, 52(6): 943–959.

16 M. Harrington. 1962. *The Other America: Poverty in the United States*. New York: Macmillan.

17 Note that Estonia is not included in this analysis as no data on income were available.

18 M. McPherson, L. Smith-Lovin, and M. E. Brashears. 2006. 'Social isolation in America: changes in core discussion networks over two decades', *American Sociological Review*, 71(3): 353–375; N. Savikko, P. Routasalo, R. S. Tilvis, T. E. Strandberg and K. H. Pitkälä. 2005. 'Predictors and subjective causes of loneliness in an aged population', *Archives of Gerontology and Geriatrics*, 41: 223–233; L. C. Hawkley, M. E. Hughes, L. J. Waite, C. M. Masi, R. A. Thisted, and J. T. Cacioppo. 2008. 'From social structural factors to perceptions of relationship quality and loneliness: the Chicago Health, Aging, and Social Relations Study', *The Journals of Gerontology, Series B; Psychological Sciences and Social Sciences*, 63: S375 – S384.

19 My paper cited above attempts to clear away the confusion: Yang, 'Individual social capital and its measurement in social surveys'.

20 Focusing on older people in a few European countries, the following studies have confirmed the benefits of social capital to the reduction of loneliness: F. Nyqvist, M. Cattan, L. Andersson, A. K. Forsman, and Y. Gustafson. 2013. 'Social capital and loneliness among the very old living at home and in institutional settings: a comparative study', *Journal of Ageing and Health*, 25(6): 1013–1035; F. Nyqvist, C. Victor, A. Forsman, and M. Cattan. 2016. 'The association between social capital and loneliness in different age groups: a population-based study in Western Finland', *BMC Public Health*, 16(1): 542; J. Domènech-Abella, J. Mundó, E. Lara, M. Moneta, J. Haro, and B. Olaya. 2017. 'The role of socio-economic status and neighbourhood social capital on loneliness among older adults: evidence from the Sant Boi Aging Study', *Social Psychiatry and Psychiatric Epidemiology*, 52(10): 1237–1246; L. Coll-Planas, G. Valle Gómez, P. Bonilla, T. Masat, T. Puig, and R. Monteserin. 2017. 'Promoting social capital to alleviate loneliness and improve health among older people in Spain', *Health & Social Care in the Community*, 25(1): 145–157.

Chapter 8

National disposition towards loneliness

When examining the relationship between age and frequent loneliness in Chapter 3, I made a promise of coming back to the effect of national context and give it a more concentrated discussion in this chapter. As we saw in that chapter, the way in which age related to loneliness varied considerably across a large number of nations, and the relationship was highly stable over time for a particular nation. More generally, I call such a stable pattern of loneliness at the national level 'national disposition towards loneliness'. Seeing loneliness as an individual-level problem alone has led to an oversight of the problem's societal origins and contexts. As de Jong Gierveld et al. aptly observed, 'Empirical studies have focused on individual-level determinants of loneliness. Much less attention has been paid to the ways in which social isolation and loneliness are patterned socially.'[1] Below I shall explain the source of inspiration for this concept and present further evidence for its existence. Once the presence of the national disposition towards loneliness is established, the more challenging task is to make sense of it – why is loneliness more prevalent in some countries than in others? Or, what are the possible factors at the national level that will lead to higher or lower levels of loneliness? As our analysis moves up from the individual to the nation or the country, we shall search for and examine the effects of some macro-level factors. It will be a much bigger challenge to draw sensible connections between these factors and the prevalence of loneliness at the national level than drawing the same connections at the individual level, because the mechanisms that connect the two together at the higher level usually remain elusive – usually people do not pay much attention to how macro-level factors such as cultural norms affect their daily lives. However, that is exactly the value of such analysis – it will reveal some connections that so far have been missing in the studies focusing on psychological or individual factors. In this chapter, I shall use the following words interchangeably: nation (or national), country, society (or societal), culture (or cultural), macro-level, and others.

In multiple ways the shift from individuals to societies will advance our understanding of loneliness. First of all, the national variation of the prevalence of loneliness strongly suggests that whether people feel lonely or not depends to a large extent on the country in which they live. Therefore, societal factors, such as the level of economic development and cultural values, should be examined in addition to the ones at the individual level. These factors may not exercise immediate influence on any individual's psychological experience and individuals may not consciously realize their influence, but these macro-level factors constitute the context of individual life and may exert powerful effects in the long run. Second, as loneliness results from the perceived discrepancy between existing and desired social relations, it is crucial to understand how people recognize and evaluate the desirability of their social relations. More importantly, such cognitive evaluations are ultimately embedded in social structures and cultural norms. It is only by shifting our attention from individual-level factors to societal and cultural factors that we could identify some long-term and fundamental sources of loneliness. The third and perhaps the most important reason for focusing on societal factors for loneliness is that individual-level research on loneliness may prevent us from answering some important questions. As we discovered in Chapter 4, although it is widely perceived that loneliness is a natural outcome of the ageing process, the prevalence of loneliness among younger people in one country could be actually higher than that of older people in another country.[2] In other words, some patterns or regularities among social phenomena will emerge only when we stand back and take a look at 'the forests' rather than 'the trees'. As Babones points out when explaining the key benefits of the Durkheimian approach for quantitative macro-comparative studies (QMCS), 'It is meaningful, or even preferable, to correlate macro-level properties of societies with other macro-level properties of societies without recourse to the micro-level realities that must underlie them.'[3]

We shall start by examining the prevalence of 'frequent loneliness' among a large number of European countries, again drawing on the data collected from the European Social Survey (ESS), in order to confirm the existence of 'national dispositions towards loneliness'. Then we discuss a popular explanation for such national variation of loneliness, that is, the cultural norms represented in the dichotomy of individualism versus collectivism. I would argue that this explanation is limited and therefore we should explore other national level factors. And we carry out the exploration in the next section. To complement these statistical studies of the overall picture, I shall make some focused analyses on loneliness in Russia and eastern European countries, comparing them with some western and northern European countries.

National disposition towards loneliness

Émile Durkheim (1858–1917) is one of the 'founding fathers' of sociology. One of his major contributions was that he made a strong case for seeing individual and psychological problems from a societal perspective. He advised that 'it is with society that the sociologist must begin' because 'in so far as man is a product of society, it is through society that man can be explained'.[4] Illustrating such an approach with his study on suicide, Durkheim observed that '*each society has a particular disposition* towards suicide at any moment in its history'.[5] When I was observing the national variations of the prevalence of frequent loneliness presented in Chapter 4, Durkheim's notion of 'a society's mental disposition' came to my mind: if each society had a disposition towards suicide, why couldn't it have a particular disposition towards loneliness as well? That is the origin of the notion 'national disposition towards loneliness'. The concept refers to the relatively stable prevalence of frequent or severe loneliness within a particular nation; in this chapter, it is measured by the percentage of adults who could be classified as being 'frequently lonely' or a similar indicator out of the whole adult population.

When studying the prevalence of loneliness in Europe, some researchers have found a gradient of variation,[6] which could be taken as a preliminary representation of national disposition towards loneliness: the percentages of residents feeling frequently lonely were the highest in southern European countries, then decreased in western European countries, and finally reached the lowest in northern European countries. There are a few exceptions to this pattern, however; for example, Stevens and Westerhof found no significant difference between Germany and the Netherlands.[7] Later, Christina Victor and I expanded the scope of analysis and discovered that the adult populations in Russia and eastern European countries, particularly Ukraine, had the highest rates of loneliness in Europe,[8] a finding confirmed by a study focusing on the older people in Europe.[9]

With more recent data made available to us, we could find out whether this gradient pattern remains true. Recall that in the ESS, respondents were asked to choose one of the following four options when answering the question 'How much of the time during the past week you felt lonely': 'none or almost none of the time', 'some of the time', 'most of the time', and 'all or almost all of the time'. While the percentages of all four values are presented in Table 8.1,[10] the percentage of respondents who chose either 'most of the time' or 'all or almost all of the time' is used as the measurement of the 'national disposition towards loneliness' among the adults in each country, because these two categories are usually defined as 'severe loneliness' or 'frequent loneliness' in the literature. For Austria, Croatia and Greece, the data were collected in Round 5 (2010); for Latvia and Romania, the data were collected in Round 3 (2006). Data for all other nations were collected in Round 6 (2012) of the European Social Survey.

The countries are ranked based on the column 'most + always' (the sum of the percentages of 'most of the time' and 'always/almost always'); that is, 'the prevalence of frequent loneliness'. A pattern of variation in the prevalence of loneliness emerges from this 'league table of loneliness in Europe', which is similar to the 'gradient pattern' discussed previously: most northern European countries enjoy the lowest rates of loneliness, followed by most of the western and then southern European countries, and the highest levels of prevalence of loneliness are found in most eastern European countries and Russia. The qualifier 'most' is necessary here, first because the classification of European regions is not indisputable; for example, the UK could be classified either as a northern or a western European country; moreover, there are a few exceptions to the 'gradient pattern': geographically, Lithuania, Estonia and Latvia are northern European countries,

Table 8.1 Prevalence (%) of loneliness among adults in 33 European nations.

Nation	Level of loneliness					n
	Never/almost never	Sometimes	Most of the time	Always/almost always	Most + always	
Norway	81.4	16.4	1.5	0.7	2.2	1618
Denmark	83.8	13.2	1.9	1.1	3.0	1647
Iceland	77.9	19.0	2.5	0.5	3.0	747
Switzerland	76.8	19.5	2.7	0.9	3.6	1490
Finland	77.9	17.8	2.8	1.5	4.3	2194
Ireland	74.3	21.3	2.6	1.8	4.4	2618
Netherlands	78.0	17.5	3.3	1.2	4.5	1843
Germany	76.6	18.8	2.9	1.7	4.6	2951
Sweden	75.4	19.9	3.1	1.6	4.7	1846
UK	74.2	20.2	3.9	1.7	5.6	2284
Slovenia	78.2	16.0	4.2	1.6	5.8	1255
Kosovo	52.7	40.5	5.4	1.3	6.7	1278
Lithuania	54.3	38.5	6.3	0.9	7.2	2076
Croatia10	55.8	36.7	5.4	2.0	7.4	1601
Portugal	70.5	22.1	5.2	2.2	7.4	2148
Slovakia	57.8	34.7	5.7	1.8	7.5	1838
Israel	70.2	21.8	5.7	2.3	8.0	2486
Belgium	70.4	21.4	5.4	2.8	8.2	1867
Estonia	63.6	26.9	6.6	2.9	8.5	2370
Spain	68.1	23.4	5.2	3.3	8.5	1885
Cyprus	67.5	23.6	5.3	3.6	8.9	1114
Greece10	53.4	36.9	6.1	3.6	9.7	2704
Poland	70.9	19.1	5.8	4.2	10.0	1885
France	66.4	23.4	5.9	4.3	10.2	1968
Italy	58.6	31.2	6.3	3.9	10.2	952
Albania	54.5	34.5	7.2	3.8	11.0	1199
Austria10	62.3	26.0	9.2	2.5	11.7	2204
Latvia06	42.8	45.4	9.3	2.4	11.7	1930
Bulgaria	59.5	28.1	8.1	4.4	12.5	2242
Czech Rep	57.0	30.1	9.3	3.6	12.9	1953
Romania06	56.6	30.2	9.3	3.9	13.2	2072
Russia	52.5	32.6	12.5	2.4	14.9	2434
Hungary	56.9	28.0	10.6	4.6	15.2	2000
Ukraine	46.6	32.9	14.7	5.8	20.5	2117

but their rates of frequent loneliness are higher than those of many other European countries. Also, Belgium, France and Austria are usually classified as western European countries but have higher prevalence of frequent loneliness than some southern European countries.

Indeed, in the first decade of the twenty-first century the prevalence of loneliness among the adult populations in Europe varies remarkably from the lowest 2.2% in Norway to the highest 20.5% in Ukraine. In two geographical directions this study has verified the gradient pattern of loneliness found in previous studies: the prevalence of frequent loneliness increases from the north to the south and from the west to the east in Europe. The repeated identifications of this pattern over the past two decades in Europe have firmly established 'national dispositions towards loneliness'. This 'social fact' – an important sociological concept by Durkheim – should be taken seriously.

On the other hand, we have identified a few important exceptions to this regularity; therefore, some caveats against taking this fact rigidly are in order. First of all, to which European region a particular country belongs could be a controversial matter; for example, the Republic of Ireland could be classified as an either northern or western European country, and whether Latvia should belong to the northern or the eastern Europe could also be disputable. Furthermore, even if there is a consensus on the region of each country, classifications based on factors other than geographical locations could be more useful; for example, although Latvia and Estonia are normally classified as northern European countries, their rates of loneliness are higher than some southern or eastern European countries, such as Italy and Albania; therefore, it seems more informative to put the members of the former USSR together when understanding the prevalence of loneliness, although to explain why these countries have some of the highest rates of loneliness is beyond this study. All in all, while the identified pattern appears more distinctive at each end of the spectrum of loneliness prevalence, they become less consistent among the countries with intermediate rates of prevalence (about 5–11%).

Culture and loneliness

How should we make sense of the above society-level variations in the prevalence of loneliness? Some have argued that 'the normative climate' – the norms and values with regard to obligations and duties in social relations – played an important role.[11] Loneliness is most commonly defined as the discrepancy between the desired and the existing social relations; if so, it then follows that, *ceteris paribus*, people with high expectations of social relations suffer from higher prevalence of loneliness. A culture with higher expectations of social relations is usually referred to as 'collectivist', as opposed to 'individualistic'.[12] Analysing the data collected from World Values Surveys, Stack showed that loneliness was more prevalent in Italy and Japan, two highly collectivist countries, than in the US and Canada, widely perceived as highly individualist.[13] Following this logic, one may hypothesize that northern European countries enjoy the lowest rates of loneliness because people in these countries have been socialized to expect comparatively less from their social relations, which make them more resilient to loneliness. Johnson and Mullins (1987) emphasize the effect of a nation's value system on loneliness with the following model: cultural values → personality expectation of social interactions → loneliness. They create the concept 'loneliness threshold' to describe the 'the minimal level of social contact that is needed for a person to avoid the subjective experience of loneliness'.[14] If such a threshold does exist, a nation with a lower loneliness threshold would have a higher percentage of people reporting loneliness. However, these authors did not say how we could determine this 'minimal threshold' for a particular nation, let alone comparing nations with regard to that threshold. Jylhä and Jokela explained the unusually high level of loneliness reported by Greek elders by pointing out that the concept of 'privacy' so central to Anglo-Saxon culture was alien to older people in Greece.[15]

Some researchers asserted 30 years ago that 'among the important factors affecting the individual's experience of loneliness are the culture and the family in which he/she develops'.[16] However, existing studies have generated somehow contradictory findings on the connection of this cultural dimension to the prevalence of loneliness. On the one hand, in a series of studies that aim to detect the effect of cultural differences on loneliness, Rokach and his colleagues found that the Canadians, who represent the individualist North American culture, scored consistently higher on almost all loneliness dimensions than the Spanish,[17] Czech Republic,[18] and Croatia,[19] which represent the collectivistic culture. In other words, according to these studies, a collectivist country is expected to have a lower rate of loneliness than an individualist one. However, in a more recent study on European countries, Lykes and Kemmelmeier have found that the European countries with higher scores on collectivism suffer from higher rates of loneliness.[20]

For two major reasons, I find it difficult to entirely adopt the above cultural perspective to explain national variations of loneliness. The first is that this approach seems to focus solely on the expectation of social interaction. It is now well established that loneliness arises when there is a perceived deficit or dissatisfaction of the quality or the quantity of social interactions. Thus, expectations alone cannot explain loneliness; it is the perceived gap between the expected and the actual social relations that accounts for loneliness. Even if we could determine the threshold, we must take great care when comparing nations with regard to the threshold because it is an individual-level measure and its intra-nation variation may not necessarily be smaller than the inter-nation variation. Another difficulty with the cultural approach is that while we appreciate the intention to explain an individual-level phenomenon with a factor at the higher national level, it is very difficult to isolate the mechanisms through which the higher-level factor brings about the individual feeling or behaviour.

It would be more fruitful to identify nation-level factors that make individual residents become more or less satisfied with their social relationships. The results reported in the previous section prompt us to ask the following question: what are the common features among nations such as Russia, Ukraine, Hungary, Romania and Latvia that could be meaningfully connected to worsening social relations and further to a frequent feeling of loneliness?

We could hypothesize two mechanisms by which economic and political changes would create a deficit of desired social relations and therefore loneliness. The first is that the transformations experienced by the above nations have forced people, especially the younger and middle-aged groups, to move away from their social relations in pursuit of a better material life somewhere else. At the operational level, we would expect a statistically significant effect of migration within a nation on the percentage of people feeling lonely, which has been confirmed by a study on loneliness among older people in China, another transitional nation that has been experiencing dramatic social and economic changes.[21] Of course, whether this mechanism applies to Russia and eastern European nations remains to be investigated. The other mechanism is less observable, that is, political and economic transformations mean that social relations have to be re-defined with new rules, including those related to code of behaviours, status and privileges. In other words, previously intimate social relations now become strained and it is now more difficult to establish friendly and trustworthy relations. These changes may be reflected in people's perceptions of others surrounding them, which in turn will make people feel more or less lonely.

However, it is advisable to be cautious when employing such dichotomy of cultural values to explain the prevalence of loneliness, as their relationship may not be straightforward. For example, while the residents of Nordic countries may be 'individualistic' in a certain way, they enjoy rich community life as well; in this sense, these countries are both individualist and collectivist. In some cases, people of an individualist culture could be even lonelier than those of a collectivist one, as found by Rokach and his associates in a comparative study of Canadians and Croatians: the Canadians, presumably individualistic, were actually lonelier than their counterparts in Croatia, who are supposedly collectivistic.[22] Clearly, these exceptions to the relationship between loneliness and the individualism versus collectivism dichotomy beg for further research, but they do suggest that the dichotomy does not seem to be as effective or strong as some researchers have believed in explaining loneliness.

Beyond individualist or collectivist cultures, researchers studying loneliness among older people in Europe have examined the following factors: living arrangements, family structures, health conditions, social networks, and others.[23] The variation among European societies in the prevalence of loneliness suggests that human development factors such as economic conditions, education, and cultural values may play important roles as well, but these connections are rarely, if ever, examined. It is therefore useful to clearly spell out the sensible relationship of the prevalence of loneliness to each of the potential country-level factors with brief explanation, which is the task of the next section.

Further national level factors for loneliness

The shortage of research on macro-level factors for loneliness and the limitations of the individualism versus collectivism dichotomy mean that we need to move on by exploring the existing measures of culture and other national indicators. For cultural effects on the prevalence of loneliness at the national level, let's examine the six cultural dimensions developed by Geert Hofstede, who created a framework of measuring national cultures when studying how national culture affected values at workplaces.[24] Since then this scheme has been expanded[25] into six cultural dimensions that 'represent independent preferences for one state of affairs over another that distinguish countries (rather than individuals) from each other',[26] and further more specific definition of each dimension shall be provided below. So far the relationship of each dimension with loneliness remains unexplored; however, as all six dimensions broadly relate to norms of social relations, it should be reasonable to expect cultures with less suppressing social norms to enjoy lower prevalence of loneliness.

Next, the reader may have already noticed in the above-mentioned gradient of loneliness in Europe that economically more developed countries tend to have lower rates of loneliness. More specifically, the relationship between gross domestic product (GDP) per capita and the prevalence of loneliness is expected to be negative. Indeed, people living in economically deprived regions are found to be prone to experiencing social exclusion and more intense loneliness.[27] In addition, the percentage of GDP that a country spent on social spending (welfare and benefits) is expected to be negatively associated with the prevalence of loneliness as well. The underlying mechanisms remain to be explored and confirmed, but it could be that economic support offers people more opportunities to establish and enjoy social relations.

Two other economic factors are expected to be associated with the prevalence of loneliness as well. First, countries with higher unemployment rates are expected to have higher rates of lonely people, probably because adults have to sacrifice their social life in searching for, or maintaining, employment. Second, the prevalence of loneliness is expected to be higher in more unequal countries,[28] probably because inequalities induce various forms of social isolation.

Finally, three socio-demographic factors are expected to be associated with the prevalence of loneliness at the country level. As loneliness is widely perceived as a problem for older people,[29] a country with a higher percentage of older people is expected to have a higher rate of loneliness, and children were not eligible for participating in the survey from which the dataset analysed in this study (see below). In addition, it seems sensible to expect a positive association between the divorce rate and the prevalence of loneliness. Lastly, countries with higher net migration rates are expected to have higher rates of loneliness, as the quality of life in a country with positive net migration rate should be lower and migration is detrimental to social life, which in turn increases loneliness.

Listed below are the risk factors (or explanatory variables) expected to be associated with the prevalence of loneliness at the country level. Normality of each factor's distribution was tested because it is desirable for Pearson's correlation coefficients although not necessary for constructing regression models. When a variable's distribution is not normal, a transformed value is tested and used if found normal; otherwise, Spearman's rank correlation coefficient is used. Normality was tested with the Shapiro – Wilk statistic: if its corresponding p-value is above 0.05, then the variable's distribution is perceived as normal. To start with, here are the definitions of Hofstede's six cultural dimensions, extracted from their website:[30]

- *Power distance index (PDI)*: 'the degree to which the less powerful members of a society accept and expect that power is distributed unequally'.
- *Individualism versus collectivism (IDV)*: 'individualism can be defined as a preference for a loosely-knit social framework in which individuals are expected to take care of only themselves and their immediate families. Its opposite, collectivism, represents a preference for a tightly-knit framework in society in which individuals can expect their relatives or members of a particular in-group to look after them in exchange for unquestioning loyalty.'
- *Masculinity versus femininity (MAS)*: 'The Masculinity side of this dimension represents a preference in society for achievement, heroism, assertiveness and material rewards for success. Society at large is more competitive. Its opposite, femininity, stands for a preference for cooperation, modesty, caring for the weak and quality of life. Society at large is more consensus-oriented.'
- *Uncertainty avoidance index (UAI)*: 'the degree to which the members of a society feel uncomfortable with uncertainty and ambiguity . . . Countries exhibiting strong UAI maintain rigid codes of belief and behaviour and are intolerant of unorthodox behaviour and ideas. Weak UAI societies maintain a more relaxed attitude in which practice counts more than principles.'
- *Long term orientation versus short term normative orientation (LTO)*: 'Societies who score low on this dimension . . . prefer to maintain time-honoured traditions and norms while viewing societal change with suspicion. Those with a culture which scores high . . . take a more pragmatic approach: they encourage thrift and efforts in modern education as a way to prepare for the future.'
- *Indulgence versus restraint (IND)*: 'Indulgence stands for a society that allows relatively free gratification of basic and natural human drives related to enjoying life and having fun. Restraint stands for a society that suppresses gratification of needs and regulates it by means of strict social norms.'

The scores for each dimension range from 0 to 100, and they are relative, not absolute. Of these dimensions, only IDV has been studied and found significant in affecting loneliness.[31] Cyprus is excluded from analyses of these dimensions due to the unavailability of its scores. Four of the six dimensions have passed the Shapiro – Wilk's normality test, but IDV and IND did not ($p = 0.026$ and $p = 0.024$, respectively), and no transformed values were found normal.

Here are the details of other factors and the respective sources of data:

- *GDP per capita (thousand US dollars; World Bank)*: Its distribution does not pass the normality test (Shapiro – Wilk statistic = 0.907, p = 0.008), so the logarithm with base 10 was taken to make it normal (Shapiro – Wilk = 0.962, p = 0.293).
- *Percentage of GDP on social spending (2012–2013)*: The data come from the Organisation for Economic Co-operation and Development, except for Albania, whose data come from International Monetary Fund (2015). Unfortunately, no reliable statistics about this variable can be found for Ukraine. This variable has passed the Shapiro – Wilk's normality test.
- *Unemployment rate (the share of the labor force without work but available for and seeking employment; World Bank)*: This variable did not pass the Shapiro – Wilk test for normality (0.893, p = 0.004) due to the high rate of unemployment in Spain (25.2%) as an outlier. Without Spain, the distribution becomes normal (0.965, p = 0.368). Later, separate association statistics are to be presented with and without Spain.
- *Gini coefficient as an indicator of inequality*: The figures for most countries come from Eurostat; those for Albania, Russia and Ukraine come from the World Bank. No Gini coefficient for Israel is available for 2012 and therefore is substituted with the figure for 2010. The distribution of this variable is barely normal (Shapiro – Wilk = 0.941, p = 0.073) but highly normal with natural logarithm transformation (0.968, p = 0.415).
- *Human Development Index (HDI; United Nations)*: Designed for measuring non-economic indicators of human development, HDI is the geometric mean of normalized indices for each of the following three dimensions: long and healthy life, being knowledgeable, and have a decent standard of living. It has a normal distribution.
- *Net migration rate (the difference between the total number of immigrants and the total number of emigrants; World Bank)*: The figure for each country is an estimate for the five year period of 2010 to 2015, standardized by the country's population size of 2012 and then multiplied by 1000 in order to make the figures in the range comparable with other variables. The transformed variable has a normal distribution.
- *Percentage of people aged 60+ (United Nations)*: This variable has a skewed distribution to the lower end and therefore does not pass the normality test (p = 0.004), and no transformation could improve normality.
- *Divorce-to-marriage ratio (various sources)*: The ratio of the crude divorce rate to the crude marriage rate came from Divorce Demography, which was compiled from government statistics offices. Note that the year of ratio for each nation varies from 2008 (Greece) to 2013 (Ireland). Further data for this variable were extracted from Divorce Science that compiled 'Updated World Divorce Rates, 2012' for seventy countries. The figures for UK, Iceland, Italy, Israel, and Cyprus are for 2011, and the figure for Greece is for 2008. This variable has a normal distribution.

For the relationship between the prevalence of loneliness and each of the risk predictors, Table 8.2 presents the Pearson's (or Spearman's) correlation coefficients (r) alongside the descriptive statistics of each predictor.[32] The last column clearly shows that the strongest and statistically the most significant correlations are found between the prevalence of loneliness and the following two predictors: log(GDP per capita) and HDI. That is, the wealthier the country, or the higher the country's human development score, the lower its prevalence of frequent loneliness, and the strength of the associations is very high (above 0.7).

Four out of Hofstede's six cultural dimensions – PDI (power distance index), IDV (individualism versus collectivism), UAI (uncertainty avoidance index) and IND (indulgence versus restraint) – are strongly associated with the prevalence of loneliness. The mildly strong association between PDI and loneliness suggests that the more tolerant the people in a country of unequal distribution of power, the higher the prevalence of loneliness. Similarly, the association between IDV and loneliness is also mildly strong but negative; that is, the more individualist a country's culture, the lower the prevalence of loneliness. Next, the strong and positive relationship between UAI and loneliness means that stronger commitment to rigid beliefs and behavioural principles as a way of avoiding uncertainty comes with a higher level of prevalence of loneliness; in other words, a culture

Table 8.2 Descriptive statistics of potential predictors and bivariate correlations.

	Domain	Mean	s.d.	Pearson's r with loneliness
Prevalence of loneliness	(2.2, 20.5)	8.52	4.14	
Log(GDP per capita)	(0.59, 2.01)	1.39	0.35	−0.771**
% GDP on social spending	(14.0, 32.8)	22.41	5.31	−0.307
Unemployment rate (with Spain)	(3.2, 25.2)	9.50	4.32	0.095
Unemployment rate (without Spain)	(3.2, 15.6)	9.01	3.32	0.125
Ln(Gini coefficient)	(3.11, 3.76)	3.39	0.16	0.330
HDI	(0.74, 0.96)	0.86	0.05	−0.747**
1000 × (standardized net migration rate)	(−56.74, 47.80)	2.18	22.16	−0.285
% 60+	(14, 27)	22.22	3.2	−0.077
Divorce/marriage	(13, 71)	43.88	14.94	0.097
PDI	(11, 100)	52.37	24.51	0.570**
IDV	(20, 89)	56.22	19.10	−0.424*
MAS	(5, 100)	44.47	25.74	0.251
UAI	(23, 100)	69.97	21.42	0.646**
LTO	(24, 83)	56.69	17.64	0.302
IND	(13, 78)	41.68	20.43	−0.684**

**: Correlation is significant at the 0.01 level (2-tailed).
*: Correlation is significant at the 0.05 level (2-tailed).

Table 8.3 Simple linear regression models on the prevalence of loneliness.

	b	Standardized b	s.e.	95% CI	R^2	Adjusted R^2
Log(GDP per capita)	−9.11	−0.77	1.35	(−11.87, −6.35)	0.59	0.58
HDI	−57.28	−0.75	9.15	(−75.94, −38.61)	0.56	0.54
PDI	0.10	0.57	0.03	(0.05, 0.15)	0.33	0.30
IDV	−0.09	−0.42	0.04	(−0.17, −0.02)	0.18	0.15
UAI	0.13	0.65	0.03	(0.07, 0.18)	0.42	0.40
IND	−0.14	−0.68	0.03	(−0.20, −0.09)	0.47	0.45

more tolerant of different beliefs and moral codes would enjoy a lower level of loneliness. Finally, as a higher score of IND means suppression of basic human needs, it is not surprising to see the strong and negative correlation between this predictor and the prevalence of loneliness.

Results of the simple linear regression models (Table 8.3) add further and more accurate information about the effect of each risk factor on the prevalence of loneliness. Both GDP per capita and HDI have the highest impact on the prevalence of loneliness, shown in both standardized as well as unstandardized coefficients, and they explain more than 50% of the national variation of loneliness. In comparison, the cultural factors, particularly PDI and IDV, are less powerful in explaining the prevalence of loneliness.

Here we have put the individualism versus collectivism dichotomy in a much wider context by bringing in other nation-level factors. A key finding of the above analysis is that compared with some other cultural factors (PDI, UAI and IND), the individualist/collectivist dichotomy actually has a weaker association with the prevalence of loneliness. Therefore, other cultural dimensions deserve more serious attention from researchers in searching for macro-level effects on the prevalence of loneliness. First of all, UAI and IND are discovered to have the strongest associations with the prevalence of loneliness, and they are highly correlated between themselves – to avoid uncertainty requires restraint. How do they help us understand the prevalence of loneliness? While the discovery and confirmation of the actual mechanisms have to be left to future studies, a theory could be proposed here: a society of low UAI and high IND scores offer a *socially liberal* environment in which its residents could establish and enjoy social relations more freely without having to worry about potential retributions, which in turn will reduce their chance of feeling lonely. A socially liberal culture will enjoy lower prevalence of loneliness by allowing its members to obtain the social relations they desire.

The dimension of PDI also describes the environment in which social relations are obtained and maintained, but in a different way. It refers to the relations between the powerful and the powerless, as it measures the level of acceptance of unequal power distribution by the less powerful members. Note that the meaning of 'power' is intentionally broad here, including not merely political power but other forms of power, such as parents' authority over children or any status-based forms of power. In this sense, a culture of higher power distance would restrict the chance of setting up social relations, thereby eventually increase the prevalence of loneliness. Let's summarize the situation as the following theoretical proposition: *a culture that emphasizes status-based power relations among its members will experience higher prevalence of loneliness.*

That GPD per capita and HDI are the two factors most strongly associated with the prevalence of loneliness is another important finding of this study. When researchers see loneliness as an individual and psychological problem, economic and human developments would not even appear on their radar. While it is the task for future research to identify the working mechanisms that causally connect economic and human developments and loneliness, the results of this study suggest a plausible explanation: these development indicators might be associated with a particular form of culture which in turn is associated with the prevalence of loneliness at the country level. To illustrate, Table 8.4 presents the correlation matrix of these factors.

Given that GDP per capita is a component of HDI, the strong correlation between the logarithm of GDP per capita and HDI is not surprising. On the other hand, it indicates that people in economically more prosperous countries enjoy other human development benefits (longer life expectancy, better education, etc.) as well. We have found *a new benefit of living in an economically more prosperous country: lower prevalence of loneliness.*

Furthermore, economic and human developments are found to be strongly associated with a particular form of culture. The most outstanding cultural dimension is IND, which has a correlation coefficient higher than 0.8 with each of the two development indicators. This means that people in economically more developed countries can indulge themselves with an enjoyable life not merely in the materialist sense *but also in the social sense of not having to worry about restrictive social norms.* PDI is also strongly correlated with the development indicators,

Table 8.4 Correlation matrix of selected factors associated with the prevalence of loneliness.

	Log (GDP per capita)	HDI	PDI	INV	UAI	IND
Log (GDP per capita)	1	.952**	−.708**	.658**	−.515**	.859**
HDI		1	−.723**	.663**	−.503**	.817**
PDI			1	−.638**	.584**	−.650**
INV				1	−.588**	.520**
UAI					1	−.555**
IND						1

**: correlation significant at the 0.01 level (2-tailed).

but unsurprisingly in the negative direction; clearly, this is because PDI and IND are strongly and negatively correlated (−0.65). In other words, a culturally liberal and tolerant society would see much shorter power distance among its members. Together, the strong correlations among these factors mean that developmental and cultural factors tend to cluster together in representing a particular social and cultural environment. It seems highly plausible that their collective effects are behind the national prevalence of loneliness, at least for the case of Europe.

It might be obvious but still important to point out that the results and analyses presented in this chapter depend on the selected variables and the data collected to realize these variables. Concerned with other theoretical or substantive issues, other researchers may select different variables or different measures of the same variables. Next, whether the studied cases (European countries in this study) are independent of each other is an important issue (or assumption) in quantitative analysis. For a variety of reasons (either historical or cultural), some European countries are more strongly related to one another than with other countries. I could neither deny nor dismiss the likely dependence among the studied European countries in terms of the selected variables; in fact, it has generated some evidence for certain clustering of these countries. It is however beyond our analysis here to find out whether some countries are dependent on each other so heavily that it becomes statistically inappropriate to employ the statistical methods used here. The meaning of statistical significance is another widely reported and debated issue, particularly when the data do not come from a probability sample of a population.[33] It should be made clear that the 33 countries in this study do *not* constitute a probability sample of the population 'European countries'. Without going into further details, suffice it to add that statistical significance could still be meaningful in such circumstance, although its meaning may be somewhat different from what is usually understood. Finally, no causal claims are made here, not simply because of the well-known caveat 'correlation is not causation' but more fundamentally because the variables used in such macro-level studies 'have no causal power in themselves' as they 'merely reflect concrete, micro-level phenomena that are causally related'[34]. When the causal relations and processes at the micro-level are intractable, macro-level regularities are all what social scientists could study. To discover the mechanisms through which the country level factors identified above affect the chance of loneliness at the individual level in a reliable way, further qualitative case studies on particular social contexts would be very useful.

Why are the Russians and eastern Europeans so lonely?

Results presented in the previous section have offered more clues to the varying national disposition towards loneliness. While they demonstrate the connections between some important factors and the prevalence of loneliness at the national level, they remain unsatisfactory in certain ways: the variables are restricted to those for which we could collect relevant information, it is difficult to understand how the effects of those factors translate into impacts on people's daily lives, and they may have missed many causes of loneliness that are specific to a particular nation, region, or social groups. In terms of the national prevalence of frequent loneliness, the contrast between Russia and some eastern European countries (Ukraine, Hungary) on the one hand and the Nordic countries on the other is particularly remarkable. Unfortunately, the resources currently available are so limited that it would not be possible for researchers to provide a convincing solution to this puzzle. My search for reports on loneliness in Russia and eastern Europe has been very disappointing: it is an irony that there are more academic studies about loneliness in western and northern European countries, where, as we have seen, loneliness is much less prevalent, than in Russia and eastern European countries, who have suffered from much higher rates of frequent loneliness. Perhaps this is not surprising. As healthy people are more likely to pay serious attention to their health, the countries with lower levels of loneliness are the ones that take loneliness more seriously, either because these countries could afford to doing so, or because they have already paid serious attention to loneliness for some time. What I shall do in this section is to present some plausible theories or hypotheses by drawing on either logical reasoning or supporting results produced by other researchers.

In searching for the macro-level factors for the various rates of frequent loneliness in Europe, we cannot help but thinking its history after the Second World War. While western and northern European countries enjoyed decades of political stability and economic growth, which in turn dramatically improved ordinary people's quality of life, countries of the former Soviet bloc suffered from political upheavals, suppressions of individual liberties, and economic stagnations and even deteriorations. After the collapse of the former USSR, the breakdown of the Berlin Wall, the unification of the former two Germanys, and the expansion of the European Union, the situations in Russia and eastern European countries have improved. In many ways, these macro-level dramatic changes have induced further changes to individual citizens' lives, which are expected to have changed their physical and psychological wellbeing. The trouble is that to a large extent we can only speculate but cannot be specific about how these have happened. For example, with many people at employment age being able to search for opportunities relatively richer countries in the European Union, their social relations should have undergone some strains, which then should make them more likely to be lonely. Disappointingly, we do not have much good data to demonstrate that this is indeed the case.

William Cockerham, a well-established medical sociologist, was facing the same problem when he was trying to explain why life expectancy in Russia and eastern Europe declined. More generally, the overall health conditions of people in Russia and eastern Europe have declined when the whole system of the former Soviet Union was starting to crumble. He described the irony of the situation in these countries at the beginning of his book:

> One of the most significant developments in world health in the late twentieth century is the decline in life expectancy in the former Soviet Union

and Eastern Europe. This situation is without precedent in modern history. Nowhere else has health worsened so seriously in peacetime among industrialized nations. Ironically, these countries sponsored a communist ideology of socioeconomic equality that theoretically should have promoted health for all. However, the reverse occurred, and life expectancy for many people has been declining for over three decades.[35]

Since the publication of Cockerham's book in 1999, the situation has improved. According to the data of World Bank, Russia's life expectancy has reached a record high of 70.91 years. On the other hand, Russia still lags behind other industrialized nations such as the US and the UK, where life expectancy is 78.74 and 81.60 years, respectively. Other members of the former Soviet bloc have about the same story, although the extent of improvement varies; for example, Ukraine has experienced the least improvement while Poland has been doing exceptionally well, catching up with the US at the moment.

Life expectancy is only one indicator that reflects the overall health condition of a particular country for a particular time period. Related to life expectancy is a whole series of living conditions that affect people's physical and mental health. It is next to impossible to imagine that people remain emotionally healthy when they experience a series of difficulties in their lives: shortages of food and fuel, an ineffective, bureaucratic, and even corrupt administrative system, restrictions on many areas of daily activities, suspicion and mistrust among people. These and other institutional and societal factors are responsible for how healthy a population could be; they are the social origins of health. Cockerham resorted to the concept of 'social stress' to capture the social aspects of psychological stress, which seems to have two meanings. The first is that people of different classes have differing capabilities to cope with stress, but it is the second meaning of 'social stress' that I have found particularly useful:

> While much of the research concerning stress focuses on small group interaction or micro-level stressors that affect individuals in their everyday life, macro-level stressors originating in the wider society also promote stress. That is, society can create stressful situations that force people to respond to conditions not of their own choosing.[36]

As stress is expected to be correlated with loneliness, it should be useful for our purposes to study these 'macro-level stressors'. In his book, Cockerham wrote a section on 'social stress' about each of the following countries: Russia, Hungary, Poland, The Czech Republic and Slovakia, Romania, Bulgaria, and East Germany. Unfortunately, he repeatedly complained about the lack of data that could let him show how societal phenomena, particularly economic failures, political turmoil, structural constraints on personal aspirations, and the lack of freedom, had made people stressed. It remains a hypothesis that these macro-level events have made people in Russia and eastern Europe much lonelier than those in western and northern Europe – we still have a long way to go in understanding the process of how events and processes at the macro level change people's health on the ground, but I believe most readers will find it a plausible hypothesis.

Here let me offer a theory of how macro-level events listed above make ordinary people lonely. Perhaps we could call it *the embarrassment theory of loneliness*: assuming that it is embarrassing for people to talk about their difficulties in life to others, and that the need to talk to others in hope of obtaining support is the stronger when people face difficulties, the suppression of such need for fear of embarrassment makes people feel lonely. If this theory is correct, then the higher prevalence of frequent loneliness in Russia and eastern Europe could be explained by the higher number and severity of difficulties in ordinary people's lives, which have been brought about by political conflicts, economic stagnations, social inequalities, structural unfairness, and other macro-level problems. More specifically, these national level difficulties represent themselves as daily difficulties for ordinary people: low wages or even unemployment, lack of access to healthcare when being ill, administrative barriers to setting up and running a private business, and many more. When people experience any of these difficulties, they feel stressed, perhaps even depressed. However, they would find it very difficult to talk to anybody about their situations and feelings, either because the people they could talk to, such as their family members, are not able to help, or because they cannot talk to those who could help, mainly those in powerful and resourceful positions. The sense of hopelessness of resolving their difficulties by talking to someone is a major source of loneliness in these countries. There is no doubt that this theory realizes itself in many different ways in real life, depending on the nature and the level of the difficulty, the strength of the embarrassed feeling, and the relations between people, but it is my hope that the reader will find it a useful tool for understanding the high prevalence of loneliness in Russia and eastern Europe.

This theory has another corollary, which I hope the reader will find sensible and useful: *loneliness rarely comes on its own; it usually comes with other negative emotions*, such as anxiety, depression, sadness, sorrow, and hopelessness. We can use this theory in two ways, or in other words, if this corollary is correct, we would expect that the following two hypotheses are also true: (1) Russia and eastern European countries are among the countries that have highest rates of unhappy people in Europe; (2) within Russia or an eastern European country that has a high prevalence of loneliness, being lonely is highly correlated with other forms of psychological problems, such as anxiety or depression.

First, it is reasonable to expect a correlated but not deterministic relationship between loneliness and happiness. It is incredible to expect people to be happy when they are lonely, but it is possible that some people are not lonely but unhappy at the same time. At the country level, this means that countries whose citizens are happy should have low prevalence of loneliness, but on the other hand, countries with high prevalence of loneliness may not rank very low on happiness although they should not rank high on happiness. As happiness has become an increasingly important issue across the whole world, we now draw on the well-prepared World

Happiness Report. The most recent report (2017) includes a ranking of one hundred and fifty-five countries in terms of happiness based on data collected from 2014 to 2016.[37] We can see almost the same pattern as we saw in the pattern of the prevalence of loneliness previously – here, we focus on European countries in order to compare with our previous findings: Seven northern European countries are at the top ten happiest (plus Canada, Australia and New Zealand), followed by most western European countries (the UK, Germany, Belgium, Luxemburg, etc.), then the southern European countries (Spain), and finally Russia and eastern European countries (Poland). Similar to the situation of loneliness as pointed out before, there are a few exceptions. Of the eastern European countries, the Czech Republic fares best, ranked the 23rd in the world, and of western and southern European countries, France and Italy do not rank as high as expected. Russia was in a higher position than expected, while as expected, Hungary ranked very low among European countries. My theory expects Ukraine to rank low in happiness, but it was a big surprise to see that it was actually worse than expected: it was 132nd out of the 155 countries.[38] It should be very clear that the Ukrainians are not just lonely, they are very unhappy. And the sources of their unhappiness go far beyond individual attributes such as gender, age, or even physical health; things much bigger and at the macro level – political uncertainties, lack of safety and security, unemployment, lack of supply of daily essentials – are at work.

Second, let's take a look at the relationship between loneliness and other emotions in these countries. Luckily, alongside the question measuring the frequency of loneliness, the seventh round of the European Social Survey (2012) also included several questions about the respondent's psychological wellbeing. Here, we focus on the questions that asked the respondents 'how much of the time during the past week' they felt 'depressed', 'happy', 'sad', 'anxious', or 'calm and peaceful'. As shown previously in Figure 3.5, Hungary, Russia and Ukraine had the highest levels of frequent loneliness in that survey, so we study the relationship between loneliness and these emotions in these three countries. Here, it would be rather cumbersome to use percentages to demonstrate the relationships; instead, I shall employ gamma, a statistic that is designed particularly for measuring the strength of the relationship between two ordinal variables – all of the variables analysed here have four values in a ranking order: 1 = 'none or almost none of the time', 2 = 'some of the time', 3 = 'most of the time', and 4 = 'all or almost all of the time'. The results are presented in Table 8.5.[39]

The values of gamma range from −1 to +1, with 0 indicating no relationship. Absolute values – with the sign ignored – around 0.5 suggest strong relationship in the social sciences. And the three stars – a common practice in quantitative social science publications – tell us how unlikely the value calculated from this sample could not be about the same as the value for the whole population. Clearly, these numbers lend very strong support to the theory that loneliness rarely comes by itself as a negative emotion; more often than not it comes with other unpleasant emotions listed above, and the list is certainly not complete, perhaps not even comprehensive. Note that the strong relationship between loneliness and each of

Table 8.5 Gamma for respective pairwise relationship between loneliness and other emotions in Hungary, Russia and Ukraine, 2012.

	n	Depressed	Happy	Sad	Anxious	Calm
Hungary	1,996	0.587***	−0.518***	0.696***	0.564***	−0.411***
Russia	2,405	0.643***	−0.404***	0.697***	0.575***	−0.395***
Ukraine	2,083	0.638***	−0.365***	0.709***	0.632***	−0.313***

***: $p < 0.001$.

the other emotions is very likely true in other countries as well, although not as strong as they are in these three countries. What makes these strong relationships matter is the implication of these numbers: these three countries had the highest levels of frequent loneliness in Europe in 2012, and because the lonely people are very likely to be depressed, unhappy, sad, anxious, and not calm at the same time, we could understand why they were so lonely if we could understand why they were experiencing other negative emotions. I would even venture to argue that many ordinary people in these countries might not even realize what kind of negative emotion they had; they only know they were feeling very bad, and they only became to realize the exact nature of their emotions when being asked to consider each emotion separately by the survey interviewer. As one painful emotion could trigger another, any macro-level event bringing about any of these emotions would bring about the sense of loneliness. Without relevant and reliable data, this is the explanation for the relatively high prevalence of frequent loneliness in Russia and eastern European countries that I could offer at the moment.

Notes

1 J. de Jong Gierveld, T. van Tilburg, and P. A. Dykstra. 2006. 'Loneliness and social isolation', in A. Vangelisti and D. Perlman (eds), *Cambridge Handbook of Personal Relationships*. Cambridge: Cambridge University Press, p. 491.
2 I have presented some results in a paper produced with Professor Christina Victor: K. Yang and C. Victor. 2011. 'Age and loneliness in 25 European nations', *Ageing and Society*, 31(8): 1368–1388.
3 S. Babones. 2013. *Methods for Quantitative Macro-Comparative Research*. Thousand Oaks, CA: Sage Publications, p. 6.
4 É. Durkheim. [1909] 1982. 'The contribution of sociology to psychology and philosophy', *The Rules of Sociological Method*, ed. with an introduction by S. Lukes, trans. W. D. Halls. New York: The Free Press, p. 237.
5 É. Durkheim. [1897] 2006. *On Suicide*, trans. R. Buss. London: Penguin Books, p. 24. The emphasis was added.
6 M. Jylhä and J. Jokela. 1990. 'Individual experiences as cultural: a cross-cultural study on loneliness among the elderly', *Ageing and Society*, 10: 295–315; G. Sundström, E. Fransson, B. Malmberg, and A. Davey. 2009. 'Loneliness among older Europeans', *European Journal of Ageing*, 6(4): 267–275; A. Walker and T. Maltby. 1997. *Ageing Europe*. Buckingham: Open University Press; G. C. Wenger, R. Davies,

S. Shahtahmesebi, and A. Scott. 1996. 'Social isolation and loneliness in old age: review and model refinement', *Ageing & Society*, 16(3): 333–358.

7 N. Stevens and G. J. Westerhof. 2006. 'Marriage, social integration, and loneliness in the second half of life: a comparison of Dutch and German men and women', *Research on Aging*, 28: 713–729.

8 Yang and Victor, 'Age and loneliness in 25 European nations'.

9 J. de Jong Gierveld and C. Tesch-Römer. 2012. 'Loneliness in old age in Eastern and Western European societies: theoretical perspectives', *European Journal of Ageing*, 9(4): 285–295.

10 The percentages were calculated with design weight for each country except for Austria, Latvia, and Romania where no design weight is available.

11 De Jong Gierveld et al., 'Loneliness and social isolation'.

12 P. Johnson and L. Mullins. 1987. 'Growing old and lonely in different societies: toward a comparative perspective', *Journal of Cross-Cultural Gerontology*, 2: 7–27.

13 S. Stack. 1998. 'Marriage, family and loneliness: a cross-national study', *Sociological Perspectives*, 41: 415–432.

14 Johnson and Mullins, 'Growing old and lonely in different societies'.

15 Jylhä and Jokela, 'Individual experiences as cultural'.

16 N. Medora, J. Woodward and J. Larson. 1987. 'Adolescent loneliness: a cross-cultural comparison of American and Asian Indians', *International Journal of Comparative Sociology*, 28: 205.

17 A. Rokach, T. Orzeck, M. C. Moya and F. Expósito. 2002. 'Causes of loneliness in North America and Spain', *European Psychologist*, 7(1): 70.

18 A. Rokach. 2007. 'The effect of age and culture on the causes of loneliness', *Social Behavior and Personality*, 35: 169–186.

19 A. Rokach, T. Orzeck, J. Cripps, K. Lackovic-Grgin and Z. Penezic. 2001. 'The effects of culture on the meaning of loneliness', *Social Indicators Research*, 53: 17–31.

20 V. A. Lykes and M. Kemmelmeier 2014. 'What predicts loneliness? Cultural differences between individualistic and collectivistic societies in Europe', *Journal of Cross-Cultural Psychology*, 45(3): 468–490.

21 K. Yang and C. Victor. 2008. 'The prevalence of and risk factors for loneliness among older people in China', *Ageing & Society*, 28(3): 305–327.

22 A. Rokach, T. Orzeck, and F. Neto. 2004. 'Coping with loneliness in old age: a cross-cultural comparison', *Current Psychology*, 23: 124–137; A. Rokach and F. Neto. 2005. 'Age, culture, and the antecedents of loneliness', *Social Behaviour and Personality*, 33: 477–494; A. Rokach. 2008. 'Coping with loneliness in North America and Spain', *Psychology Journal*, 5: 51–68.

23 P. A. Dykstra. 2009. 'Older adult loneliness: myths and realities', *European Journal of Ageing*, 6: 91–100; T. Fokkema, J. de Jong Gierveld, and P. A. Dykstra. 2012. 'Cross-national differences in older adult loneliness', *The Journal of Psychology*, 146(1–2): 201–228.

24 G. Hofstede. 1980. *Culture's Consequences: International Differences in Work-Related Values*. Beverly Hills: Sage.

25 G. Hofstede. 2001. *Culture's Consequences: International Differences in Work-Related Values*, 2nd edition. Beverly Hills, CA: Sage; G. Hofstede, G. J. Hofstede, and M. Minkov. 2010. *Cultures and Organizations: Software of the Mind: Intercultural Cooperation and its Importance for Survival*. New York: McGraw-Hill.

26 See their website at https://geert-hofstede.com.

27 A. M. O'Rand. 2001. 'Stratification and the life course: the forms of life-course capital and their interrelationships', in R. H. Binstock & L. K. George (eds), *Handbook of Aging and the Social Sciences*, 5th edition. New York: Academic Press, pp. 197–213; T. Scharf, C. Phillipson, and A. E. Smith. 2004. 'Poverty and social exclusion: growing

older in deprived urban neighbourhoods', in A. Walker and A. Hennessy (eds), *Growing Older: Quality of Life in Old Age*. Maidenhead: Open University Press, pp. 81–106.

28 Scharf et al, 'Poverty and social exclusion: growing older in deprived urban neighbourhoods'.

29 C. Victor, S. Scambler, and J. Bond. 2009. *The Social World of Older People*. Maidenhead: Open University Press.

30 See https://geerthofstede.com/culture-geert-hofstede-gert-jan-hofstede/6d-model-of-national-culture.

31 Lykes and Kemmelmeier, 'What predicts loneliness?'.

32 Bivariate scatterplots are better tools for examining such relationships, but to save space, they are not presented here.

33 See Babones, *Methods for Quantitative Macro-Comparative Research*, pp. 108ff.

34 Ibid., p. 8.

35 W. C. Cockerham. 1999. *Health and Social Change in Russia and Eastern Europe*. New York: Routledge, p. 1.

36 Ibid., p. 41.

37 The full report can be found at http://worldhappiness.report/ed/2017.

38 Professor Richard Rose reported some statistics about happiness in some countries of the Russian Federation in 2003: R. Rose. 2003. *Health, Money, and Wellbeing: Subjective Responses to Post-Soviet Transformation*, Studies in Public Policy series no. 380, Centre for the Study of Public Policy, University of Strathclyde, available online at www.abdn.ac.uk/socsci/documents/Rose_2003.pdf. The data came from 'an eight-nation survey in autumn, 2001 of Living Conditions, Lifestyle and Health (LLH) in the Commonwealth of Independent States (CIS), covering the Russian Federation, Armenia, Belarus, Georgia, Kazakhstan, Kyrgizstan, Moldova, and Ukraine . . . In each country a minimum of 2000 respondents were interviewed face-to-face by national research institutes between 25 October and 6 December 2001 . . . ' (p. 6). It was found that 21% were very happy, 43% fairly happy, 17% not very happy, 8% very unhappy, and 12% don't know (p. 8). It is difficult to put these results into any context as no country-level statistics were presented and the measurement might be different from those used in other surveys.

39 Statistics in this table were calculated with design weight.

Chapter 9

Tackling loneliness
Messages to the lonely and the non-lonely

In the previous chapters I have tried to answer the following questions: what loneliness means, who as groups are lonely, and what make them lonely. This chapter is very different: it is about what we can do about loneliness as a social problem. It may be impossible to eliminate loneliness – or any other social problem such as crimes and conflicts – completely, but that should not mean we cannot reduce the chance or the level of loneliness. Again, I emphasize the word 'social' in the sense that it is not merely a psychological or individual problem; it is a social problem because different social groups suffer from it at different degrees and for different reasons, and ultimately, such uneven distributions relate to issues such as inequality and injustice. Loneliness goes far beyond any particular individual's mind; its origins are social: broken families, immigrations, discriminations of one social group against another, bullying and abuse, stigma, ostracism, exclusion, or other forms of social hostility and antagonism. If so, isn't it logical, if not completely obvious, that we should tackle loneliness as a social problem? This does not mean, of course, that we should not offer psychological or psychoanalytic support and help to lonely individuals. It means that such individual-focused support is far from sufficient or efficient. If a large number of people suffer from loneliness for a common reason at the societal level, surely it should be more effective and efficient to deal with that societal reason. The absence of suggested solutions to loneliness at the social level (groups, classes, nations, cultures) is reflected in the publications in the category of 'self-help'. We are not short of books that offer advice to the lonely individual;[1] tackling loneliness should not be a task only for the lonely individual, but few self-help books, if any, have delved into the causes beyond the individual and thus offer strategies and tactics to be employed by the lonely individual. Loneliness should not be just a problem for the lonely; to maximize our chance of eradicating this special form of mental suffering, the non-lonely must do something as well. Loneliness is not just a problem for any individual; some strategies and solutions can only be implemented by society as a whole.

Following these principles, here is what I shall do in this chapter. I will go too far in the opposite direction if I completely ignore what a lonely individual should do, so I will start with some strategies and practices that I have found particularly useful for growing out of loneliness. Then I shall try to identify and suggest any possible solutions or actions that different groups of the non-lonely could take to help the lonely. I will do so as if I am writing a personal message directly to the respective individual or group of people. And the reader will see that each of my messages targets a particular group of people who have been identified as being vulnerable to a higher risk of frequent loneliness in one of the previous chapters.

I trust that the reader will understand that by no means this is a complete list of actions or solutions, and each will be working smoothly in practice; as shown in the previous chapters, loneliness could mean so many things, for so many reasons, and so many different groups of people suffer from it. Loneliness comes in many different sources and forms; it could even be specific to a particular individual at a particular moment of life. It is therefore next to impossible to come up with strategies and solutions that are effective to all of its forms. Similarly to tackling any other problem, it is all about managing the tension between generic and customized strategies. General principles and guidance may be offered, but adaptations, either straightforward or ingenious, are always desirable or even required when following them. I can only offer some advice in this chapter as both an academic who have done research on loneliness for more than ten years, as well as someone who has been lonely many times in life.

So far in this book I have avoided talking about my personal experience and feelings. In some parts of this chapter, however, I will share some of them with the reader. I admire the courage and generosity of authors like Olivia Liang and Tony Selimi, who presented the details of their life events and feelings in their books. I know this is not what academics are supposed to do; they should keep their personal values and emotions far out of the way of their work; otherwise, they become biased, and a result, the quality of their research will be compromised. I tried to keep that kind of objectivity and neutrality of my research in the previous chapters, but as I said, this one is different. After examining the 'social facts' as coldly as possible, I cannot escape from the following question anymore: 'What would you say to those you have studied, the lonely, the not lonely, those around them, those who want to help them, the government, and the general public?' It is my sincere hope that they will find something sensible and helpful, even only a little bit.

To a lonely child

I know feeling lonely is no good; I was lonely many times when I was a boy, and I know many children are lonely – some told university lecturers like me, others told their parents, and still others contacted charities either by phone or online. Actually, it is not just many children who may be lonely; many adults are lonely as well. Perhaps you already know another child or an adult who was lonely. If you are lonely, you are not alone! You feel sad, bored, and you want to get out of this kind of feeling as soon as possible.

Before you do anything, it's a good idea to calm down for a moment and think about what has been going on; this kind of thinking or reflection itself is good for you, and it's good for making what you do later more helpful. Now you have some time alone, and that's good for keeping yourself calm and doing some thinking. You see, being alone is not necessarily, definitely not always, a bad thing; it actually can be a very good thing – you can do something you choose to do without interruption! While you are growing up, you may need a number of such moments of being and thinking alone; it's something you go through to become an adult.

Now let's find out what has happened. When did you start to feel lonely? What happened so that you suddenly felt lonely? Different people feel lonely for different reasons, and the same people may become lonely for different reasons. While talking to you, I now remember some moments when I was a boy that I felt lonely, even though I might not use the word 'lonely' or 'loneliness' to describe my feeling, but now I know that was my feeling at that time. I would like to share those moments with you.

While I was at a primary school, every day I came home to find that nobody was at home: my parents worked long hours, my mother worked three shifts per week, my big sister was living in a different place, and my two brothers were in secondary schools. I was the first to come home, to find it locked, to open it without actually wanting to enter. If I was hungry, I searched for any leftover, a bun, a pancake, some noodles, or anything else.

At school, I was a shy boy; I rarely started chatting with any other child. I enjoyed learning but, strangely enough, not the breaks, because I had to think hard about how I should kill the time. I walked around the playground in a hope to find something interesting, I tried to do different things on an iron bar, or I drew something different each time with a tiny piece of chalk, very likely thrown away by a teacher. Occasionally, I was able to exchange a few words with another boy from my neighbourhood, but I didn't find that enjoyable at all. What I did enjoy was homework, particularly drawing and calligraphy. Perhaps by the genes of my father, I enjoyed producing nice and neat writings. Regardless of the subject, my work was always nicely presented. So I become what today's children would call 'a teacher's pet'. While that brought some self-confidence to me, it made some other children very unhappy; they made me even more isolated. Sometimes they even tried to bully me after school, on my way back home, so I had to find another longer route. It could be a fearful and lonely journey.

Your story could be different, of course. However, I expect it to be somehow similar to mine. Loneliness, no matter how different the way it represents itself, is always about the difficulty of connecting with others. Sometimes it happens 'naturally' because the others like your parents, siblings or other children have to do certain things that make you feel lonely but they don't realize that, such as my parents had to leave me alone at home for a few hours after school, or other children were occupied among themselves without realizing that I wanted to play with them.

Is something similar happening to you? If so, one thing you should and can do is to let your parents or any other adult family member know your feeling. I know this is much harder to do than say. When you feel lonely or isolated, you seem to have lost the energy to make the effort of talking to people; you want to stay as you are now, to be alone, to keep it to yourself. But think about what will happen if you take no action: obviously, you will keep being lonely, and that could be very bad for your health. It may sound strange, but it is indeed the case for many people that they find it not easy at all to talk to their family members about their unhappy feelings. That perhaps is more saddening than the sad feeling itself. Many children worry about how others, including their family members, will react – they may think of you in a negative way, and you may feel embarrassed as a result. No one could guarantee that they will react in a way that you like. But if they are your parents, your family members, or anyone you feel close, that is, anyone who cares about you, they will help you in the end. There is no need to make yourself look always good in front of them. Talking to someone you trust or feel comfortable is the best way to get out of loneliness.

If you feel lonely because you were bullied, it is even more important to talk about it to your parent, your guardian, your teacher, or any adult you can trust. Again, you may find it very hard to do. You may want to keep the terrible experience as a secret only to yourself. Please understand: keeping the secret itself will make you even lonelier, because by keeping the secret, you isolate yourself even more from others. You will be stressed to keep a bad experience only to yourself; you must be alert all the time, as if guarding something from attacks from all directions. Think about which situation you would prefer: talking to someone about what happened, or keeping yourself bullied? I trust you want to stop being bullied. Talking to someone about it should be much easier.

As you are alone and have a lot time now, it's a good idea to take stock of what relations you have: starting with your family members, and extending to others in your life, who they are, when you can talk to them or do things with them. And then think about what things you would prefer to do on your own. It is likely that only for a short time that you have to be alone, and that should be very bearable. Try to figure out a daily schedule in which you do things with others in some slots while on your own in other slots. If so, you may even appreciate the time being alone.

To parents

A couple of months ago, a parent of a student at my university contacted me because she found out that I did some research on loneliness. Her son, a young adult living in a college with many other peers, being supported by a team of tutors and supporting staff, and having access to many activities, social events, and facilities, had fallen into loneliness for a while. This prompted her to do some research on the Internet to find out how unusual her son's case was. While she did not find much systematic research about loneliness among university students, she did see a number of reports, either on mass media or university web pages, that depicted a worrying picture. For me as an academic in this area, I think these anecdotal stories justify the need for a more systematic approach. However, I haven't been able to find any useful data for examining how bad the situation is: there is simply no existing datasets that contain useful information about loneliness among university students; those datasets with information about loneliness did not target university students, while datasets targeting university students did not ask about loneliness. To study this issue properly, we need to collect new data.

Clearly, the mother was shocked to find out her son's loneliness. Here is a general lesson that parents may want to take from the above situation: do not assume that your child, no matter how mature you think they should be, is fine with their social and emotional life. To keep informed about their social and emotional life, however, is a big challenge. With two teenage children, I know a thing or two about how difficult it could be to communicate with them, and it is an even greater challenge to be their confidante, and I am very certain that my children are not among the most difficult ones. But if they do not make themselves accessible to you, there is a risk that sooner or later you may be shocked as the mother was. Living with peers, having support of staff members, living a life with many activities, all these, unfortunately, cannot guarantee a healthy emotional life. I would think that those parents who have little difficulty in communicating with their adolescent or young adult children are the most successful or the luckiest. But not all parents could be so capable or lucky. The bottom line is, do not assume everything is fine with your child's mental state, try as much as you can to make them like you and thus talk to you. You may be tired after work and household chores, or you don't want another issue on your mind in addition to others in your life, but your child's social and emotional life should be something at the back of your mind. Keeping alert will help you pick up the earliest signs and minimize the cost to pay in the future.

As we have learnt from a previous chapter, having a confidante is a highly effective anecdote to loneliness. I trust you would want to be a confidante of your child. But again, I can tell from my experience that although this is my intention, I don't think my children have always seen me as one. In our daily life, we give priority to many things other than our relationship with our children: deadline of delivering a piece of work, keep our job secure or get promoted, dealing with health issues of our own or our ageing parents, repairing a leaked roof or toilet, switching to a new service provider (gas, electricity, broadband), and some others. Having quality time with our children comes only after we have dealt with all these 'more important and urgent issues'. And when we do have time with our children, their homework, exams, extracurricular activities, very likely will take most if not all of it. Enhancing our relationships with our children seems to have become a luxury! If so, not feeling lonely is a luxury as well.

I also want to say a word particularly to those parents who have been experiencing a difficult time with their spouse or partner. Once I was talking to a 10-year-old boy in a pilot study about loneliness. During the conversation, he mentioned that he didn't see his dad much. Attempting to find out why, I mentioned a few possibilities: is he very busy with his work? Does he travel a lot? Then he started to try very hard to hold the tears in his eyes, telling me it was because his dad moved out after having a row with his mother. While this did not come to me as a surprise – I know how high the divorce rate is in the UK and how researchers have shown how lonely children of divorced parents were – to see a child so lonely, sad, confused, and helpless in front of me gave me another opportunity to feel the human costs of loneliness. It doesn't help simply to blame his parents or any parents in that kind of situation – no parents would intentionally inflict such pain on their children, and they may feel the whole process is out of their control. All I can say is this: please keep the emotional wellbeing of your child in mind; they will be very lonely during and after each row, and this sense of loneliness may accompany them to their adulthood and do some harm to their health.

To non-lonely siblings

Soon after my daughter was born, my wife and I decided to have another child. We realized that for my daughter to grow up happily, our love may not be enough – she will need a different kind of love, and we cannot take care of her throughout her entire life. About two years later, we had our son. We assume, or we hope, that our two children will enjoy each other's company, a relationship that we as parents cannot replace. Most of the times we are right; in fact, I felt so happy, satisfied, even self-congratulatory when seeing them play together, prepare presents under the Christmas tree together, and help each other with homework. It's not always like that, unfortunately. When they fought, particularly when one made the other one cry, I felt frustrated, miserable, and angry. I knew I should not take such fights too seriously, but when they occurred several times in a row, I started to question whether we were still that wise to have two children. These extremely different moods came to me many times during their childhood. And I know both from the people that I personally know as well as life stories that siblings could indeed be either a blessing or a trouble. Those living together have the opportunity to become either the best friends or the worst adversaries.

The question is: if you have a sister or brother, do you want to be their best friend or their worst adversary? You might say that depends on how your sibling treats you. What would your brother or sister say? I guess they will say the same. You see, we all want to be treated in the same way as we treat others, particularly our equals (siblings are our equals). I trust you would want to be in good terms with your siblings, because everybody would be happy. And because the relationship is mutual, like a loop, someone must start it off by being nice first so that the relationship will run like a happy circle; if someone starts to be mean first, the relationship will run like a sad circle, and at least one of you will be sad and lonely. I trust everyone would want the happy circle, and you will feel very good when you start it off.

To other children

We humans need different types of relationship. It was reported that an 11-year-old boy was very lonely because he did not have any friend to invite for his birthday party, even though his mother loved him very much; there are quite a number of things that he would only do with other children, his friends. He was lucky: once his story was posted on social media, many people sent him birthday presents, cards, and comforting words, which are really nice. I wonder, however, whether his mother will do that again when his next birthday comes. Even if that happens again next year, how about his daily life? I also wonder why his mother had to put his story on social media to let so many other people know; why couldn't the children in his neighbourhood come and celebrate his birthday? Why not the children in his school? What made him believe that nobody would come if he invites other children?

If you have ever been lonely, you may be able to understand how that boy felt when he thought that nobody would come to his birthday party. If you have never been lonely, you may want to think about what you would do if that boy lives near you or is in your class. You may even know some children who might be lonely as they tend to stay alone during breaks or lunch hours, sit alone on the bus of a trip, wait alone in the playground after school, or have a difficult time finding another child to work with for a group task in the classroom. We cannot say for sure that they are lonely; they may not be; they may even like to be alone at that time. But for a child, that is very unusual, so the chance that they are lonely is quite high. I trust that you, like most other children would like to be nice to other children and help them if they need it. I understand that if you have never been lonely, you may have never thought about it, until now. From now on, if you notice another child who is alone and looks down, it is very likely that they are lonely. The trouble is, few would admit it, because admitting it will make them look bad in front of others. So, you will need to be subtle a bit – avoid asking them directly 'Are you lonely?'; instead, simply talk to them about anything children normally talk about, such as a TV show, a game, a fun place, and jokes. Talking can be very powerful; it can cure, like medicine. You will feel good after helping anybody lonely.

In case you don't think it is your job to help any lonely child, at least please do not treat them badly, let alone bully them. Better still, please try to stop bully whenever you see it. I know your teacher may have already talked about this many times. I mention bullying again for a different reason: I have found that more children feel lonely if they have been bullied than those who haven't. So if you can stop bullying, you have stopped the bullied child from becoming lonely. If you can not stop it yourself, tell a teacher, a parent, or any adult you know.

Lastly, if you have bullied any other child, you should realize what you have done by now – what you have hurt others in a way that you cannot see, the damage on other children's mind, which could be much worse than a bruise or even a cut. Perhaps it was because you were bullied before by others that you think it is fine to bully other children. If so, please realize that the logic does not make sense: you cannot stop bullying by bullying others; bullying will only bring about more bullying. Or, you may feel good when you bully others – you feel you are so powerful! But keep in mind that being good is much more important than being powerful, because most people like to be on the side of the good, not necessarily the side of the powerful. Many powerful persons were the bad guys in history. The powerful may win for a while, but the good ones will win for long. In the end, do you really enjoy hurting others, making them sad, lonely, and helpless? If you don't want that happen to you, better do not do it to others.

To lonely older people

It is in vain to refuse to acknowledge the biological process of ageing: except for the very few who live an active life until the moment of leaving this world, most experience the decline of biological functions of the human body. Eyesight becomes blurred, hearing becomes a struggle, knees get weaker, lifting a bag of potatoes is a strenuous test, and many other daily life activities appear a daunting task. It would be even more frustrating if a chronic illness adds to the list. There is a great variation, of course, of how much people above a certain age suffer from these outcomes of biological ageing: some are healthier than others by either genes, disciplined self-improvement, or both. Nevertheless, for the majority, sooner or later the weakening of physiological functions is simply a fact of life. It's wiser to accept it, face it, and find ways to minimize the undesirable consequences it brings to us.

For two major reasons, this process may make you and some other older people lonely. First, your social life has changed once your biological age has reached a certain point. It is absolutely arbitrary to determine when people should retire; to make their life easier, however, governments and organizations would prefer a universal retirement age. Few of them take seriously what will happen to your social life after retirement, or they assume that you are able to live an enjoyable social life after retirement. Again, this may be true for a minority; for the majority, the size of their social circle has definitely shrunk and the number of social activities has reduced after retirement.

Second and perhaps more importantly, your social circle becomes smaller and smaller, which happens to occur alongside your biological ageing process. Starting with those older than you are – your parents, your uncles and aunts, your senior colleagues, your teachers, and then followed by those of your generation – your cousins, siblings, even your spouse, close friends, schoolmates, colleagues, the news that they are not part of your social connections anymore becomes part of your life. On the other hand, it has become a cultural norm, at least in modern Western societies, that the young adults do not live with their parents and grandparents anymore. Your adult children may still be in contact with you or visit you a few times during the year, but the frequency of their direct interactions with you has been much lower. Their children – your grandchildren – have the potential of balancing out some of your loss of social relations, but that potential will only be realized if they become a part of your daily life, which is rarely the case in many countries. On balance, you have a deficit of social relations while your biological age passes a certain point, and that is no less serious a problem than the decline of your biological functions.

Clearly, these two kinds of problem reinforce each other: on the one hand, your shrinking social network may induce some negative emotions to you – sadness, loneliness, even depression, which in turn will induce further problems in your physical health; on the other hand, your declining physical health will make it harder for you to maintain existing social relations and set up new social relations. To fight against this from developing into a vicious cycle is a major struggle of ageing.

How do you fight this battle if you are an older and lonely person? Consider the following tips by Mr Derek Taylor, a 90-year-old man from London who felt lonely and isolated following the deaths of his wife and sister. These tips were published in a booklet by Manchester City Council. Although it is very easy to find his list on the Internet, I put them here for the reader's convenience and for further considerations:

1 Make an effort to make new friends.
2 Join a hobbies club.
3 Visit your local community or resource centre and find out what's on offer.
4 Learn to use a computer at your local library.
5 Seek help from your local social services.
6 Consider taking in a lodger or paying guest.
7 Use your telephone more often to contact people; don't wait for people to contact you.
8 Contact friends and relatives you haven't spoken to recently.
9 Make friends with your neighbours.
10 Do voluntary work if you are able to.

Note that every tip starts with a verb. In this sense, all ten tips could boil down to just one: do something, do not just wait for someone to contact you – being passive or withdrawing from others is the worst of all for tackling loneliness. Take actions, initiate interactions, revive old relations, or establish new ones, make use of the resources in your community – many communities and local authorities have already realized the importance of loneliness and have started some programmes for helping the lonely, so some opportunities got to be there already for you to be social with others. So as long as you do something to help yourself, it does not really matter what you do; your list of actions does not have to be this long; it may have only one or two items, which is absolutely fine.

Another important point implied in Mr Taylor's list is this: try to establish new social relations naturally. When you are lonely and in need of human interactions, you cannot start a new social relation with anybody on the street; it might be obvious but it is important to point out that the construction of social relations is heavily regulated by many rules, although some of these rules are unspoken or informal. Your attempt to set up new social relations would be counterproductive if you ignore or break these rules. It would be more effective to contact others not for the sake of establishing a social relationship but for some other purposes: such as sharing a hobby, volunteering to help a noble cause, asking a neighbour for a small favour, or learning a skill together with others. In these occasions, social interactions are a by-product of some other interactions, which is the meaning of 'naturally' as you will not feel awkward socially; you don't even have to tell anybody that you are lonely. You may feel difficult for the first time, but once you start it off, new social relations will follow. The will power of getting out of loneliness is the first condition for following Mr Taylor's tips.

There is another condition: at the advanced age of 90, he was fit both physically and mentally. Not every person of that age is so lucky. If you have a chronic illness or any illness that prevents you from going out, you won't be able to join a club or take a part-time job as a volunteer at a local charity. Indeed, in my research I have found that it is the combination of being widowed and having a chronic illness that is a condition most likely to make older people lonely. Such combination deprives one's ability to revive social life and expand social circle. What tips could we give to this group of older people? Here are a few that I can think of.

1   *Take stock of your existing social relations.* Your social circle may have become smaller, but in social relations, quality is much more important than quantity. One confidante with whom you can discuss any personal matters is more valuable than ten acquaintances you can only have a brief chat. Consider carefully the ones that you can call, have dinner together, or discuss important matters in your life. Make a list of them with their contact information (if you don't know, try to find out through other people), and think about when it might be an appropriate time or occasion for you to contact them.

2   *If you don't know yet, learn to use today's communication technologies* that help you keep existing social relations or even establish new relations, such as mobile phone, email, Skype, or better still a social media app. Skype is particularly useful – you can contact anybody in most parts of the world, you can either make a call or leave a message. Modern technologies could somehow make up the loss from physical separations and distances.

3   *Make use of services provided by charities, local communities and authorities.* As mentioned previously, many charities, communities and local authorities, at least in the UK, have realized the importance of loneliness and created some programmes to help the lonely; for example, Springboard (Cheshire), Seniors Network (Leeds), Community Wellbeing Practices (Halton), Social Prescribing Scheme (Rotherham), Living Well (Cornwall), Village and Community Agents (Gloucestershire), Time for Life (Devon), Touchstones (Yorkshire), and Carers Centre – Male Carers Social Support Group (Brighton and Hove).[2] You are lucky if you live in such an area, and you definitely should try to make use of such service. Contact your GP (doctor) or local council about your desire to participate in the programme. If your local area does not provide such service yet, you can still tell your GP about your experience of loneliness, and he or she should be able to refer you to some kind of help. More importantly, keep in mind that you are fortunate if you live in a country

like the UK, where several nationwide charities have been set up with their mission (or part of their mission) of helping the lonely, including the Campaign to End Loneliness, Age UK, Independent Age, The Silver Line, The Co-Op, The Red Cross, and FoodCycle. Each offers somewhat different forms of support, including helping you find a regular visitor, talking to you over the phone when you want to, bringing out to a social activity, and altogether you have a variety of opportunities to set up new relations with others that ultimately bring you out of loneliness. Nothing should prevent you from seeking for help from them.

4   *Be social at home*. Chronic illness and a certain level of disability have been found to be two of the most common risk factors for loneliness, because they seriously reduce one's ability to engage in social interactions and activities with others. But, not all people with chronic illness or disability are necessarily lonely. Besides making use of the available supports mentioned above, there are a number of things you can do at home that keep you out of loneliness. Inviting people to your home rather than joining them somewhere else will keep your social life active, particularly if you could share a hobby with them, such as watching sports or a movie. You could also keep yourself socially active by using the Internet, such as tweeting or commenting on an event or an article, or even writing a blog, this way you are interacting with others online by writing. Similarly, sending people emails or texts is a great way of keeping in touch with others; you won't interrupt their life as they don't have to talk to you immediately. The key is to keep writing to others; if you don't write them, they are not going to write back to you.

5   *Enjoy being alone*. See the section 'Turn loneliness into solitude' below.

To those unemployed and struggling with financial constraints

It might be obvious, but is worthwhile to realize that being out of work or in poverty for a long time is not simply a financial constraint; it has serious social and psychological implications as well. As physical frailty could seriously constrain one's social life, unemployment or living with a very tight budget may make you mentally down and reduce your ability to live a richer social life. Being aware of such impacts is an important first step; to know what's going on is a condition for doing something about it. Being out of work or living hand to mouth is bad enough; to minimize its damage on the mental health of your own and those around you should be your top priority. To live a healthy social life with a low income, especially in today's Western societies, is not something unachievable. If you can manage it, it will be a great achievement in your life.

An irony that I have observed among people with a small amount of disposable income is that some of them tend to spend a higher proportion of their money on items that damage their health than those who have more money, such as cigarettes, cheap alcohol drinks, and unhealthy fast food. This is understandable – one's spirit is easily low when being constrained by a low disposable income, and expects to ease the mental pain by consuming these unhealthy items. But this is an illusion: they will only make you even unhappier; this way of life will trap you in a vicious cycle of poor health, inability to work, and forms of mental suffering such as depression, loneliness, and low self-esteem. The wisest thing you can do is to replace these unhealthy items with things that can help with your social life. It certainly will require some will power, but will power, by definition, is simply a matter of thinking in a certain way, which could be the easiest or the hardest thing for people to do. A better social life is not just about having a chat or having some fun with others; it does a lot of good to your mind and body, because it keeps you out of negative mental states such as depression and loneliness. If you could switch your consumption from cigarettes, alcohol, and ready meals to outdoor activities with friends and cooking healthy meals at home, your life will be on its way to turn around for the better. Replace smoking with gardening or any other hobby, alcohol drinks with tea or coffee, and ready meals with cooking with fresh ingredients.

Many simple social activities – a picnic with friends at a park, a barbecue in a garden, a day trip to museum or a nearby tourist site, etc. – do not cost a lot of money. And many places in western Europe, such as local colleges and leisure centres, offer discounts of classes to those unemployed or with a low income. Taking educational or sport classes will not only give you the opportunity to improve yourself but also, as mentioned before, a natural occasion for you to be social with others. Having lived in several countries in North America and Europe, I have always been amazed by the small number of people who make use of public resources (libraries, sport facilities, parks, local colleges, etc.), most of which are free or extremely affordable.

To an immigrant soon after arriving in a new nation

Having moved from one country to another for four times in my life, I know a thing or two about the loneliness as an immigrant. In two of these four countries, I knew nobody and had little money on my arrival; for the other two, I knew one or two people that I could talk to but knew that I could ask little favour from them. All those who knew me and would support me were back in the country that I just left. When one moves from one country to another, the changes of the physical environment are much less significant than the changes in our social life. Literally, you feel you are an outsider, you are different, in my case physically, from those who are already there, at least at the beginning, you need help on almost everything but you know so few who could or would answer your questions or give you a hand: where should I shop? Which bus or subway goes from A to B? Where is the building that I should go to get something done? How much money do I need for a month's expenses? What is the appropriate way of talking to people? Where can I find a job? Even when you have already landed a job before moving to the country, you need so much physical energy and strength to cheer yourself up and keep going. 'Cultural shock' is not an accurate description; 'settling anxiety' is better – what you desire so much is to settle down with your daily life, physically but more mentally, so that you are not anxious about so many important matters anymore. To do that, you need social relations, which could be exactly what you are short of, the reason why you are vulnerable to loneliness. And it is not simply these specific daily matters that make you feel so much in need of social contacts; it is also some vague anxiety or frustration of not belonging to the place you plan to live for a long time, as it is so uncertain when you can feel at home; as you are not familiar with the life of the new place, you are not confident of your expectations of what will happen. You need information and people that could help you increase the certainty, better predictability, of things around you, and make you feel to be part of an even very small group of people; all these take time; before all of these are settled, you are most likely to be lonely.

Most of the countries that immigrants see as their destinations today – the US, Canada, Australia, etc. – have been immigrants' destinations for centuries. And economically advanced European countries have become much more liberal in taking immigrants, although there are always a proportion of their residents who do not want to do so anymore. As a new immigrant, you could not help feeling that you are the only immigrant in the hosting country; if you realize that tens of thousands have moved here over the years and you are just one of them, you will not feel so separated apart from the existing residents anymore.

Many immigrants feel lonely because they cannot help reinforcing the artificial distinction between immigrants and local residents; they keep thinking themselves being very different from local residents, they are very suspicious that local residents will be nice to them, they feel it too daunting, even hopeless, a task to become one of the locals. Most immigrants I personally know or have studied have moved their body to the new country, but their mind still stays with the place they are from; they find the food in the new country not as tasty as theirs, the weather more miserable, the language difficult to understand or speak, local people's behaviours and values at odds with what they have believed. In short, they come to the new country not to become a part of it but just to make money; they want to lead their original way of life while physically staying in the new country. If you think like this, you will always be an immigrant, and you are more likely to be lonely, because you do not make effort to remove a barrier separating yourself from the locals.

Unless you are prepared to leave the hosting country in a near future, it is wiser to embrace what is new to you. You do not have to become a local, but at least try to feel what being a local looks like: what do they eat every day? Try and see whether you like any. Where do they bring their children to play? I find waiting to pick up my children in the playground of the schools a very effective way of becoming to know some of the parents. They may not want to talk about you, but they would not refuse to talk about the children, both theirs and yours. And inviting their children to your house to have tea or a party would be a great way of helping your children make friends. What TV programmes are popular? Watch one or two and be prepared to talk about them. What is in the newspapers? What are the locals concerned about? What do they do after work? What are the popular local events (festivals and fairs)? Try to join them. If you do not have a job yet, try to learn where the locals find jobs, and talk to those at the job centre. If you have a job, try to participate in all corporate events, and better still invite some colleagues to dinner. These may sound common sense but they raise your awareness of actively developing your social life in the new country. Finally, to repeat my suggestion made earlier, in most European and North American countries, public resources are underused; if you look, you will find events, classes, facilities, and support that bring you closer to others and ultimately reduce your chance of falling into loneliness.

Turn loneliness into solitude

Mr Taylor's overall strategy is to reach out to others. If loneliness is an emotional reaction to the perceived lack of desired social relations, setting up new relations as substitutes seems to be the natural solution. Indeed, this is the general idea underlying all strategies and practices adopted by charities and professional services for helping the lonely – you are lonely because you do not have someone to talk to, or you do not have a friend, so we make someone for you to talk to or to become your friend (befriending).

The trouble is, this idea does not always work. First of all, the person who is assigned by a charity or has volunteered to be your friend is unlikely to be the same as the one you have lost or you really need. The volunteer should be of some help, but while you may expect interactions with others will alleviate your loneliness, there is no guarantee that they will work, because becoming someone's friend requires much more than having a chat regularly. Even if the volunteer does become a close friend to you, they cannot be with you anytime you want; there must be some time you may have to stay alone. 'For who not needs shall never lack a friend' (Hamlet): while the friendship of others will certainly help, you cannot rely on it all the time; the best strategy is to be your own friend. If it is too much to be completely self-sufficient, at least we can try to be as independent as we can so as to minimize our dependence on others.

An alternative (if not better) strategy is to turn your lonely experience into something productive, even enjoyable. If we can call Mr Taylor's the strategy of reaching out, this is a strategy of *tuning in*. Perhaps the most effective is to use both strategies in combination, alternating from one to the other depending on the situation. In other words, whenever you cannot, or do not want to, be with others, try to enjoy aloneness. As mentioned in early chapters, some have argued that such solitude is a necessary condition for spiritual development or artistic creativity.[3] Nevertheless, creativity requires talents as well, something not all of us possess. If you are lucky enough to have such talent, by all means make use of the lone state of life to create something valuable. If you are not so lucky, here are a few things that you might want to do to turn a potentially lonely state into an enjoyable solitude. The key is to realize that being alone gives you the opportunity to do anything you would prefer to do alone rather than with others.[4]

Meditate

I used to have migraines frequently in my high school and university years, perhaps due to the long hours of strenuous study. To help me out, my father introduced meditation to me. At the beginning, I found it almost impossible to concentrate, let alone to enjoy any effects. However, after taking a few classes, I was able to have a taste of what it was like to be in the meditative state. Combined with some physical exercises, meditation has eased the pain during my postgraduate studies. And its effects are more than ameliorating the migraine; meditation is also a process of training my mind to calmly deal with the issues in my life. My experience shows that it is very helpful to combine reading some classics such as *Meditations* by Marcus Aurelius with the practices of Tibetan meditation. The former adds substance to the latter, while the latter regulates and stabilizes the thoughts. This is clearly not the place for me to go into the details. The point is that if you start to meditate, you would appreciate the time alone; not only you will not feel lonely, but you will even feel grateful and joyful when and after meditating. There are many resources on meditation you can use, such as local meditation classes, online meditation classes (such as the one I took on Coursera),[5] books and DVDs, and free videos on YouTube. These may lead you into the field of meditation, but it is important to remember that you need to meditate and make meditation a part of your daily life on your own. When you feel healthy and your head clear, it is very unlikely you will feel lonely, even if you are physically alone.

Make gentle physical exercises part of your daily routine

Many scientific studies have converged on the same wisdom: physical health and mental health are closely connected. An effective way of improving the health of your mind is to improve the health of your body. And many physical exercises do not require a large space or outdoor, such as yoga, simple t'ai chi, or body workout schemes. Clear up a small space in any room, put a piece of rug, a sitting cushion, an exercise ball, and anything you may want to use. Come to this place at about the same time every day. The routine is very important, as it will make your mind peaceful. If you have a chronic illness or partly disabled, think about which parts of your body you can still control and move, and then develop a simple exercise scheme for those body parts. After my mother had a stroke many years ago, she couldn't move the right half of her body anymore, so I made up a few simple movements for the left part of her body and her head. The principle is: move any part of your body that you can move.

Do or learn something creative

As Anthony Storr illustrated with many examples in his *Solitude*, creative people (novelists, artists, composers, etc.) prefer solitude to social interactions. If you desire to express yourself in any way, the time being alone gives you the precious opportunity to do so. It does not have to be artistic or impressive; many simple activities could be creative, such as gardening or even trimming a plant in a pot, decorating a room, repainting a wall, woodcarving, fixing a piece of furniture or carpentry in general, knitting, tailoring, playing a music instrument, learning a new language, writing comments under a news report or editorial, etc. As long as you keep doing it, you will get better at it, and you will start to be happy about what you do, and both your mind and your body have been occupied in a healthy activity.

Read and write

This could be an example of the previous point, but I list it separately, because it is perhaps the easiest thing to do when one is alone – all you need is a pen and a piece of paper (or a computer), and it is both therapeutic and creative. What I like reading and writing the most is the interaction between what you think and what you see on paper: you have a thought, you express it on paper, but you have another thought to make it better, and you see the improvement. Create a list of books that you truly want to read. Do not put more than ten books on it, and rank order them in priority. Then start reading in that order. Read very carefully, ideally you are not aware that you are reading, you forgot what time it is, you find yourself emotional, you can't lay back in your seat anymore. Or, read a challenging book that you must think very hard to understand what is going on, such as Dostoyevsky's *The Brothers Kamarazov*, or what the author was trying to say, such as those by Kafka or Sartre. It is hard – you have to spend a lot of time thinking in order to understand and appreciate it, but that's exactly what you want to do! Compared with watching a video or movie, reading will do much more good to your mind, to remedy your loneliness, because you are more active, not simply passively receiving the images coming to you. Your mind should be healthy when it is working actively. Robinson Crusoe did not go mad while living alone on an island for more than twenty years, because most of the time his mind was actively busy of thinking about things of great importance to him: how to keep himself safe, how to grow crops, how to cook without any utensils, how to turn a wild animal domestic, how to keep food fresh, etc.

It's seldom that people read something classic without any thoughts coming to mind. More often than not, comments, ideas, evaluations, suggestions, wishes, emotions, etc., will come to you while you are reading. Put them down in writing. You don't have to write after reading the classics, of course. Write down anything you feel you can write about, because writing freely can be therapeutic. I kept a diary when I was alone, but found it a dilemma: I didn't have something worth writing about every day, but I wouldn't 'keep' the diary if I didn't write every day. A notebook is better than a diary: write about anything whenever it comes to you mind, ideally about a particular topic, paying close attention to the flow of your thoughts and emotions. A writing session like this is a recorded meditation.

Keep a pet

Some researchers have demonstrated the positive effects of keeping a pet on reducing the chance of loneliness. Lynch reported that 'Pets appeared to alleviate the cardiac patients' sense of isolation and loneliness in a way that substantially enhanced their chances for long-term survival'.[6] I have mixed feelings about this strategy, which is why I put here at the end. Obviously, keeping a pet, particularly a dog, requires investments and commitment, so it may not be everyone's cup of tea. Consider trying easier and more low-maintenance animals such as fish and chicks. It would be even better if the pets could bring some people to you, such as children and people with the same kind of pet. I am also concerned with the emotional reactions to the death of the pet – you enjoy the pet's company, which may make you lonelier once they die.

To charities, professional services, and governments

In mid-January 2018, following a wish of the late MP Jo Cox, the UK's prime minister Theresa May appointed Tracey Crouch as the minister for loneliness. By setting up this ministry, the British government is the first in the world to have taken loneliness seriously. Soon afterwards, Valentina Matviyenko, speaker of Russia's Federation Council (upper house of parliament), has proposed the creation of a Ministry of Loneliness in Russia, arguing that 'Loneliness of older people is a very important problem. They need daily attention. Not so much money as attention.'[7] Clearly, her proposal has fallen on deaf ears. Ironically, as we saw previously, loneliness is much less prevalent in the UK than it is in Russia. More generally, nations with lower prevalence of loneliness have taken loneliness seriously – most research on loneliness has been conducted in, and on, North America, northern and western Europe, and most charities for helping the lonely are in these countries as well. Is it because they take it seriously that the prevalence in these countries is low?

The British and other governments take loneliness seriously because they realize that not only loneliness itself is a painful experience, but more importantly, if loneliness could trigger other more serious illnesses, tackling loneliness would save a lot of taxpayers' money from the costs of treating those illnesses. Following the same logic, the next important question would be: what triggers loneliness? As shown before, so far researchers have identified a long list of these triggers, including an advanced age, widowhood and divorce, living alone, low socio-economic status, chronic illness, disability, ethnic minority, immigration, etc. Practically, for tackling loneliness, this list is expected to serve the purpose of helping health professionals to identify the lonely individuals so that they and charities could take remedying actions.

In my view, a few weak links remain in connecting the dots of the above approach. First of all, the connection between loneliness and illness remains obscure and therefore needs specification. Put in the form of a question: exactly how lonely one has to be so as to suffer from a particular illness? As I argued previously, health professionals and medical researchers have the task of establishing more specific connections between a much better measured loneliness and a specific medical illness. Scientific confirmation of these connections is the foundation of all other programmes of work.

Second, how the risk factors work remains highly uncertain. I am not expecting any causal relationship supported with ample empirical evidence between a risk factor and a certain level of loneliness. More realistically, we need to know whether a risk factor alone will suffice to make some people very lonely, or it has to work with other risk factors to do so, and whether the combined effects work differently for different groups of people. I have started to work on this issue but the results are clearly limited.[8] Eventually, we need to develop a profile of the lonely – a description of how multiple factors work together – and a set of corresponding strategies.

Third, almost all risk factors listed above are demographic, socio-economic, or health-related attributes of an individual. They are useful for identifying the groups of people who are most vulnerable to loneliness. What I have tried to remind government officials, health professionals, charities and others of, is some factors at the societal level for loneliness. These *societal risk factors for loneliness* include, not exclusively, socio-economic inequality, poverty, collective or large-scale conflicts, large-scale immigration, cultural or religious norms that suppress individual liberties for social contacts, low level of generalized trust of institutions and the others, etc. Seen in the light of these macro issues, policies and practices for tackling loneliness based on individual attributes appear insufficient or even superficial – there are a number of higher level and more fundamental courses of loneliness. On the other hand, it is perhaps too much to ask governments and other institutions to tackle these issues as part of their campaigns against loneliness. Compared with these, loneliness is a much less serious and urgent issue, and strategies based on individual attributes will soon reach their limits.

To the non-lonely members of society

People working for the institutions mentioned in the above section take it as their responsibility to help the lonely. To win the battle against loneliness, however, what they do is not sufficient; their resources are limited, and most likely they will target the loneliest to maximize the effectiveness of their resources. That loneliness is a social problem means that all members of a society should be prepared to contribute to the reduction of its scale and severity.

If you are reading this book, then you have already learnt about the importance of loneliness. Obviously, such awareness of the problem is a precondition of doing something about it, but the importance of loneliness may not be so obvious to those who are not lonely. When I told others, some being academics, that I was doing research on loneliness, they looked surprised; they had a question in their mind but thought it impolite to ask me: is it really worthwhile to spend your time and effort on loneliness? They are right: most people have been lonely at some point, but they are fine because, although it is not pleasant, loneliness is not unbearable. What they are not right about is that a problem's transience and mildness can justify our neglect of it. A key message from health researchers of loneliness is very clear: the psychological could turn into something medical, so better deal with it before it turns medical. For me as a sociologist, loneliness is also a social problem in at least two ways: the distribution of loneliness is not even – some social groups suffer more from it than others, and some fundamental factors at the societal and cultural level are responsible for the prevalence of loneliness in a society. All researchers who work on loneliness will very much appreciate if you could pass these simple points to those who still take loneliness lightly.

With the importance of loneliness established, the next question for you is: why should I care? I think it is safe to assume that as you are reading this book, particularly this chapter, you would like to help the lonely, either someone close to you or people you do not know personally. But not all would agree. Indeed, this is a difficult question of moral philosophy: should the non-lonely help the lonely? Or more generally, should those better off help the less fortunate? Loneliness is a special case of this general question because its solution requires social relations; that is, unlike tackling the problem of poverty, where the better off do not have to, the non-lonely must be directly or personally involved in helping the lonely. At the moment, it is clearly not an obligation for the non-lonely to help out the lonely; even if it is widely perceived as an obligation, some could refuse to fulfil it with no undesirable consequences. As for all other charitable actions, all we can expect is a certain level of compassion and empathy; in other words, as one of the better off (not lonely), you have the choice of either helping out the less fortunate (the lonely) or not, although it is socially approved, even promoted, to help.

Given you would like to help the lonely, the next question is, how? For the lonely, to grow out of loneliness could be an enormous challenge because they do not know how to interact with others, they are concerned with, even afraid of, negative responses from others (rejections, cold shoulders, abuses, etc.). With about a century's development of sociology and social psychology, there have been no effective ways of revising existing social relations or constructing new social relations, although some training of developing social skills could be offered. It is therefore impossible to compile a list of actions that you can take to help the lonely.

On the other hand, if you are compassionate, you can always find the opportunities. Besides becoming a volunteer for charities (Campaign to End Loneliness, Age UK, NSPCC, etc.), you may consider what William Wright suggested in his

Ted Talk.[9] He has set up a charity to 'digitize empathy'. I have found his idea stimulating: rather than complaining about how modern technologies have alienated ourselves, why not use the modern technologies (mobile phone, the Internet, social media, etc.) to show you care about the lonely? Send a message to anybody who you know or suspect is lonely, telling them that you care, you want to check out they are fine, and you are there to be with them if they need you, offer a coffee together, watch a movie together, or just a chat over the phone for a few minutes. It should not be a big effort for you to make, but it will make a big difference to the lonely. And that's the beauty of social relationships.

Notes

1 Here are a few that interested readers may want to start with: J. Page. 2012. *Freedom From Loneliness: 52 Ways To Stop Feeling Lonely*. CreateSpace; T. J. Selimi. 2016. *#Loneliness: The Virus of the Modern Age*. Carlsbad, CA: Balboa Press; K. Floyd. 2015. *The Loneliness Cure: Six Strategies for Finding Real Connections in Your Life*. Avon, MA: Adams Media Corporation.

2 For further details, see the report by Campaign to End Loneliness and Age UK. 2015. *Promising Approaches to Reducing Loneliness and Isolation in Later Life*, available online at www.campaigntoendloneliness.org/wp-content/uploads/Promising-approaches-to-reducing-loneliness-and-isolation-in-later-life.pdf.

3 See, for example, A. Storr. 1997. *Solitude*. London: HarperCollins Publishers.

4 I must add that some may prefer to be in contact with others *all of the time*; that is, it is difficult for them to be alone for even a short period of time. For example, I know a researcher from Spain who found it unbearable to be alone even for a few hours; he had to talk to someone either on the phone or on Skype while he was having meals, and he must go out to be with others after dinner or during weekends. I believe it is close to be a psychological disorder but haven't found the terminology for it.

5 See www.coursera.org.

6 A. Lynch. 2000. *A Cry Unheard: New Insights into the Medical Consequences of Loneliness*. Baltimore, MD: Bancroft Press. And he cited the following studies: E. Friedmann, A. Katcher, J. J. Lynch, and S. Thomas. 1980. 'Animal companions and one-year survival of patients discharged from a coronary care unit', *Public Health Reports*, 95: 307–312; A. H. Katcher, E. Friedmann, A. Beck, and J. J. Lynch. 1983. 'Looking, talking, and blood pressure: the physiological consequences of interaction with the living environment', in A. Katcher and A. Beck (eds), *New Perspectives on Our Lives with Companion Animals*, Philadelphia, PA: University of Pennsylvania Press.

7 Reported at Russia Beyond on 4 February 2018: see www.rbth.com/lifestyle/327485-politician-proposed-creating-ministry (accessed 23 February 2018).

8 For interested readers, please see K. Yang. 2016. 'Causal conditions for loneliness: a set-theoretic analysis on an adult sample in the UK', *Quality & Quantity*, 52(2): 685–701.

9 See his talk on YouTube at www.youtube.com/watch?v=ruh6rN5UrME. However, I cannot find further information about his charity on the Internet.

Chapter 10

Conclusions and reflections

In this last chapter I highlight the key points that I have made in the previous chapters, elaborate on them with further reflections and discussions, and suggest what should be done to tackle loneliness as both an academic and a practical problem.

We need better research on the connection of loneliness to its medical consequences

When I started working on loneliness over ten years ago, loneliness remained very much an academic issue among a small circle of psychologists, health researchers, and social gerontologists. In the past few years, a few signs have arisen to suggest that it has come into the centre of attention of the mass media and the general public: reports about loneliness appeared more frequently in major media outlets, many people left their comments and reactions online, existing and new charities have launched their campaigns against loneliness, a few TED talks were given about loneliness, and some books with an explicit aim of helping the lonely have been published for the general public. Even as a latecomer to the field, I have been asked to contribute to raising the public awareness of loneliness by participating in interviews with media agents, attending public meetings about how to cope with loneliness, and writing articles for the general public. As an academic working on this issue, I have been thrilled to see the growing public attention to loneliness.

However, in the meantime I cannot help but wonder what was behind this rapid and wide growth of interest in loneliness. It is not hard to find the answer: because some scientists have claimed that loneliness is very bad for our health. Or perhaps the scientists would prefer to tone down the certainty a bit: loneliness *could* damage our health. Indeed, many articles about loneliness, including some of those written by myself, start by presenting the scientific findings that connect loneliness to a series of illnesses that we all would try to avoid as much as we can. The readers who have forgotten or have not read could go back to the incomplete list of these illnesses in Chapter 1. The connection between loneliness and these illnesses is an issue of fundamental importance: much of academic research and almost all of the public discourse about loneliness rely on the establishment of such connection.

Unfortunately, the connection is not as well established as I would have hoped, which is why I start this book by asking the question 'Is it a problem?'. I cannot answer this question by myself as I am not a medical researcher, and even if I were, I would not be able to answer it all alone. At some point we must reply on other researchers' work. After reading a literature on this question, which could by no means be exhaustive, I have come to the conclusion that there has been sufficient evidence for treating loneliness seriously as a high risk factor for a number of illnesses. Put in a different way: loneliness is not a straw man.

For a number of reasons, however, the above conclusion comes with a few but important uncertainties and controversies. The first question is whether loneliness *per se* is a problem. In his book *Loneliness*, John Cacioppo, the leading expert in the field of loneliness that we mentioned many times in previous chapters, says repeatedly that loneliness itself is *not* a problem:

> But once again, loneliness itself is not a disease; feeling lonely from time to time is like feeling hungry or thirsty from time to time. It is part of being human . . . But once again, even *chronic* loneliness is not a 'mental disorder,' although it can put us at risk for depression.[1]

As I introduced in Chapter 1, some religious scholars hold a similar view, taking loneliness as normal as other daily experiences and feelings. I have found myself unable to accept such view, at least not completely. True, loneliness may be as common as hunger or thirst, but hunger or thirst is a very unpleasant feeling. Moreover, like hunger or thirst, loneliness is not a problem only if the degree is not high, or the feeling does not last long, and some kind of solution is supplied soon enough to ease away the unpleasant feeling; when the feeling lasts long enough, it means something seriously wrong with our body – we might suffer from malnutrition or dehydration. Loneliness itself could be a highly painful experience, thus a problem, either when its intensity is very high, or when it lasts for a long time, or both. It is understandable not to take loneliness as a disease or disorder when it is transient, or mild, or both, but why don't we treat it as a problem when it is a highly painful feeling that people suffer from? In fact, some psychoanalysts, such as Frieda Fromm-Reichmann, Melanie Klein, and more recently Arlene Kramer Richards and Lucille Spira, treated patients suffering from loneliness, which means that they did take loneliness as a serious mental disorder.[2] I would accept that *not all* loneliness is a disease or mental disorder, but certain types of loneliness are. It is clear that what kinds of loneliness should be treated as a mental disorder or a form of psychosis is a complicated issue. I shall say a bit more about this below, but eventually it is an issue that could only be resolved by the community of psychologists, psychiatrists, and psychoanalysts.

To take a step back for now: if what makes loneliness a problem is not the unpleasant feeling itself, then it must be the illnesses as those listed in Chapter 1 that it causes, either alone or together with other causes. The amount of evidence for the connection between loneliness and these illnesses is, at least in my judgement, compelling; otherwise, most of subsequent research on loneliness including mine would be ill-conceived, even pointless. However, I do not think the connection has been established as firmly as it should be, because the claimed relationship between loneliness and each particular illness remains somewhat imprecise or obscured in a black box. When many articles and presentations about loneliness report that loneliness increases the chance of developing a particular illness (heart attack, dementia, etc.) by a certain factor (30%, twofold, etc.), what do they exactly mean by 'loneliness'? It would be absolutely too farfetched to claim that as long as one feels lonely, one will be subject to that level of risk. If so, how lonely does one have to be so that the level of risk of having a disease should be taken seriously by medical professionals? Disappointingly, most authors or presenters simply use the word 'loneliness' without any qualification, leaving their readers or audience with the impression that all loneliness is that bad, which is clearly not the message the psychological or neurological specialists would want to pass around. Again, I accept the general claim that loneliness is a contributing factor to the development of many illnesses, but we need more precise scientific findings that describe how loneliness works as specifically as possible. I appreciate that this may be already a tall order; the least researchers can do is to measure loneliness and its association with a specific illness, either physical or mental, as precisely as possible.

So far the importance of loneliness has been supported by the medical implications that it may bring about. It is important to realize that loneliness could have serious social consequences as well. What kinds of things do lonely people tend to do? And how do people not lonely treat the lonely? For example, loneliness seems to be responsible for having an extramarital affair. In the BBC drama about the Brontë sisters, *To Walk Invisible*, their brother had an affair with a married woman, and his excuse was, 'She was lonely!'. Similarly, in another and more recent BBC drama, *The Split*, Nathan's justification for his extramarital affair was the same: 'I was lonely!'. It turns out that these fictional experiences represent the stories in real life. In a large scale survey conducted on an extramarital dating site, as many as 30% of the website's female users described themselves as lonely, and women who described themselves as 'lonely' and 'virile' were found more likely to cheat.[3] We need to apply some caution when interpreting these results due to the nature of the website and the potential bias of the sample, but it is clear that more systematic and rigorous academic research is needed to discover the nature and the scope of the social consequences of loneliness.

We need more precise definition and classification of loneliness

In order to make the connection between loneliness and any particular illness as specific and precise as possible, we need more precise definitions and measurements of different types and sub-types of loneliness. However, among researchers working on loneliness, most have been far more interested in modelling on loneliness as either an exogenous or an endogenous variable, assuming that the issues surrounding its meanings, its nature, its classifications, and its measurements have all been settled properly. I do not mean to suggest that we should abandon existing definitions and measurements; there is no doubt that they have been very useful. I do want to argue, however, they could be improved.

This is a good place for me to emphasize one point that I made in the previous chapters. The existing most widely used definition of loneliness by Peplau and Perlman focuses on the absence of desired social relations. While it covers a large range of situations, it misses two general situations in which one could be very lonely, because it assumes the past existence of desired social relations or that the lonely person knows what social relations they desire to have, although in most cases these two are the same (the person knows which social relation is desirable because it existed before). In some situations, it could be the case that the person may desire a new social relationship but has no clear idea of what it is; or in some other situations, the person could feel that no social relation, either in the past or in the future, is desirable, because they simply feel lost, alienated, confused, or hopeless. In these cases, the lonely individual may not be able to identify the solution to their problem. In addition, the presence of undesirable social relations such as bullying, discrimination, purposeful isolation or alienation, hostile attitudes, etc., could be another major source of loneliness. Researchers would make significant contributions to our understanding of loneliness by studying these two further general situations of loneliness.

The more general point is that loneliness has a variety of sources and thus represents itself in various ways. At the beginning of her piece on loneliness, Frieda Fromm-Reichmann had to painstakingly exclude all other meanings of loneliness before being able to focus on her own 'real loneliness'.[4] In their 'sourcebook' of loneliness, Peplau and Perlman listed eight different approaches to studying loneliness.[5] In addition to the requirement of specifying the connection between loneliness and illness, these struggles with the conceptual clarity of loneliness strongly suggest that we need clearer and more systematic classifications of the lonely experience so that we know which specific type or level of loneliness we are referring to when we make a claim about loneliness and a particular consequence.

Clearly, it will take quite some time to develop such classifications and to make them acceptable by the research community at large. Here I would venture to offer an initial thought about the attributes of loneliness which may help us develop a scheme of classification of loneliness. Like any emotion, loneliness has three dimensions: *intensity* (how strong it is), *frequency* (how often it occurs), and *duration* (how long it lasts once it has occurred). Obviously, each dimension can be measured at different levels. Even at the most crude level, that is, to assign binary values to each dimension – for intensity, intensive versus mild loneliness; for frequency, frequent versus seldom; and for duration, transient versus chronic loneliness, we shall have eight possible combinations, each of which indicating a

Table 10.1 A three-dimensional classification of loneliness.

Type	Meaning	Note
1	Intensive, frequent, chronic	Most worrying
2	Intensive, frequent, transient	Regular passing bouts
3	Intensive, seldom, chronic	Sudden bouts of suffering
4	Intensive, seldom, transient	Specific to particular event
5	Mild, frequent, chronic	Long-term but manageable
6	Mild, frequent, transient	Manageable and specific to event
7	Mild, seldom, chronic	Low level but long term suffering
8	Mild, seldom, transient	Least worrying

certain type of loneliness and together constituting a continuum in terms of level of seriousness of loneliness (Table 10.1).

In light of this scheme of classification, existing measurements of loneliness appear to be less than comprehensive as they tend to focus on only one of these three aspects. Currently there are two widely used measurements of loneliness. The first is a multi-item scale, including the UCLA loneliness scale[6] and the one created by de Jong Gierveld.[7] Scores produced with these scales measure the *strength* (or the *intensity*) of loneliness *at the time when the measured are taken*; therefore, they do not contain any information about the frequency nor the duration of the feeling. The second widely used measurement is a single-item measurement that requires respondents to report on the frequency of loneliness ('always', 'often', 'sometimes', 'never'), normally during the past week of the survey date. It is obvious that this scale does not measure the intensity or the duration of loneliness. So far there have been no measurements that cover all three dimensions of loneliness. Finally, Robert Weiss made the distinction between emotional and social loneliness, which is employed in some studies.[8] Essentially, a person will suffer from 'social loneliness' if an engaging social network, such as is provided by friends and like-minded members of community groups, is absent, and it will be 'emotional loneliness' if a close emotional attachment, such as is provided by a spouse, is lost. Note that such distinction is only a simple classification of the causes of loneliness and as such it does not capture any attributes of loneliness.

Essentially, loneliness is about the relationship between an individual and other members of society

Both the existing definitions and the measurements of loneliness aim to discover the source, the nature, and the level of loneliness by tapping into the relationship between the studied individual and others, because essentially, the problem of loneliness is a specific representation of the more general problem of the relationship between the individual and the society. It must be added that the distinction is analytical, not realistic, as the two are always intertwined in reality. Still, there are several versions of individualism in academic discourses, but they share an important starting point: as each individual human being is biologically separated from another, it is only in extreme cases – slavery or totalitarian societies coming to mind – that their being as independent social entities has been completely overwhelmed by other individuals or the society as a whole. In most contemporary societies, they influence each other, but in principle, their thoughts, feelings, and actions are distinctive from those of others.

That is only half of the story. That human beings are social animals has become a cliché. Even biologically, human beings are not self-contained – from the very moment of being born into this world, each of them relies at least partly on other human beings in order to be able to grow up into adulthood. It is certainly true that as a species, human beings must work together in order to survive and thrive. As Talcott Parsons, an influential American sociologist, pointed out, each person's striving for gratification must be directed towards other people from the very outset.[9] More relevant to our interest, Norbert Elias conceptualized human beings' emotional needs as fulfilling the function of bonding people together as a family, a community, or a nation.[10]

Yet again, that description has missed some important features of social life among human beings. We may not like them but have to accept the following points about human relations. First, it is possible albeit unpleasant for one person to live alone for a very long time without becoming seriously ill, as Robinson Crusoe or Chuck Noland in *Cast Away* or any real stories of men living in forest after war for many years, who may even find it difficult to adapt after returning to the society they left many years ago. At least for some human beings, the ability of living alone could be stretched to the extreme. Second, many times and for many reasons some people do not want to live with some other people; that is, it is simply not true that *any* human beings will necessarily prefer to live with *any* other human beings; they only want to live with *certain kinds of others*. Some may not know what kinds of people they want to live with, but they know what kinds of people they do not want to live with. For those who know, their desire for only some special types of social relations is a fundamental course of loneliness, because the probability of having some others they do not like around is high while on the other hand the probability of having the others they like around is low. That may sound disheartening, but I think it is very much true, and I would think many readers will find it true as well. Those who do not know what kinds of people they want to live with are in an even worse situation; they are lonely because they are lost, they do not know who will help them grow out of loneliness, they become hopeless. In short, what human beings truly want is *being both alone and social at the same time*; put differently, they want to *control when they are alone and when they are social*; they want to *be alone whenever they want but not lonely as a consequence*. It is indeed a tall demand. How a society – that is, a large number of people living in a certain geographical area and sharing a set of rules – manages to make its members at least not dislike one another, ideally like one other, should be one of the biggest question for sociology or social sciences in general.

In this sense, living alone is not an issue; regularly and constantly being alone is. Many young, single, and professional urban dwellers want to live alone but do not want to be alone all the time. They want to live alone so that they can be alone not only whenever they want to be alone but also when they can be social with others. This control is the key to their feelings, either loneliness or joy. Living alone affords them privacy and autonomy but could induce isolation and loneliness. On the other hand, they enjoy the sense of belonging, care and support of others but do not expect to give at least part of themselves away to social obligations and commitments. Under some strong conditions, living alone may increase their chance of enjoying the best while avoiding the worst of the two worlds. It is not so easy to satisfy these conditions, however – if everyone is trying to make use of the best of both worlds, the chance of making everybody happy is very low, unless some kind of organization is in place, but organization means rules, obligations, commitments, loss of control and autonomy. In the end, to be alone or to be with others *whenever one wants to* remains an ideal; sooner or later, something we would not like to have from either aloneness or togetherness will come to us. Life is not perfect: it may be possible but it is very difficult to achieve autonomy, freedom, privacy and avoid loneliness, isolation, estrangement at the same time. It is admirable to aim high, but it is also helpful to be realistic. A wise strategy is to nurture your ability of turning aloneness, even loneliness, into solitude, that is, the experience of refreshing and restoring yourself by yourself. Sherry Turkle has expressed this point very well:

> My own study of the networked life . . . has left me thinking about solitude – the kind that refreshes and restores. Loneliness is failed solitude. To experience solitude you must be able to summon yourself by yourself; otherwise, you will only know how to be lonely.[11]

Loneliness is unevenly distributed across social groups and societies

Throughout Chapters 3–8 I have repeatedly tried to demonstrate how the prevalence of loneliness varies across social groups and societies. These variations, I believe, constitute some strong evidence for the effects of factors at the levels higher than the individuals. In addition to the social consequences of loneliness suggested above, these aggregate and societal effects make loneliness a social rather than merely a psychological and individual problem. Shaping individual attributes and life chances in more systematic, fundamental, but invisible manners, these higher level factors may be more powerful than individual attributes in determining the individual's chance of feeling seriously lonely. For example, poor health or illness has constantly been found a significant risk factor for frequent or severe loneliness. While health or illness is indeed individual attributes, they are also strongly associated with another individual attribute, socio-economic status (SES) or class, an individual attribute that is also under the heavy influence of factors beyond an individual's control. Some societal factors, such as cultural values, social norms, political and religious ideologies, tax policies, educational resources, employment opportunities, etc., shape a society's class structure but are resistant to individual efforts of changing them. An individual could become very lonely when he or she realizes the consequences of violating these norms or rules, when they could not get a job due to being a member of an ethnic minority group but cannot prove so, when they cannot trust the people around them out of religious, social, or political isolations, or when they cannot afford to cover the costs of being social with others. Perhaps because loneliness has so long been perceived just as a psychological – thus individual – problem, or perhaps it is so difficult to do something about these societal level factors, existing research on the higher level factors for loneliness stays mostly at comparing cultural values and interpretations of loneliness. While such research is very important, it is certainly far from being sufficient for revealing how aggregate and societal level factors make a large number of people very lonely. In fact, if any of these factors could be reformed in the direction of relieving people from loneliness, it would be much more efficient than tactics and strategies targeting individuals. As long as people are hopeful and determined to change their society for the good, it is self-defeating to think that these factors are not changeable.

Perhaps here is a good place for me to explain why in the subtitle of this book I have used the word 'social' rather than 'sociological'. After submitting one of my papers on loneliness to a sociology journal, I received the reviewers' comments, and one of the reviewers suggested that I change 'sociological' in 'loneliness as a sociological problem' into 'social'. I followed the advice, but not because I think it is wrong to see loneliness as a sociological problem but because it is better to use a more inclusive word. It is not wrong to say that loneliness is a sociological problem because, as mentioned in the second chapter, some sociologists, such as Robert Weiss, David Riesman, and Norbert Elias, explicitly write about loneliness as a sociological problem. Moreover, as I have tried very hard to show in this book, loneliness can and should be studied in connection with many important sociological concepts, including social inequality, social structure, family and marriage, friendship and bullying, immigration, race and ethnicity, culture, religion and ideology. In short, there is nothing inappropriate to call loneliness a sociological problem, despite the fact that the number of sociologists who take loneliness as the focus of their research is very small.[12] I adopted the word 'social' in the end because I worried that my book would be interpreted as being written only for sociologists or students of sociology. Loneliness is a problem for academics from multiple academic disciplines, and sociology is one and only one of them.

We need to identify the loneliest

A difficulty with helping the lonely is that they do not want to tell others that they are lonely. Some charities and health professionals have urged people to constantly check with people they personally know whether they are lonely or not. While this should not be as scary as asking someone you are close to whether they have suicidal thoughts, as Dr Xand van Tulleken suggested at the end of his Horizon documentary *Stopping Male Suicide*, the lonely may not have someone who will check on them or they simply would not tell anyone they personally know about their loneliness. This is perhaps the most challenging for those who are the loneliest, but it is exactly this group who need help. In addition to all these actions that people can take to help the lonely, we need to identify the loneliest by what we know about them. More specifically, if it is possible to predict suicide with a level of accuracy as high as 90%,[13] then why don't we predict who are lonely with the same method? In a country like the UK or any country that holds its residents' health and other personal information, it should not be too much a trouble to run the working algorithm on such database in order to find the loneliest residents. But before doing that, we need to sort out two things. First, going back to a point made previously, we need to be clear about what exactly we mean by loneliness; more specifically, we need to define what kind of loneliness deserves serious attention from the health professionals, charities and the government. The second issue is ethics: we need people's consent of using their personal information and telling them that they have been identified as being subject to a high risk of loneliness.

The non-lonely should help more

The search for the causes or the risk factors for loneliness leads to two implicit but important and ethical questions: Whose fault is it when some people feel lonely? And do the non-lonely members of the society have the obligation of helping the lonely? For the first questions, Robert Weiss pointed out the culture of victim blaming in his widely cited book on loneliness: the lonely have brought the problem to themselves.

> Why can't the lonely change? . . . They must find a perverse gratification in loneliness; perhaps loneliness, despite its pain, permits them to continue a self-protective isolation or provides them with an emotional handicap that forces handouts of pity from those with whom they interact.[14]

If it is truly the lonely people's own fault, as claimed above, then researchers should have invested their valuable time and energy on something else. The fact that Weiss brought it up in his book means it might not be completely unnecessary to remind ourselves that some, hopefully a small minority, may still believe that the lonely have taken on the issue all on their own.

This is also another reason for examining the aggregate and societal sources of loneliness: loneliness is not a purely personal and private matter because others related to the lonely and even the society as whole should take some responsibility for the loneliness. While losing a spouse (or any loved one) or having to live alone is a private matter, being made redundant, immigrating to a new country, or being discriminated due to a demographic attribute is not. If so, it should be also a responsibility for the non-lonely and the society of helping the lonely.

It is important to realize that such help is not just needed *after* someone has become seriously lonely. It is still very honourable, of course, to set up an organization or be a volunteer for a charity tackling loneliness, such as the newly established b: friend[15] and the new start-up No Isolation.[16] There are two things that these and other charities, health professionals and government agents cannot do: one, to find out all those who are seriously lonely and in need of urgent help because they may not want to tell others, and two, to pre-empt the occurrence of loneliness. I made a suggestion for dealing with the first problem above. And it is the second problem that I would like to emphasize here: how could we tackle loneliness by stopping people from becoming lonely in the first place? At the moment I have not learnt any answers to this question. I would like to suggest passing the following message around to the general public, including children: if you are not lonely and would not help the lonely, *at least please do not make anybody lonely*. It is in this sense that I mean that the non-lonely should take more responsibility in the campaign against loneliness. I do not think I am overly pessimistic by saying that in most human groups and societies there are still a certain number of people, including children, who do not mind or even enjoy isolating or bullying others without an understandable excuse. When seeing a loner who appears to be lonely, many believe it is not their job to help or it is fine to keep a loner lonely. In workplaces, employees are so busy, if not overwhelmed, with so many matters that not making a colleague lonely, let alone helping them, is rarely considered to be an issue; some would not mind punishing colleagues with social isolation, ostracism, or discrimination. In pursuing their own interests and objectives, how many would care that they have made some others lonely, either purposefully or inadvertently? Without transforming the way people think about and treat each other, we have a long way to go to win the battle against loneliness.

Notes

1 J. Cacioppo and W. Patrick. 2008. *Loneliness: Human Nature and the Need for Social Connection*. New York: W. W. Norton & Company, pp. 228, 230, emphasis original.
2 For the early contributions by psychoanalysts, see J. Hartog, J. R. Audy and Y. A. Cohen (eds). 1980. *The Anatomy of Loneliness*. New York: International University Press. For more recent contributions, see A. K. Richards, L. Spira, and A. A. Lynch (eds). 2013. *Encounters with Loneliness: Only the Lonely*, 2nd edition. New York: International Psychoanalytic Books.
3 See the report by Natalie Keegan in *The Sun* on 31 July 2017.

4 See F. Fromm-Reichmann. 1959. 'Loneliness', *Psychiatry*, 22: 1–15; reprinted in in J. Hartog, J. R. Audy and Y. A. Cohen (eds). 1980. *The Anatomy of Loneliness*. New York: International University Press, pp. 338–361.

5 L. A. Peplau and D. Perlman (eds). 1982. *Loneliness: A Sourcebook of Current Theory, Research, and Therapy*, New York: John Wiley & Sons, p. 31.

6 D. Russell, L. A. Peplau, and C. E. Cutrona. 1980. 'The revised UCLA Loneliness Scale: Concurrent and discriminant validity evidence', *Journal of Personality and Social Psychology*, 39(3): 472–480.

7 J. de Jong Gierveld. 1987. 'Developing and testing a model of loneliness', *Journal of Personality and Social Psychology*, 53: 119–128.

8 R. S. Weiss. 1973. *Loneliness: The Experience of Emotional and Social Isolation*. Cambridge, MA: MIT Press.

9 T. Parsons. 1954. 'Psychology and sociology', in J. Gillin (ed.), *For a Science of Social Man: Convergences in Anthropology, Psychology, and Sociology*. New York: Macmillan.

10 N. Elias. 1969. 'Sociology and psychiatry', in S. H. Foulkes and G. S. Prince (eds), *Psychiatry in a Changing Society*. London: Tavistock Publications, pp. 117–144; see also N. Elias. 1970. *What is Sociology?* New York: Columbia University Press, pp. 134–137.

11 S. Turkle. 2011. *Alone Together: Why We Expect More from Technology and Less from Each Other*. New York: Basic Books, p. 288.

12 It is somehow comforting to report that in the 13th annual conference of the European Sociological Conference in Athens in 2017, I initiated and organized a session on the sociology of loneliness. To my surprise, I received more papers than I could squeeze into the time slot for this session.

13 Approaching the end of his documentary *Stopping Male Suicide*, Dr Tulleken interviewed Dr Joseph Franklin at Florida State University, who claimed that they had developed an algorithm that could predict suicide attempts with about 90% accuracy.

14 R. S. Weiss. 1975. *Loneliness: The Experience of Emotional and Social Isolation*. Cambridge, MA: MIT Press, p. 13.

15 See https://letsbfriend.org.uk.

16 See www.noisolation.com/uk.

Bibliography

Akerlind, I. and Hornquist, J. O. 1992. 'Loneliness and alcohol abuse: a review of evidence of an interplay', *Social Science and Medicine*, 34: 405–414.

Argent, N., Tonts, M., Stockdale, A., He, C., Ye, J. 2014. 'Lonely sunsets: impacts of rural–urban migration on the left-behind elderly in rural China', *Population, Space and Place*, 20(4): 352–370.

Aydin, N., Fischer, P., Frey, D. 2010. 'Turning to God in the face of ostracism: effects of social exclusion on religiousness', *Personality and Social Psychology Bulletin*, 36(6): 742–753.

Ayis, S., Gooberman-Hill, R. and Ebrahim, S. 2003. 'Long-standing and limiting illness in older people: associations with chronic diseases, psychological and environmental factors', *Age and Ageing*, 32(3): 265–272.

Babones, S. 2013. *Methods for Quantitative Macro-Comparative Research*. Thousand Oaks, CA: Sage Publications.

Bauer, E. and Thompson, P. 2006. *Jamaican Hands across the Atlantic*. Kingston: Ian Randle.

Becker, G. 1964. *Human Capital: A Theoretical and Empirical Analysis, with Special Reference to Education*. New York: National Bureau of Economic Research.

Bellah, R. et al. 1985. *Habits of the Heart: Individualism and Commitment in American Life*. Berkeley, CA: University of California Press.

Bennett, J. and Dixon, M. 2006. *Single Person Households and Social Policy: Looking Forwards*. York: Joseph Rowntree Foundation.

Berkman, L. F. 1995. 'The role of social relations in health promotion', *Psychosomatic Medicine*, 57: 345–254.

Berkman, L. and Breslow, L. 1983. *Health and Ways of Living: The Alameda County Study*. New York: Oxford University Press.

Berkman, L. F. and Syme, S. L. 1979. 'Social networks, host resistance, and mortality: a nine year follow-up study of Alameda County residents', *American Journal of Epidemiology*, 109(2): 186–204.

Boyne, J. 2014. *A History of Loneliness*. London: Transworld Publishers.

Brennan, T. 1982. 'Loneliness at adolescence', in L. A. Peplau and D. Perlman (eds), *Loneliness: A Sourcebook of Current Theory, Research, and Therapy*. New York: John Wiley & Sons.

Burris, C. T. Batson, C. D., Altstaedten. M. and Stephens, K. 1994. '"What a friend . . .": loneliness as a motivator of intrinsic religion', *Journal for the Scientific Study of Religion*, 33(4): 326–334.

Cacioppo, J. T. and Harkley, L. C. 2005. 'People thinking about people: the vicious circle of being a social outcast in one's own mind', in K. D. Williams, J. P. Forgas, and W. von Hippel (eds), *The Social Outcast: Ostracism, Social Exclusion, Rejection, and Bullying*. New York: Psychology Press.

Cacioppo, J. T., Hughes, M. E., Waite, L. J., Hawkley, L. C. and Thisted, R. A. 2006. 'Loneliness as a specific risk factor for depressive symptoms: cross-sectional and longitudinal analysis', *Psychology and Ageing*, 21: 140–151.

Cacioppo, J. and Patrick, W. 2008. *Loneliness: Human Nature and the Need for Social Connection*, New York: W. W. Norton & Company.

Campaign to End Loneliness and Age UK. 2015. *Promising Approaches to Reducing Loneliness and Isolation in Later Life*. Available online at www.campaigntoendloneliness.org/wp-content/uploads/Promising-approaches-to-reducing-loneliness-and-isolation-in-later-life.pdf.

Cannon, W. 1942. 'Voodoo death', *American Anthropologist*, 44: 169–181.

Chatterjee, C., Ransel, D. L., Cavender, M., and Petrone, K. (eds), 2015. *Everyday Life in Russia Past and Present*. Bloomington, IN: Indiana University Press.

Clark, K. Capuchin. 1982. *An Experience of Celibacy: A Creative Reflection on Intimacy, Loneliness, Sexuality and Commitment*. Notre Dame, IN: Ave Maria Press.

Clark, R. W. 1980. *Freud: The Man and the Cause*. New York: Random House.

Cockerham, W. C. 1999. *Health and Social Change in Russia and Eastern Europe*. New York: Routledge.

Cockerham, W. C. 2017. *Medical Sociology*, 14th edition. New York: Routledge.

Cockerham, W. C. 2017. *Sociology of Mental Disorder*, 10th edition. New York: Routledge.

Coll-Planas, L., Valle Gómez, G., Bonilla, P., Masat, T., Puig, T., Monteserin, R. 2017. 'Promoting social capital to alleviate loneliness and improve health among older people in Spain', *Health & Social Care in the Community*, 25(1): 145–157.

Coric, D. and Murstein, B. I. 1993. 'Bulimia nervosa: prevalence and psychological correlates in a college community', *Eating Disorders: The Journal of Treatment and Prevention*, 1: 39–51.

Davies, R. and Elias, P. 'The application of ESeC to three sources of comparative European data', in Rose, D. and Harrison, E. (eds.) 2010. *Social Class in Europe: An Introduction to the European Socio-economic Classification*. New York: Routledge.

Deckx, Laura et al. 2015. 'Loneliness in patients with cancer: the first year after cancer diagnosis', *Psycho-Oncology*, 24(11): 1521–1528.

De Jong Gierveld, J. 1978. 'The construct of loneliness: components and measurement', *Essence*, 2: 221–238.

De Jong Gierveld, J. 1987. 'Developing and testing a model of loneliness', *Journal of Personality and Social Psychology*, 53: 119–128.

De Jong Gierveld, J. and Kamphuis, F. 1985. 'The development of a Rasch-type loneliness scale', *Applied Psychological Measurement*, 9(3): 289–299.

De Jong Gierveld, J. and Tesch-Römer, C. 2012. 'Loneliness in old age in Eastern and Western European societies: theoretical perspectives', *European Journal of Ageing*, 9(4):285–295.

De Jong Gierveld, J. and van Tilburg, T. 2010. 'The De Jong Gierveld short scales for emotional and social loneliness: tested on data from 7 countries in the UN generations and gender surveys', *European Journal of Ageing*, 7(2): 121–130.

De Jong Gierveld, J., van Tilburg, T. and Dykstra, P. A. 2006. 'Loneliness and social isolation', in A. Vangelisti and D. Perlman (eds), *Cambridge Handbook of Personal Relationships*. Cambridge: Cambridge University Press.

Dolberg, P., Shiovitz-Ezra, S. and Ayalon, L. 2016. 'Migration and changes in loneliness over a 4-year period: the case of older former Soviet Union immigrants in Israel', *European Journal of Ageing*, 13(4): 287–297.

Dolin, T. 2000. 'Introduction', in C. Brontë, *Villette*. Oxford: Oxford University Press.

Domènech-Abella, J., Mundó, J., Lara, E., Moneta, M., Haro, J., Olaya, B. 2017. 'The role of socio-economic status and neighborhood social capital on loneliness among older adults: evidence from the Sant Boi Aging Study', *Social Psychiatry and Psychiatric Epidemiology*, 52(10): 1237–1246.

Dommaraju, P. 2015. 'One-person households in India', *Demographic Research*, 32: 1236–1266.

Dunn, E. F. and Dunn, P. C. 1980. 'Loneliness and the black experience', in J. Hartog, J. R. Audy and Y. A. Cohen (eds), *The Anatomy of Loneliness*. New York: International University Press, pp. 284–304.

Durkheim, É. [1893] 1984. *The Division of Labour in Society*, translated by W. D. Halls. New York: The Free Press.

Durkheim, É. [1897] 2006. *On Suicide*, translated by R. Buss. Penguin Books.

Durkheim, É. [1909] 1982. 'The contribution of sociology to psychology and philosophy', in his *The Rules of Sociological Method*, edited with an introduction by S. Lukes and translated by W. D. Halls. New York: The Free Press.

Dykstra, P. A. 2009. 'Older adult loneliness: myths and realities', *European Journal of Ageing*, 6: 91–100.

Easton, M. 2018. 'How should we tackle the loneliness epidemic?', 11 February, available online at www.bbc.co.uk/news/uk – 42887932 (accessed 12 February 2018).

Elias, N. 1969. 'Sociology and psychiatry', in S. H. Foulkes and G. S. Prince (eds), *Psychiatry in a Changing Society*. London: Tavistock Publications, pp. 117–144.

Elias, N. 1970. *What is Sociology?* New York: Columbia University Press.

Emerson, K. G. and Jayawardhana, J. 2016. 'Risk factors for loneliness in elderly adults', *Journal of the American Geriatrics Society*, 64(4): 886–887.

Epley, N., Akalis, S., Waytz, A., Cacioppo, J. T. 2008. 'Creating social connection through inferential reproduction', *Psychological Science*, 19(2): 114–120.

Erikson. R. and Goldthorpe, J. H. 1992. *The Constant Flux: A Study of Class Mobility in Industrial Societies*. Oxford: Clarendon Press.

Ernst, J. M. and Cacioppo, J. T. 1999. Lonely hearts: psychological perspectives on loneliness. *Applied and Preventive Psychology*, 8(1): 1–22.

Ettema, E.; Derksen, L.; Leeuwen, E. 2010. 'Existential loneliness and end-of-life care: a systematic review', *Theoretical Medicine and Bioethics*, 31(2): 141–169.

Figes, O. 2008. *The Whisperers: Private Life in Stalin's Russia*. London: Penguin.

Fitzpatrick, S. 1999. *Everyday Stalinism: ordinary life in extraordinary times; Soviet Russia in the 1930s*. New York: Oxford University Press.

Floyd, K. 2015. *The Loneliness Cure: Six Strategies for Finding Real Connections in Your Life*. Avon, MA: Adams Media Corporation.

Fokkema, T., De Jong Gierveld, J., Dykstra, P. A. 2012. 'Cross-national differences in older adult loneliness', *The Journal of Psychology*, 146(1–2): 201–228.

Frantz, G. 2014. *Sea Glass: A Jungian Analyst's Exploration of Suffering and Individuation*. Cheyenne, WY: Fisher King Press.

Freud, S. 1927. *The Future of an Illusion*, translated by W. D. Robson-Scott. New York: Doubleday.

Freud, S. 1930. *Civilization and its Discontents*, translated by J. Strachey. New York: W. W. Norton.

Freud, S. 1963. *A History of the Psychoanalytic Movement*. New York: Collier Books.

Friedmann, E., Katcher, A., Lynch, J. J., and Thomas, S. 1980. 'Animal companions and one-year survival of patients discharged from a coronary care unit', *Public Health Reports*, 95: 307–312.

Fromm, E. 1993. *The Art of Being*. London: Constable.

Fromm-Reichmann, F. 1959. 1980. 'Loneliness', *Psychiatry*, 22: 1–15. Reprinted in J. Hartog, J. R. Audy and Y. A. Cohen (eds). 1980. *The Anatomy of Loneliness*. New York: International University Press, pp. 338–361.

Gambetta, D. 1988. *Trust: Making and Breaking Cooperative Relations*. New York: Wiley-Blackwell.

Gardner, H. 1993. *Creating Minds: An Anatomy of Creativity Seen through the Lives of Freud, Einstein, Picasso, Stravinsky, Elliot, Graham, and Gandhi*. New York: Basic Books.

Gardner, K. 2002. *Age, Narrative and Migration*. Oxford: Berg.

Gebauer, J. E. and Maio, G. R. 2012. 'The need to belong can motivate belief in God', *Journal of Personality*, 80(2): 465–501.

Gergen, K. 1991. *The Saturated Self: Dilemmas of Identity in Contemporary Life*. New York: Basic Books.

Gillies, C. M. 2016. 'What's the world's loneliest city?', *The Guardian*, 7 April, available online at www.theguardian.com/cities/2016/apr/07/loneliest-city-in-world (accessed 11 May 2018).

Goffman, E. 1991. *Asylums: Essays on the Social Situation of Mental Patients and Other Inmates*. London: Penguin.

Goldsmith, S. K., Pellmar, T. C., Kleinman, A. M., and Bunney, W. E. 2002. *Reducing Suicide: A National Imperative*. Washington, DC: National Academy Press.

Hansen, T. and Slagsvold, B. 2016. 'Late-life loneliness in 11 European countries: results from the generations and gender survey', *Social Indicator Research*, 129: 445–464.

Hardin, R. 2002. *Trust and Trustworthiness*. New York: Russell Sage Foundation.

Harrington, M. 1962. *The Other America: Poverty in the United States*. New York: Macmillan.

Hartog, J. 1980. 'Introduction: the anatomization', in J. Hartog, J. R. Audy and Y. A. Cohen (eds), *The Anatomy of Loneliness*. New York: International University Press, p. 11.

Hawkley, L. C., Hughes, M. E., Waite, L. J., Masi, C. M., Thisted, R. A., and Cacioppo, J. T. 2008. 'From social structural factors to perceptions of relationship quality and loneliness: the Chicago Health, Aging, and Social Relations Study', *The Journals of Gerontology, Series B; Psychological Sciences and Social Sciences*, 63: S375 – S384.

Hawkley, L. C., Masi, C. M., Berry, J. D., and Cacioppo, J. T. 2006. 'Loneliness is a unique predictor of age-related differences in systolic blood pressure', *Psychology and Ageing*, 21: 152–164.

Hofstede, G. 1980. *Culture's Consequences: International Differences in Work-Related Values*. Beverly Hills, CA: Sage.

Hofstede, G. 2001. *Culture's Consequences: International Differences in Work-Related Values*, 2nd edition. Beverly Hills, CA: Sage.

Hofstede, G., Hofstede, G. J., and Minkov, M. 2010. *Cultures and Organizations: Software of the Mind: Intercultural Cooperation and its Importance for Survival*. New York: McGraw-Hill.

Holt-Lunstad, J., Smith, T. B., Baker, M., Harris, T., and Stephenson, D. 2015. 'Loneliness and social isolation as risk factors for mortality: a meta-analytic review', *Perspectives on Psychological Science*, 10(2): 227–237.

Holwerda, T. J., Deeg, D. J. H., Beekman, A. T. F., van Tilburg, T. G., Stek, M. L., Jonker, C., and Schoevers, R. A. 2014. 'Feelings of loneliness, but not social isolation, predict dementia onset: results from the Amsterdam Study of the Elderly (AMSTEL)', *Journal of Neurology, Neurosurgery & Psychiatry*, 85: 135–142.

Homans, G. C. 1950. *The Human Group*. New York: Harcourt, Brace.

Horne, A. 1994. *The Lonely Leader: Monty, 1944–1945*. London: Macmillan.

House, J. S., Landis, K. R. and Umberson, D. 1988. 'Social relationships and health', *Science*, 241: 540–545.

Jamieson, L. and Simpson, R. 2013. *Living Alone: Globalization, Identity and Belonging*. Basingstoke: Palgrave Macmillan.

Johnson, P. and Mullins, L. 1987. 'Growing old and lonely in different societies: toward a comparative perspective', *Journal of Cross-Cultural Gerontology*, 2:7–27.

Jylhä, M. and Jokela, J. 1990. 'Individual experiences as cultural: a cross-cultural study on loneliness among the elderly', *Ageing and Society* 10:295–315.

Karlsen, S., Becares, L., and Roth, M. 2012. 'Understanding the influence of ethnicity on health', in G. Craig, K. Atkin, S. Chattoo, and R. Flynn (eds), *Understanding 'Race' and Ethnicity: Theory, History, Policy, Practice*, Bristol: Policy Press. pp. 115–132.

Katcher, A. H., Friedmann, E., Beck, A., and Lynch, J. J. 1983. 'Looking, talking, and blood pressure: the physiological consequences of interaction with the living environment', in A. Katcher and A. Beck (eds), *New Perspectives on Our Lives with Companion Animals*. Philadelphia: University of Pennsylvania Press.

Keegan, M. 2014. *The Opposite of Loneliness: Essays and Stories*. New York: Simon & Schuster.

Klinenberg, E. 2014. *Going Solo: The Extraordinary Rise and Surprising Appeal of Living Alone*. London: Gerald Duckworth & Co.

Laing, O. 2016. *The Lonely City: Adventures in the Art of Being Alone*. Edinburgh: Canongate Books.

Lamis, D. A., Ballard, E. D., and Patel, A. B. 2014. 'Loneliness and suicidal ideation in drug-using college students', *Suicide and Life-Threatening Behaviour*, 44(6): 629–640.

Lasch, C. 1979. *The Culture of Narcissism: American Life in an Age of Diminishing Expectations*. London: Abacus.

Luhmann, M. and Hawkley, L. C. 2016. 'Age differences in loneliness from late adolescence to oldest old age', *Developmental Psychology*, 52(6): 943–959.

Lykes, V. A. and Kemmelmeier, M. 2014. 'What predicts loneliness? Cultural differences between individualistic and collectivistic societies in Europe', *Journal of Cross-Cultural Psychology*, 45(3):468–490.

Lynch, J. J. 1977. *The Broken Heart: The Medical Consequences of Loneliness*. New York: Basic Books, Inc.

Lynch, J. J. 2000. *A Cry Unheard: New Insights into the Medical Consequences of Loneliness*. Baltimore, MD: Bancroft Press.

Marcus, A. 2010. 'The loneliness of fighting a rare cancer', *Health Affairs*, 29(1): 203–206.

Marcuse, H. 1964. *One Dimensional Man: Studies in the Ideology of Advanced Industrial Society*. London: Routledge.

Marshall, J. R. and Funch, D. P. 1983. 'Social environment and breast cancer: a cohort analysis of patient survival', *Cancer*, 52(8): 1546–1550.

McClay, W. M. 1994. *The Masterless: Self and Society in Modern America*. Chapel Hill, NC: University of North Carolina Press.

McClosky, H. and Schaar, J. 1965. 'Psychological dimensions of anomy', *American Sociological Review*, 30: 14–40.

McPherson, M., Smith-Lovin, L., and Brashears, M. E. 2006. 'Social isolation in America: changes in core discussion networks over two decades', *American Sociological Review*, 71(3): 353–375.

Mead, G. H. [1934] 1967. *Mind, Self & Society: From the Standpoint of a Social Behaviorist*, edited with an Introduction by Charles W. Morris. Chicago, IL: University of Chicago Press.

Medora, N., Woodward, J. and Larson, J. 1987. 'Adolescent loneliness: a cross-cultural comparison of American and Asian Indians', *International Journal of Comparative Sociology*, 28: 204–210.

Mental Health Foundation. 2010. *The Lonely Society*, London: Mental Health Foundation.

Merton, R. K. 1964. 'Anomie, anomia, and social interaction: contexts of deviant behaviour', in M. B. Clinard (ed.), *Anomie and Deviant Behaviour: A Discussion and Critique*. Glencoe, IL: Free Press.

Moustakas, C. 1961. *Loneliness*. Upper Saddle River, NJ: Prentice-Hall.

Murray, S. L., Bellavia, G. M., Rose, P., and Grifin, D. W. 2003. 'Once hurt, twice hurtful: how perceived regard regulates daily marital interactions', *Journal of Personality and Social Psychology*, 84: 126–147.

National Bureau of Statistics of China. 2018. 'National economy maintained overall stability with momentum of progress in October', available online at www.stats.gov.cn/enGliSH (accessed 14 March 2018).

National Council on Aging. 2006. 'Summary of the Survey on Attitudes to Age (March, 2000)', available online at www.ncoa.org/content.cfm?sectionID=105&detail=43.

Nazroo, J., Bajekal, M., Blane, D., Grewal, I. and Lewis, J. 2003. *Ethnic Inequalities in Quality of Life at Older Ages: Subjective and Objective Components. Research Findings: 11 from the Growing Older Programme*, available online at www.growingolder.group.shef.ac.uk/Nazroo_Findings_11.pdf, (accessed 15 May 2016).

New Zealand Ministry of Social Development. 2009. 'Loneliness', in *The Social Report 2016: Te pūrongo oranga tangata*, available online at www.socialreport.msd.govt.nz/social-connectedness/loneliness.html (accessed 15 August 2010).

Nyqvist, F., Cattan, M., Andersson, L., Forsman, A. K., and Gustafson, Y. 2013. 'Social capital and loneliness among the very old living at home and in institutional settings: a comparative study', *Journal of Ageing and Health*, 25(6): 1013–1035.

Nyqvist, F., Victor, C., Forsman, A., and Cattan, M. 2016. 'The association between social capital and loneliness in different age groups: a population-based study in western Finland', *BMC Public Health*, 16(1): 542.

O'Rand, A. M. 2001. 'Stratification and the life course: the forms of life-course capital and their interrelationships', in R. H. Binstock and L. K. George (eds), *Handbook of Aging and the Social Sciences*, 5th edition. New York: Academic Press, pp. 197–213.

Ostrov, E. and Offer, D. 1980. 'Loneliness and the adolescent', in J. Hartog, J. R. Audy and Y. A. Cohen (eds), *The Anatomy of Loneliness*. New York: International University Press, pp. 170–185.

Page, J. 2012. *Freedom From Loneliness: 52 Ways To Stop Feeling Lonely*. CreateSpace Independent Publishing Platform.

Parsons, T. 1954. 'Psychology and sociology', in J. Gillin (ed.), *For a Science of Social Man: Convergences in Anthropology, Psychology, and Sociology*. New York: Macmillan.

Paul, C., Ayis, S., and Ebrahim, S. 2006. 'Psychological distress, loneliness and disability in old age', *Psychology, Health & Medicine*, 11(2): 221–232.

Perlman, D. and Peplau, L. A. 1981. 'Toward a social psychology of loneliness', in S. W. Duck and R. Gilmour (eds), *Personal Relationships in Disorder*. London: Academic Press, pp. 31–56.

Perlman, D. and Peplau, L. A. 1982. 'Theoretical approaches to loneliness', in L. A. Peplau and D. Perlman (eds), *Loneliness: A Sourcebook of Current Theory, Research, and Therapy*. New York: John Wiley & Sons, pp. 126–127.

Phillips, D. P. 1977. 'Deathday and birthday: an unexpected connection', in J. M. Tanur et al. (eds), *Statistics: A Guide to the Biological and Health Sciences*. San Francisco, CA: Holden-Day, pp. 111–125.

Phillipson, C., Ahmed, N. and Latimer, J. 2003. *Women in Transition: First Generation Migrant Women from Bangladesh*. Bristol: Policy Press.

Pinquart, M., and Sörensen, S. 2001. 'Influences on loneliness in older adults: a meta-analysis', *Basic and Applied Social Psychology*, 23(4): 245–266.

Polo, A. J., and Lopez, S. R. 2009. 'Culture, context, and the internalizing distress of Mexican American youth', *Journal of Clinical Child and Adolescent Psychology*, 38(2): 273–285.

Portes, A. and Rumbaut, R. G. 2001. *Legacies: The Story of the Immigrant Second Generation*. Berkeley, CA: University of California Press.

Portes, A. and Zhou, M. 1993. 'The new second generation: segmented assimilation and its variants', *Annals of the American Academy of Political and Social Sciences*, 530(1): 74–96.

Putnam, R. 2001. *Bowling Alone: The Collapse and Revival of American Community*. New York: Simon & Schuster.

Reynolds, P. and Kaplan, G. A. 1990. 'Social connections and risk for cancer: prospective evidence from the Alameda County Study', *Behavioural Medicine*, 16(3): 101–110.

Rich, A. R. and Bonner, R. L. 1987. 'Concurrent validity of a stress-vulnerability model of suicidal ideation and behaviour: a follow-up study', *Suicide and Life-Threatening Behaviour*, 17: 265–270.

Richards, A. K., Spira, L., and Lynch, A. A. (eds). 2013. *Encounters with Loneliness: Only the Lonely*, 2nd edition. New York: International Psychoanalytic Books.

Riesman, D., Glazer, N., and Denney, R. 1961. *The Lonely Crowd: A Study of the Changing American Character*, abridged edition. New Haven, CT: Yale University Press.

Ripple, P. 1982. *Walking with Loneliness*. Notre Dame, IN: Ave Maria Press.

Rokach, A. 2007. 'The effect of age and culture on the causes of loneliness', *Social Behavior and Personality*, 35: 169–186.

Rokach, A. 2008. 'Coping with loneliness in North America and Spain', *Psychology Journal*, 5: 51–68.

Rokach, A. and Neto, F. 2005. 'Age, culture, and the antecedents of loneliness', *Social Behaviour and Personality*, 33: 477–494.

Rokach, A., Orzeck, T., Cripps, J., Lackovic-Grgin K. and Penezic, Z. 2001. 'The effects of culture on the meaning of loneliness', *Social Indicators Research*, 53: 17–31.

Rokach, A., Orzeck, T., Moya, M. C. and Expósito, F. 2002. 'Causes of loneliness in North America and Spain', *European Psychologist*, 7(1), 70.

Rokach, A., Orzeck, T. and Neto, F. 2004. 'Coping with loneliness in old age: a cross-cultural comparison', *Current Psychology*, 23: 124–137.

Ronald, R. and Hirayama, Y. 2009. 'Home alone: the individualization of young urban Japanese singles', *Environment and Planning A*, 41: 2836–2854.

Rose, D., Harrison, E., and Pevalin, D. 2010. 'The European socio-economic classification: a prolegomenon', in D. Rose and E. Harrison (eds), *Social Class in Europe: An Introduction to the European Socio-economic Classification*. New York: Routledge.

Rose, R. 2003. *Health, Money, and Wellbeing: Subjective Responses to Post-Soviet Transformation*. Studies in Public Policy series No. 380, Centre for the Study of Public Policy, University of Strathclyde.

Rotenberg, K. J., Bharathi, C., Davies, H., and Finch, T. 2013. 'Bulimic symptoms and the social withdrawal syndrome', *Eating Behaviours*, 14(3): 281–284.

Ruberman, W., Weinblatt, E., Goldberg, J. D., and Chaudhary, B. S. 1984. 'Psychosocial influences on mortality after myocardial infarction', *New England Journal of Medicine*, 311:552–559.

Russell, B. 1975. *Autobiography*. New York: Routledge.

Russell, D. 1996. 'UCLA loneliness scale (Version 3): reliability, validity, and factor structure', *Journal of Personality Assessment*, 66(1): 20–40.

Russell, D., Peplau, L. A., and Cutrona, C. E. 1980. 'The revised UCLA Loneliness Scale: concurrent and discriminant validity evidence', *Journal of Personality and Social Psychology*, 39(3): 472–480.

Russell, D., Peplau, L. A., and Ferguson, M. L. 1978. 'Developing a measure of loneliness', *Journal of Personality Assessment*, 42: 290–294.

Sadler, W. A. and Johnson, T. B., Jr. 1980. 'From loneliness to anomia', in J. Hartog, J. R. Audy and Y. A. Cohen (eds), *The Anatomy of Loneliness*. New York: International University Press, p. 55.

Salter, P. 1970. *The Pursuit of Loneliness*. Boston, MA: Beacon Press.

Savage, M., Devine, F., Cunningham, N., Taylor, M., Li, Y., Hjellbrekke, J., Le Roux, B., Friedman, S., and Miles, A. 2013. 'A new model of social class? Findings from the BBC's Great British Class Survey experiment', *Sociology*, 47(2): 219–250.

Savikko, N., Routasalo, P., Tilvis, R. S., Strandberg, T. E., and Pitkälä, K. H. 2005. 'Predictors and subjective causes of loneliness in an aged population', *Archives of Gerontology and Geriatrics*, 41: 223–233.

Scambler, G. (ed.). 2018. *Sociology as Applied to Health and Medicine*, 7th edition. Basingstoke: Palgrave Macmillan.

Scharf, T., Phillipson, C., and Smith, A. E. 2004. 'Poverty and social exclusion: growing older in deprived urban neighbourhoods', in A. Walker and A. Hennessy (eds), *Growing Older: Quality of Life in Old Age*. Maidenhead: Open University Press, pp. 81–106.

Schoonenberg, P. 1965. *Man and Sin: A Theological View*, translated by J. Donceel. Melbourne: Sheed and Ward.

Segrin, C. 1998. 'Interpersonal communication problems associated with depression and loneliness', in P. A. Anderson and L. K. Guerrero (eds), *Handbook of Communication and Emotion: Research, Theory, Applications, and Contexts*. San Diego, CA: Academic Press.

Selimi, T. J. 2016. *#Loneliness: The Virus of the Modern Age*. Carlsbad, CA: Balboa Press.

Selvon, S. 2006. *The Lonely Londoners*. London: Penguin Books.

Sennet, R. 1977. *The Fall of Public Man*. Cambridge: Cambridge University Press.

Sennett, R. and Cobb, J. 1977. *The Hidden Injuries of Class*. Cambridge: Cambridge University Press.

Shelley, M. [1818] 1985. *Frankenstein*. London: Penguin Books.

Shorthouse, R. 2014. 'Loneliness should be recognized as a signal of poverty in today's Britain', *The Guardian*, 26 February, available online at www.theguardian.com/

commentisfree/2014/feb/26/loneliness-signal-poverty-britain-iain-duncan-smith (accessed 15 May 2018).

Simmel, G. [1903] 1950. 'The metropolis and mental life', in his *The Sociology of Georg Simmel*, trans., ed., and introduced by K. H. Wolff. New York: The Free Press, pp. 409–424.

Sirtio, S. et al. 2016. 'Existential loneliness at the end of life: design and proposal of Existential Loneliness Detection Scale of (ELDS), preliminary results', *Psycho-Oncology*, 25(SP, S3): 56–65.

Slater, P. 1971. *The Pursuit of Loneliness: American Cultural at the Breaking Point*. London: Allen Lane.

Srole, L. 1956. 'Social integration and certain corollaries', *American Sociological Review*, 21: 709–716.

Stack, S. 1998. 'Marriage, family and loneliness: a cross-national study', *Sociological Perspectives*, 41: 415–432.

Stacy, A. W., Newcomb, M. D., and Bentler, P. M. 1995. 'Expectancy in mediational models of cocaine abuse', *Personality and Individual Differences*, 19: 655–667.

Stevens, N. and Westerhof, G. J. 2006. 'Marriage, social integration, and loneliness in the second half of life: a comparison of Dutch and German men and women', *Research on Aging*, 28: 713–729.

Storr, A. 1988. *Solitude*. London: HarperCollins Publishers.

Stravynski, A. and Boyer, R. 2001. 'Loneliness in relation to suicide ideation and parasuicide: a population-wide study', *Suicide and Life-Threatening Behaviour*, 31: 32–40.

Sundström, G., Fransson, E., Malmberg, B., and Davey, A. 2009. 'Loneliness among older Europeans', *European Journal of Ageing*, 6(4): 267–275.

Taylor, S. E. and Seeman, T. E. 1999. 'Psychosocial resources and the SES – health relationship', *Annals of the New York Academy of Science*, 896: 210–225.

Teixeira, P. (ed.). 2014. *Human Capital*. Abingdon: Routledge.

Thomson, I. T. 2000. *In Conflict No Longer: Self and Society in Contemporary America*. Lanham, MD: Rowman & Littlefield.

Tóibín, C. 2009. *Brooklyn*. London: Penguin Books.

Tolstoy, L. 2010. *The Death of Ivan Ilyich and Other Stories*, translated from the Russian by R. Pevear and L. Volokhonsky. New York: Vintage Books.

Turkle, S. 2011. *Alone Together: Why We Expect More from Technology and Less from Each Other*. New York: Basic Books.

Turner, J. H. (ed.). 2011. *The Sociology of Emotions*. Cambridge: Cambridge University Press.

Van Bergen, D. D., Smit, J. H., van Balkom, A. J. L. M., van Ameijden, E., and Saharso, S. 2008. 'Suicidal ideation in ethnic minority and majority adolescents in Utrecht, The Netherlands', *Crisis: The Journal of Crisis Intervention and Suicide Prevention*, 29(4): 202–208.

Victor, C. R., Burholt, V., and Martin, W. 2012. 'Loneliness and ethnic minority elders in Great Britain: an exploratory study', *Journal of Cross Cultural Gerontology*, 27(1): 65–78.

Victor, C. R., Scambler, S. J., Bond, J., and Bowling, A. 2000. 'Being alone in later life: loneliness, isolation and living alone in later life', *Reviews in Clinical Gerontology*, 10(4): 407–17.

Victor, C., Scambler, S., and Bond, J. 2009. *The Social World of Older People: Understanding Loneliness and Social Isolation in Later Life*. Maidenhead: Open University Press/McGraw Hill Education.

Victor, C. and Yang, K. 2012. 'The prevalence of loneliness among adults: a case study of the United Kingdom', *The Journal of Psychology: Interdisciplinary and Applied*, 146(1–2): 85–104.

Walker, A. and Multby, T. 1997. *Ageing Europe*. Buckingham: Open University Press.

Wallerstein, J. S. and Kelly, J. B. 1980. 'The effects of parental divorce: experiences of the child in later latency', in J. Hartog, J. R. Audy, and Y. A. Cohen (eds), *The Anatomy of Loneliness*. New York: International University Press, pp. 148–169.

Wei, M., Russell, D. W., and Aakalik, R. A. (2005) 'Adult attachment, social self-efficacy, self-disclosure, loneliness, and subsequent depression for freshman college students: a longitudinal study', *Journal of Counselling Psychology*, 52: 602–614.

Weiss, R. S. 1973. *Loneliness: The Experience of Emotional and Social Isolation*. Cambridge, MA: MIT Press.

Weiss, R. S. 1982. 'Issues in the study of loneliness', in L. A. Peplau and D. Perlman (eds), *Loneliness: A Sourcebook of Current Theory, Research, and Therapy*. New York: John Wiley & Sons, pp. 71–79.

Wellman, B. 1973. 'The network nature of future communities: a predictive synthesis', paper presented at 23rd Annual Meeting of the Society for the Study of Social Problems, New York.

Wells, M. and Kelly, D. 2008. 'The loneliness of cancer', *European Journal of Oncology Nursing*, 12(5): 410–411.

Wenger, G. C. 1984. *The Supportive Network: Coping with Old Age*. London: George Allen and Unwin.

Wenger, G. C., Richard, D., Shahtahmesebi, S., and Scott, A. 1996. 'Social isolation and loneliness in old age: review and model refinement', *Ageing & Society* 16(3): 333–358.

Whyte, W. H. 1957. *The Organization Man*. London: Jonathan Cape.

Wilkinson, R. and Pickett, K. 2010. *The Spirit Level: Why Equality is Better for Everyone*. London: Penguin Books.

Wilson, R. S., Krueger, K. R., Arnold, S. E., Schneider, J. A., Kelly, J. F., Barnes, L. L., Tang, Y., and Bennett, D. A. 2007. 'Loneliness and risk of Alzheimer's disease', *Archives of General Psychiatry*, 64: 234–240.

Wittenberg, M. T. and Reis, H. T. 1986. 'Loneliness, social skills, and social perceptions', *Personality and Social Psychology Bulletin*, 12(1): 121–130.

Yamagishi, T. 2001. 'Trust as a form of social intelligence', in K. Cook (ed.), *Trust in Society*. New York: Russell Sage Foundation, pp. 121–147.

Yang, K. 2007. 'Individual social capital and its measurement in social surveys', *Survey Research Methods*, 1(1): 19–27.

Yang, K. 2016. 'Causal conditions for loneliness: a set-theoretic analysis on an adult sample in the UK', *Quality & Quantity*, 52(2): 685–701.

Yang, K. and Victor, C. 2008. 'The prevalence of and risk factors for loneliness among older people in China', *Ageing & Society*, 28(3): 305–327.

Yang, K. and Victor, C. 2011. 'Age and loneliness in 25 European nations', *Ageing & Society* 31(8): 1368–1388.

Zylla, P. C. 2012. *The Roots of Sorrow: A Pastoral Theology of Suffering*. Waco, TX: Baylor University Press.

Index

Printed in Great Britain
by Amazon